Retuning Culture

DATE DUE			
			Printed in USA

RETUNING CULTURE

Musical Changes in

Central and Eastern Europe

Edited by Mark Slobin

Duke University Press Durham and London

1996

Contents

Introduction

⸬ Music is both deeply rooted and transient. It dissolves into space while simultaneously settling into individual and collective memory. Yesterday's songs trigger today's tears. Music harbors the habitual, but also acts as a herald of change. It helps to orchestrate personal, local, regional, ethnic, religious, linguistic, and national identity. Stable yet constantly in flux, music offers both striking metaphors and tangible data for understanding societies at moments of transition.

Yet the region this volume describes, the former "East bloc," was a nearly blank spot on the map of English-reading ethnomusicology. For reasons of both Eastern and Western politics, few outside scholars specialized in the music cultures of the Soviet Union and its circle of subordinated states. Musicology, anthropology, and sociology were similarly weak in their coverage of "the second world." During the communist period, not only "the sciences of man," but also cultural studies, media studies, colonial/postcolonial discourse, and postmodernist theory largely abandoned this world area to political scientists, economists, and ideologically driven analysis of all sorts. Even the burgeoning literature on postcommunism has scarcely taken music into account beyond a fascination with "rock" (Troitsky 1987, Ryback 1990, Ramet 1994), continuing a widespread scholarly disinterest in expressive culture's power to shape consciousness and organize daily life.

This volume stems from a February 1993 conference called "From Dissidence to Dissonance," convened by Mark Slobin at the invitation of Michael Holquist, Director of Yale University's Center for Russian and East European Studies. Almost all the contributors participated in the conference. Authors completed their work by January 1994, by which time several had made update journeys to Eastern Eruope. *Retuning Culture* offers the vantage points of observers who have either grown up in or have long visited and professionally specialized in, Russia, Ukraine, Hungary, former Czechoslovakia, Poland, Romania, former Yugoslavia, and Bulgaria.

Since no single angle of vision can encompass this vast geomusical territory, I suggest three perspectives that emerge from the essays: modernity, identity, and continuity. These perspectives overlap and intersect, each providing a helpful vantage point from which to view a crowded, rapidly shifting landscape.

Modernity

Communism was modernity in its most determined mood and most decisive posture; modernity streamlined, purified of the last shred of the chaotic, the irrational, the spontaneous, the unpredictable.

Communism [could not] seriously contemplate facing the challenge of the postmodern world: the world in which consumer choice is simultaneously the essential systemic requisite, the main factor of social integration, and the channel through which individual life-concerns are vented and problems resolved. — Zygmunt Baumann (1992: 170)

These two insights of Zygmunt Baumann offer a springboard for this volume's leap into a musical maelstrom. As Soviet communism settled into power as state socialism in the 1920s and 1930s, the authorities organized a framework for music-making that moved inexorably in the late 1940s to the "satellite countries" of Poland, Czechoslovakia, Hungary, Romania, and Bulgaria and that parallel universe of communism, Yugoslavia. This was a three-part system:

   1. *A rule-setting bureaucracy*. A combination of state and party administrators and activists produced a complex structure that operated at officially defined levels of the music culture. For "classical" music, the crystallizing moment was the invention of the Soviet professional artists' unions in 1932. The Composers' Union set standards for music composition, per-

formance, study, and dissemination for the entire country, with separate unions in each of the constituent republics. Cities had *filarmonia* organizations that supported and regulated local music-making, and even the smallest settlement clusters had a "house of culture" that brought national policy into every nook and cranny of the vast USSR. Everywhere in Central and Eastern Europe, networks of bureaucrats ruled the concert halls, airwaves, and record players of the socialist state, fostering and prohibiting musics, offering the carrot of patronage and brandishing the stick of censorship, even erasure, of individual voices and whole cultural traditions.

2. *A set of standardized formats and venues.* Festivals, parades, competitions, local houses of culture, and amateur troupes at various levels of support, proficiency, and national visibility provided places and moments, hooks on which to hang the acceptable forms of music-making. Music classes in ordinary and special-education music schools operated as filters for talent in the classical music realm, culminating in the international-contest prizewinner clutching a state-owned Stradivarius, a system that directly paralleled the identification and fostering of Olympic athletes.

3. *The ubiquitous presence of official repertoires.* The masters of music decided to create a shared experience of daily life and communal memory, exploiting the appeal of arranged folk songs, mass songs, movie musicals, and radio hits (the last three combinable into one package). In the USSR, Russification brought a foreign language repertoire to a large percentage of citizens and the replication of Russian genres and styles in local musical languages, under the guise of "rapprochement" and "convergence" of nations.[1] In extremely nationalist communist systems like Romania and Bulgaria, the doctrine of monoethnic identity was part of an invented homogeneity, so researchers could neither collect nor disseminate, say, Jewish, Turkish, or Roma ("gypsy") musics except indirectly.[2]

Yet every attempt to make music manageable, as if following a physical law, evokes the "chaotic and unpredictable" as a response. An important theme in the essays below is the dialectic between control and reaction, the planned and the unforced. As in the best of gardens, unwanted "volunteers" grow alongside neat rows of plants, despite constant weeding. Music is mutable, flexible, and volatile. People riff on the available chord changes, improvise on the most banal and well-known patterns, precisely because the state provides these familiar, inescapable components of consciousness. It is impossible to cleanse the spontaneous from music. Music's social and cultural role is always that of shape-changer, if not trickster. While both Plato and Stalin decried this essential nature of music, neither could absolutely eliminate it from the ideal state, hoping at best to tame it to their needs. While music will obligingly serve to animate marching men or Young Pioneers, it also anchors individual memory and group consciousness, placing them out of the reach of the state. In the most regulated of performative moments, no one can account for the multitude of meanings, responses, and attachments each individual is bringing to the experience. One of the great social virtues of kitsch, both state-spawned and commercial, is that its very anonymity of address allows for many modes of individual or subcultural anchoring. By spreading feel-good songs and movies throughout a mass culture, the state feels comfortable in avoiding danger, yet it must also close an indulgent eye to the possible meanings produced by the consumers of official culture. Local/subcultural sensibilities make full use of music's ambiguity, of which more below.

Variable interpretation is part of any system, but free choice is another matter. Disallowed and regulated, musical diversity sprang up increasingly in the late 1970s in various forms and flowered in the 1980s as part of the breakthrough of grassroots discontent that culminated in song-filled demonstrations stretching from 1970s Poland to regionwide breakthrough demonstrations in the late 1980s. As early as the Khrushchev cultural "thaw" of the late 1950s and early 1960s, tastemakers ranging from the Russian singer-songwriter "bards" to classical composers began to circumvent and ignore official music culture. In Poland, contemporary music festivals and compositions flourished as Stalinism waned, while Hungary was able to draw continuously on a highly developed tradition of musical modernism. The import of Anglo-American rock increased the possibilities of consumer choice as citizens became directly or indirectly aware of what the West calls "the sixties," a liberatory moment in Euro-American culture. Yet the brief opening of such windows provided only a tantalizing whiff of fresh air, as they were soon slammed down in the "stagnation era" under Brezhnev. Alfred Schnittke, a Russian composer particularly attuned to world musical currents, recalls the moment:

1968 was a time of colossal enthusiasm . . . we thought then that some mighty convulsion lay ahead which would propel us on to yet another plane of thought, intuition, and God knows what else. But it didn't happen. For artists in other countries, 1968 was a time of powerful subjective impressions. For us it was the start of an era of stagnation, and instead of attaining that higher reality . . . these changes merely continued to be reflected in our own personal lives. (in Kagarlitskaya 1990: 71)

In the 1970s, some members of the intelligentsia turned instead to local sources, creating small-scale formations that bridged the gap between the individual artist and the ethnic/national community. In Russia, Hungary, and the Baltic lands, intellectuals started amateur folk music collecting and performing groups that went behind the back of the state to contact villagers directly.[3] Around the same time, grassroots-oriented youth gravitated toward the West's "folk revival" movement. This started in the United States in the 1940s and 1950s and spread to Europe mostly through personal, noncommercial means: personalities (like the members of the Seeger family in America and England), folk festivals, and the ceaseless wanderings of youth across seas and continents in search of identity. The ripple effect of this restless roots-seeking eventually reached Central and Eastern Europe. By the time major cultural transition began in the mid-1980s, this urge for global networking was not just confined to youth, as another quotation from Schnittke, soon to leave Russia, shows:

As for the accelerated pace of our lives today . . . ! One has only to switch on the wireless and wander over the airwaves to embrace a vast world of sound. I've come to feel that one shouldn't resist this but should relate to it as a fact of modern life. The problem is how to hang on to one's individuality within this vast world of polystylism. (in Kagarlitskaya 1990: 71)

Meanwhile, everyday consumers and musicians took advantage of economic loopholes to invent and spread vernacular musical styles. In the 1970s, the regulators of the partly privatized Yugoslav economy defined a space called "newly composed folk music" that served as an alternative to official styles by adjusting rural roots music to the tastes of urbanizing audiences. A bit later in Bulgaria, Roma musicians literally electrified the atmosphere by plugging into updated sound technologies and importing

Western musical constructs. These homegrown adaptations coexisted with the spread of Anglo-American rock music. Rock provided an imported system of expression that not only offered a substitute aesthetic but also came with the trappings of commodification and stardom even before state-run economies could offer major financial rewards. The literal packaging — records, bootlegged tapes — epitomized the inaccessible, triggering all the local longings for consumerism, while the song's sounds and texts offered a rich array of possible meanings for music beyond the anodyne atmosphere of official music. To what extent rock was actually subversive of state social-ism is debatable. Pekacz (1994) has argued that in most cases, rock did not actually lead to the overthrow of communism, as some cultural critics have claimed. Like other cultural forms, rock was caught in the web of state patronage even as it proclaimed its marginality. Yet Vaclav Havel has al-ways pointed to American rock and the suppression of a Czech band, Plastic People of the Universe, as catalysts for the creation of the crucial anti-government Charter 77 group, telling evidence for rock's local importance in crystallizing dissent.

In summary, the "modernity angle" suggested by Bauman is a helpful perspective because it situates musical manipulation and yearnings within the larger context of a global pattern that started in Western Europe and the United States and spread out in vast concentric rings to the rest of the world. In Central and Eastern Europe, music was understood by cultural bureau-cracies as a powerful tool in their social management schemes and was pursued with an almost maniacal hypersensitivity and discipline. Consum-ers anticipated the eventual release of the pent-up pressure of state pa-tronage by finding channels for choice in forms of musical expression, either participatory or mediated electronically. Interesting here is the two-sided nature of "choice." Some turned to the romantic-heroic world of rock, with its intimations of commodification, most evident in the actual market created in Yugoslavia. Others looked to tradition defiantly, searching for both homegrown roots and internationalist ties in musical styles associated with precommunist days — an entirely different, though still somewhat ro-mantic, version of modernity. In some cases, the two approaches blended, as in the superstardom of Bulgarian Roma wedding bands.

Yet modernity offers only a partial viewpoint on the transitions that overtook the region around 1990. For people did not just act individually, or as small consumer subcultures, against an unmovable state patronage system. They also banded together as collectives, rallying around forms of ideology and identity politics that coexisted with communism. All these social formations featured strong musical underpinning, so looking at their activity provides another lens for surveying the crowded cultural scene.

Identity

Modernity alone tells only part of the tale of transition. The essays below foreground varieties of identity that are intimately intertwined with the political and ideological implications of musical change ranging from the largest claims of emergent and triumphant nationalism to the small-scale assertions of subcultures.

The state offered an overarching identity: nationalism, but of a rather conflicted variety. As Verdery says, "national ideology disrupted the Marxist discourse and thus — despite the Communist party's apparent appropriation of it — was a major element in destroying the Party's legitimacy" (1991a: 4) An anecdote she cites is illuminating:

When I suggested that [the] villagers saw their "old customs" as "for public display only" rather than as an integral part of the life cycle still being practiced, the officials became (to my view, inexplicably) irate. Only later did I begin to realize that I had stabbed close to the heart of nation-building. (Verdery 1983: 23)

This passage displays conflicting forms of collective identity. The villagers acknowledge the showcase nature of their public display, which they keep separate from a still extant body of voluntary local practice. Meanwhile, the bureaucrats are angry that a visitor has noticed the discrepancy between top-down and grassroots identities. Toward the end of state socialism, "local custom" began to be co-opted by political groups bent on wresting power away from collapsing power structures and forming new ones. In case studies such as those of Bosnian Muslims and Ukrainians below, it is the *ritual appeal* rather than the entertainment appeal of music that advocacy groups exploit, providing a very public alternative to the more traditional forms of state-sponsored public performance. The mass energy found at parade grounds or in soccer stadiums can be channeled through music into new political formation-building when community begins to be redefined. For the USSR, Aves, Duncan, and Hosking have noted the emergence and power of the "informals" in Soviet political life, who "did more to reshape and eventually destroy the Soviet Union than the Communist Party leadership" (Aves, Duncan, and Hosking 1990: 204–5). The power of the "informals" drew strongly on a sense of place, of local allegiance as the key to power:

The informals' success in reflecting broader moods depended in part on their ethnic closeness to the population . . . they could deploy national symbols, flags, emblems, and folk-songs . . . and they could impart an ethnic coloring to issues which aroused strong emotions, but which were not in themselves ethnic, such as the environment and the economy. (Aves et al.: 105–6)

In fact, the Baltic peoples' drive for self-determination was called "the Singing Revolution" in which "many participants of the folk music revival movement played leading roles" (Boiko 1994: 54).

Labeled regionally, ethnically, linguistically, or religiously (usually a mixture of two or more), infranational microsystems proved extraordinarily resilient through the toughest times of totalitarianism. Despite Stalin's strenuous efforts to redefine, relocate, or legislate out of existence whole peoples, his work was swept away by collective memory. Across Eastern Europe, enough levels of music-making remained to sustain nonnationalist forms of identity. Parodies of mass songs abounded and survivals of older layers of repertoire provided some small sense of continuity.

Musical activity, then, became a battleground contested by local oppositional forces and entrenched centralized bureaucracies, since both had a stake in promoting musical identity as a key component of citizens' consciousness. Within the mind of each citizen, this translates into a multilayered musical consciousness in which youth-group patriotic songs, national pop tunes, dissident songs, and local survivals coexist and compete, all grounded in personal moments and memories. "Identity," as always, is layered. Yet looking at it only in terms of immediate, shifting sensibilities can be limiting, since in Central and Eastern Europe, continuity and turbulence interact as part of a complex calculus of cultural politics and personal positioning.

Continuity

Each hegemonic thrust and subcultural parry are just episodes in a long fencing match on the battlefield of culture. Looking at the local is particularly critical in examining top-down societies, since it counters the sometimes facile tendency to look for the ways that powerful fists rearrange and even crush regional and ethnic landscapes. Yet, as Balzer points out, one has "to fracture one's perspective into multiple views" as a way of redefining "what is 'central' and 'peripheral' " (1994: 59). The Soviet state offers an extraordinary example of how control misfires: "almost everything the Soviet leadership tried to do in the area of nationality relations led to heightened, not repressed, ethnic consciousness" (Balzer 1994: 85). Music was often the crucible of controversy. Take, for example, the controversy in the 1960s over the survival of the Bukharan court music (*shashmaqam*) in Central Asia. As a remnant of the "feudal" past, the Russian authorities felt, this tradition was negative and should be silenced. Yet the logic of the social order of the republics left a space for local cultural management, and the *shashmaqam* not only survived but was even enshrined as a key component of Uzbek identity in the cultural renaissance of the late Soviet period, allowing it to survive into the postcommunist period. As Balzer says, "the ironic consequence of Soviet ethnic policies was a heightened awareness of ethnicity" (1994: 85). This local pride coexisted with a commitment to modernization, showing how interactive the perspectives of modernity, identity, and continuity can be in musical systems. When I interviewed Uzbek musical leaders in 1968, I was surprised that they trotted out a student playing the Mendelssohn Violin Concerto on the modernized Uzbek fiddle, since I thought of the updating of their musical instruments as intrusive Russification. But they saw it as a positive development, strengthening their claim to being a fully modern Asian people.

Everywhere, national musical forms served and continue to function as resources, ready on short notice to be reintegrated into a current context. The Baltic "Singing Revolution" drew on a tradition of choral festivals that dates back to the nineteenth century, when in Estonia it was an oppositional move in the face of the dual German and Russian cultural hegemonies. In 1988, a group of visiting American ethnomusicologists touring the Latvian

Ethnographic Open-Air Museum was greeted by a group standing in front of a sample peasant house and singing *ligo,* summer festival songs. To the Americans, this looked like a completely normal "heritage" performance. Yet the singers explained that this was the first year that *ligo* songs had made a comeback, since they had been considered too nationalistic. Gorbachev's Minister of Culture had called and practically ordered the Latvians to start the custom again. This made it easier to understand why the group was an informal, mixed-generation ensemble of a few older people (who knew the songs) and some cultural activists with their children, who were learning the tradition anew.

In early postcommunist music cultures, the parties to a current conflict are often stands-in for generations of such negotiations over authority and expression. To take examples cited below, a group as small and powerless as the Russian religious sect, the Molokans, or as extensive and influential as the Hungarian intelligentsia have been persistent in holding or molding ideologies for a very long time. True, the Molokans might now use American songs for their liturgy. The Hungarian intelligentsia might confront an upstart form of working-class rock 'n'roll rather than scorning "inauthentic" urban Gypsy music. Yet the Molokans' penchant for adaptability and the Hungarian intelligentsia's claim to moral and cultural leadership have remained unchanged. Deep, longheld fears like the Serbian and Bulgarian view of the "Turkish threat" are always available for a ruling group to mobilize in a quest for power. The fault lines of Russian ambivalence about European culture run just as precipitously under the surface of political and cultural life as ever. Every national debate echoes the rhetoric of the loud slogans of yesteryear.

As former communists have returned to power in several countries, older cultural habits have shown their durability as the bureaucratic train, derailed temporarily, has moved back onto its accustomed tracks. In Poland in 1994, the newly elected Minister of Culture slashed the budget of the internationally recognized Center for Contemporary Art, since he "favors traditional and folk art [and] has expressed disdain for the Center, leaving it with virtually no money for new art shows" (*New York Times,* 16 Sept. 1994). In any case, in Poland the communist-style folk festival had been maintained under regional management as part of local pride. Similarly, the devolution of power in Bulgaria has had the effect of enhancing various forms of post-official, but still managed, representations of culture supported by local governments and private patronage.

This new localization coexists with the persistence of the national folk troupe concept as an export item, as witnessed by this blurb for a Slovak ensemble appearing in New York in 1994:

Lucnica makes its first New York appearance with dazzling folk dances, music and songs of Slovakia . . . Lucnica is renowned throughout the world for its exuberant and joyous performances — highlighted by breathtaking acrobatic dances — expressing the poetry, lyricism and passion of the Slovak people, their history and culture. It has been led for decades by noted choreographer Stefan Nosal. (World Music Institute brochure, fall 1994)

So a troupe understood in Czechoslovakia as a representation of regional official culture "for decades" can become the showcase of newly independent Slovakia — in the words of the brochure, "a country which lies in the heart of Europe where the cultures of Eastern Europe and the Balkans meet." This sentence boosts a newly identified nation and culture by referring to the well-known charms of the more famous official ensembles, like the Soviet/Russian Moiseyev dancers, while simultaneously evoking the atmosphere of New York's well-established amateur and "ethnic" Balkan song-and-dance groups. The country changes, while the choreographer remains. The strategy worked; *New York Times* reviews gushed over the precision and professionalism of the Slovak troupe in exactly the same terms once used for communist-era "folk" ensembles.

Such transitional moments show how important it is to look for continuities as for disjunctures, reflex behavior as well as innovation. For music is layered into consciousness in three strata: current, recent, and long-term — all of which occur simultaneously in the present. The *current* is always at the forefront of attention, claiming primacy through policy or persuasion. Everywhere, a turn of the radio dial most commonly yields "the latest." The *recent* is the seedbed of the current. Right now, recent might mean "since the advent of rock music," a moment that extended in concentric circles around the globe from its heartland in Anglo-America.[4] The *long-term* operates at another level of memory in this archaeology of music cultures. It is, of course, just as immediate as the others, since music history is reborn every day as a clustering of available sound resources. Yet long-term resonance is felt, marketed, and interpreted as distant echoes of earlier vibrations rather than as the shock waves of the latest hit or the soothing sounds of the songs of our youth. By highlighting how music, a powerful expressive resource, moves along these three axes, this volume hopes to make a distinctive contribution to the understanding of a region in transition.

The essays below offer a wide range of viewpoints, from tightly framing a small group or a demarcated moment that displays condensed, powerful activity to offering a wide-angle panorama of decades or generations that unfolds a long continuum of musical practice. The essays are case studies of specific musical milieus, which have implications for larger social, cultural, and historical patterns. They can be read geographically or topically. Their ordering here reflects a topical approach:

Levin, Beckerman, Frigyesi, Lange, and Rasmussen particularly point out the intricate ways in which the intelligentsia interacts with music-making. Since sometime in the nineteenth century (depending on region), an educated elite has had the power to shape, respond to, and sometimes even create local musical taste, styles, and repertoires. Levin, Beckerman, and Frigyesi focus on "traditional" (i.e., peasant-origin) musics, while Levin and Frigyesi report on the "revivalism" of the 1970s to 1990s. Lange and Rasmussen explore the response to urban popular music styles disapproved by the intelligentsia. Czekanowska points toward the situation in mid-1990s Poland in which the intelligentsia is not particularly involved in the shifting, ad hoc relationship of "tradition" to the emerging postcommunist culture.

Lausević and Wanner present case studies of musical moments when formerly local/"ethnic"/"national" forms are reshaped, reinterpreted, and performed as part of a strong drive for autonomy — among Bosnian Muslims and Ukrainians, respectively. They discuss how political groupings seek power through metaphoric musicality, genres, and songs that represent emerging national identity. Popa brings us the voices of Romanian folk artists who create new songs even while they are experiencing the brutal shock of social change that is far from metaphoric: the 1989 revolution.

Rice, Buchanan, and Silverman offer dovetailing studies on the positioning of minority musics in communist and postcommunist states, with an emphasis on the perseverance and power of Roma ("gypsy") music. Mazo augments this perspective with a study of the Molokans, a small sect of Russian Christians that stresses the continuity of their musical vision both at home and in diaspora.

Geographically, the contexts of the essays are as follows: Bulgaria: Buchanan, Rice, and Silverman; Czech lands: Beckerman; Hungary: Frigyesi and Lange; post-Yugoslav Macedonia: Silverman; Poland: Czekanowska; Romania: Popa; Russia: Levin and Mazo; Ukraine: Wanner; prewar Yugoslavia: Lausević and Rasmussen.

Notes

1. Space constraints do not allow a presentation of Soviet musical colonialism; for quick reference to the communist and postcommunist situation in Central Asia, see Slobin 1968 and Levin 1993.

2. One should not forget the indefatigable folklorists and ethnomusicologists who circumvented official directions and collected a broad range of popular expressive culture anyway, much of which is now being recuperated and reevaluated as a part of the push for local, regional, and national identity in the postcommunist nation-states.

3. Still another tack was taken in one particularly West-leaning country, Poland, where ethnomusicology graduate students were actually sent abroad, to destinations from India to Peru, rather than to the Polish countryside for their dissertation fieldwork.

4. Earlier, style currents like the waltz or the tango went from "current" to "recent" as they became domesticated in local surroundings everywhere. It is important to think of the present "postmodern transnational" situation as not necessarily all that different in some ways from prior patterns of the transmission of technologically driven and/or commodified forms of music.

THEODORE LEVIN

Dmitri Pokrovsky and the Russian Folk Music

Revival Movement

> To a friend of the enlightenment the word and conception "the folk" has always
> something anachronistic and alarming about it; he knows that you need only tell a
> crowd they are "the folk" to stir them up to all sorts of reactionary evil. What all has
> not happened before our eyes — or just not quite before our eyes — in the name of
> "the folk" though it could never have happened in the name of God or humanity or
> the law! — Thomas Mann, *Doktor Faustus*

The phone rang in the austere one-room apartment that Dmitri Pokrovsky, founder and artistic director of the Pokrovsky Ensemble, subleases
on the fourteenth floor of a nondescript high-rise in central Moscow. Boris
Yeltsin's office was calling. Would the Pokrovsky Ensemble be available to
perform Russian folk music at a party celebrating Boris Nikolayevich's
inauguration as President of Russia? And just one request: could the ensemble please be prepared to sing Boris Nikolayevich's favorite song, "Ural-
skaya Ryabinushka" ("The Ural Rowan Tree," a sentimental worker's song
from Yeltsin's native Ural region)?

"I'm sorry, we don't have that song in our repertory," Dmitri Pokrovsky
told the caller from the Kremlin.

The caller pleaded, "But if you'll just learn it, this one time . . . "

"I'm sorry," Pokrovsky repeated. "You don't understand. We don't sing
such songs."

Pokrovsky chuckled as he recounted the story in a conversation that took
place in June 1994. "They found some other musicians who agreed to
perform "The Ural Rowan Tree." Everyone sang along, and Yeltsin played
the spoons. It was all fine, but I'm glad I didn't agree to do it. I don't want to
be a court musician to the czar of the new Russian empire. And after refus-

ing to sing Yeltsin's favorite song, I'm sure they won't invite me back again soon."

The imperial culture from which Pokrovsky felt estranged had been amply displayed on Moscow television the evening prior to our conversation. The occasion was Russian Independence Day, 12 June (1994), and a gala celebration had been organized in the Rossiya Concert Hall, with President Yeltsin in attendance. "It was a performance that conformed to the norms of Stalin's time, not to mention czarist times," Pokrovsky commented. "It used to be that they would hang a portrait of Stalin in the background. But in the Rossiya Hall, instead of Stalin, they had Don Cossacks carrying an icon of St. George, and everyone had to stand and sing Glinka's "Slava!" ["Glory"] chorus from [the opera] *A Life for the Czar*. In the opening part of the concert, there was grandiose classical music: the Alexandrov Russian Army Choir, a symphony orchestra, opera arias performed by singers from the Bolshoi Theater. After that, there was a transition to national folk culture: the Krasnoyarsk Dance group, the Kuban Cossack Choir, Nadya Babkina — all with a lot of military pomp on stage. Those sorts of imperial ensembles are the only kind of folk or national cultural group that can be successful now. Our ensemble wouldn't fit in. We wouldn't be successful. We wouldn't be invited, and I wouldn't go. Artists are going to have to make a choice: to be part of the imperial system, or to say 'no' to it."

Pokrovsky's acerbic antiestablishment sentiments might have come as a surprise to some of his Russian critics — and these days there is no shortage of them. "Pokrovsky has become too slick; he's lost touch with his roots," is one commonly heard jab. "He's responsible for a lot of the ugly nationalism that's crept into performances of traditional folk and sacred music" is another. "He's sold out and become a rich capitalist by spending all his time touring in the West," goes a third. Pokrovsky is alternately annoyed and amused by the criticism. "My ensemble and I are doing very much the same thing now that we were doing twenty years ago," he retorts. "We're just doing it more professionally and more seriously. We're not the ones who have changed; what has changed is people's interpretation of what we do."

How and why have those public interpretations changed? Why has Dmitri Pokrovsky, the leader of a small Moscow-based music ensemble, become such a celebrated and controversial public figure in Russia? Why does folk music, and the hermeneutics of folk music performance, matter so much in Russia? Why has folk music so often been forced to be more than itself, to assume a purpose beyond the aesthetic, as an *art engagé,* in which artists become, or are beheld as, the victim, handmaiden, or shill (or some of each) of politicians and bureaucrats?

I sought answers to these questions in a series of conversations with Dmitri Pokrovsky, whom I have known since early 1986, the dawn of the glasnost age, when Pokrovsky was just beginning to emerge from a lengthy period of official disfavor. The vicissitudes of Pokrovsky's career and his changing relationship to the *vlast'* — the "power," as all levels of government are so often collectively referred to in the former Soviet Union — are instructive for what they reveal about the to and fro of cultural politics, and about how Russians continue to redefine and reimagine their sense of nation, national past, and perhaps, national future.

Pokrovsky's experiences as a cultural activist and folk music revivalist challenge the chaste image of traditional folk song, still common in the West, as music filled with an unambiguous moral power rooted in an authentic "spirit of the people" and accepted at face value by listeners. In fact, Pokrovsky's career demonstrates, to the contrary, that meanings and associations attributed to folk music in Soviet and post-Soviet Russia have been eminently protean. And if a conventional representation of Soviet cultural politics has it that abstract and expressionist art and music were held at bay while folk art, folk music, and artistic production derived from folk sources were made to flourish, then the roller-coaster saga of Pokrovsky's artistic life must again serve as a caveat against such easy generalizations. During most of the Soviet era, authentic Russian village music, with its weird dissonances, bawdy textual innuendos, and fervent religious undertones, was considered as ill-suited for the aesthetic and ethical development of the "Soviet" citizen as the much maligned music of the avant-garde.[1]

I asked Pokrovsky, who was born in Moscow in 1944, to tell me about his musical life, about how he had come to the idea of forming his ensemble, and about how the ensemble has evolved over the twenty years of its existence. Our conversations were in English, which Pokrovsky has learned to speak with astonishing fluency during the last half-dozen years of intensive touring in the West. The quotations that follow are Pokrovsky's own words, with minor style editing.

"In the mid-1960s, I was a student at the Gnessen Institute, in Moscow. I played the balalaika and was interested in authentic instruments, but I thought I wanted to be an opera conductor. I became an unofficial student of Alexander Yurlov, the head of the choir conducting department, because I figured that I ought to learn how to conduct a choir as well as an orchestra. Yurlov was a young and energetic person, and during those years, he had opened a department of folk choir conducting. He invited Russia's leading folklorists to come to the Institute and teach authentic folklore. It took three or four years to get the idea of teaching authentic folklore through the bureaucracy. It started in the time of the Khrushchev thaw. I became involved, and soon I was arranging expeditions to villages.

"I started thinking about why people in different regions of Russia sing differently, and came to the conclusion that it's due to an unconscious connection with acoustics. My hypothesis was that singing is basically like a kind of long-distance connection. Different kinds of singing had to be developed in different kinds of acoustic conditions: forest, steppe, river valleys, mountains — they all have different acoustics, and folksingers use their mouth and throat differently than do academic singers because of the different acoustic demands. It seemed so obvious, and I began to organize expeditions to show this. I became immersed in research and started taking x-rays and using equipment for working with the deaf that allowed me to see on a screen not just frequency spectrums but different aspects of speech sound. Finally, I developed a theory. I didn't have a singing voice, but I had to find out whether I was crazy or whether I was right. So I gathered together some friends, and we started to do experiments. We didn't tell anyone what we were doing. Our first rehearsal was on September 16, 1973.

"In the beginning, none of the musicians in my ensemble was a singer, and they had nothing to lose by trying to develop their voices in a certain way. I took them to villages, and they got really involved. But we started from nothing. We didn't know what we were doing it for. Three or four months after we started, we sang in a Georgian restaurant in Moscow. Everyone applauded. 'It's wonderful; sing more,' the customers said. That was exciting. They thought we were Georgians. After that, I decided to go to the Folklore Commission [of the USSR Union of Composers] and tell them that we had this group, but I was afraid that they wouldn't like it. So instead of telling them that I already had a group, I told them that I wanted to start one, and asked them how I should do it. Their suggestions turned out to be exactly what we'd already been doing. I was relieved. These days, a lot of people are singing the way we do, but can you imagine that at that time no one was singing like that outside of the villages. You can't just start to improvise this sort of singing. You have to know how to use your voice, how to sing together in a particular style. A style is based on a certain kind of sound, and you have to be able to create that sound. For example, if you try to sing northern songs with the sound of southern songs, you won't be able to do it.

"Up until the late 1920s, there were commercial folklore ensembles that sang absolutely authentic folk music — for example, the Piatnitsky Choir. But in the 1930s, everything changed. On the recordings, you can hear the year and the moment when it changed. Stalin ordered the creation of official Soviet folklore. The Piatnitsky Choir was a good institution to do it, and so they were ordered to create this folklore; and all other folk choirs became like clones of Piatnitsky."

Mitrofan Piatnitsky (1864–1927), the son of a Russian Orthodox sexton, had been an amateur singer and a member of the Moscow Society of Amateur Scientists, Anthropologists, and Ethnographers. In the first years of the twentieth century, he had assembled a large collection of ethnographic costumes and musical instruments, and made some of the early phonograph recordings of Russian folk songs. In 1910 he organized a choir of peasant singers that became a sensation in Moscow and other cities, riding a wave of interest among urban Russians in "national" folk art and folk music. However, it wasn't until the beginning of collectivization, in 1929, that ethnographic interest in Piatnitsky's work metamorphosed into a political program. "All politics changed at that moment," said Pokrovsky, "and the folk choirs were affected along with everyone else. There were two stages. In the first stage, singers maintained an authentic style, but changed the words of their songs. They started to put political messages in the texts so that the songs became propaganda for the Soviet system. In the second stage, composers were invited to write new music — so-called 'mass songs' (*massovie pesni*), and these songs became the main repertory of the folk choirs."

Gradually, peasants were replaced by trained singers. "The professional folk choirs with their composed and arranged songs have continued down to the present. But in the 1960s, under Khrushchev, there was a strong idea that art done by amateurs would replace professional art; that professional artists and writers would be replaced by a whole population that would become artists. It's a very Bolshevik idea. The Khrushchev 'thaw' was a time whose main symbol became restoring Lenin's system of Communism, which had been ruined by Stalin. It wasn't that Khrushchev was anti-Communist; he wanted to return to Lenin's path. So all the ideas of 1917 and 1918 became central ideas again in the state system. It was at that time that the Folklore Commission was established, and that they added the position of "folklore specialist" (*metodist po folkloru*) in all of the "houses of folk art" (*doma narodnogo tvorchestva*) run by the Ministry of Culture."[2]

Pokrovsky became one of those folklore specialists. As he explained it, the job of the folklore specialist was to support the amateur groups in the villages that sang authentic folklore. "Another of their jobs was to make sure that thirty percent of the authentic folklore would be fakelore. That is, thirty percent had to be songs about the Soviet system and how great it is, about collective farms, tractors, and so on."

I asked, "Were the folklore specialists only in the Ministry of Culture's houses of folk art or were they also in the Union of Trade Unions' houses of amateur arts?"

"No, the trade union houses didn't have them. Instead they had people who worked with patriotic workers songs. Workers are workers; they're not supposed to have anything to do with folklore. Peasants are peasants; they *have* to have folklore. Even if they don't have it, they have to have it. So every village had to have a folklore choir. The folklore specialists who ran them did a good job; mostly, they were real folklorists, and they supported folklore, not fakelore. They were often amateur composers as well, and they'd write the thirty percent Soviet stuff. They knew folk music, so a typical love song became a song about the Twentieth Congress of the Party. They just changed the words. It's really easy to change the words of a folk song, especially because no one can understand them anyway." (Despite the lyrical stereotype of Russian folk songs like "Stenka Razin" — actually a composed folk song from the end of the nineteenth century — or "Kalinka" — a composed song from the beginning of the twentieth — traditional singers do not perform "songs" in the sense of setting fixed texts to fixed melodies; rather, short segments of text and melody are spontaneously and variously combined during performance, and may lead toward any one of a number of different subjects or images. In this process of musical extemporization, words may be chopped up, stretched out, or accentually distorted to fit the rhythmic scheme of a melody, not to mention that nonsensical sequences of phrases frequently make texts incoherent in any case. Hence, substituting particular segments of song text for other segments would not in principle have been considered outside the norms of tradition.)

"I remember Yurlov's course for choir masters," Pokrovsky recalled. "I remember their graduation exam. The first song they sang was about two falcons on an oak tree. The falcons represented Lenin and Stalin. It was a fake song from the 1950s. They still had to sing it in the mid-1960s, but by that time, there was, of course, only one falcon on the tree. That song was published as folklore by folklorists. To publish any collection of folk songs at that time, you had to have a song about Stalin at the beginning; a song about electricity, a tractor; and after that, you could have your love songs, calendar songs, or whatever. After a while, no one looked at the first few pages of those books.

"All that I've said about fakelore and the system that supported it is to show why, outside of the villages, no one was doing what we were doing in the early 1970s; why it seemed so strange and subversive. For the first five or six years, we were an unofficial group, and beginning in 1974 or 1975, the KGB prohibited our performances. It wasn't really because of us. It started when we were scheduled to perform in some house of culture, and that very day the KGB used bulldozers to destroy an art exhibit in an empty lot [in Moscow]. Probably they just cancelled everything that day that wasn't absolutely official. For us, the cancellation was fortunate; it was the beginning of our success. We were supposed to have performed with Evgenii Bachurin and some other singer-songwriters. They had a small but pretty avant-garde audience, and when people came to the theater and found that the concert had been cancelled, Bachurin said, 'Let's all go to my studio.' There were only thirty or so people. I'm not sure the concert would have been successful, but when we all got to the studio and people started to perform, and after someone came and told us about what had happened on the streets — about the art show being bulldozed — we all started to feel a real camaraderie. We got involved with this group of people whose performances were being prohibited, and afterwards, the KGB started to prohibit our performances, too. As a consequence, people got interested in us, and we started to get invitations to sing.

"We became an underground ensemble. We didn't try to create this image. But from the very beginning, we were prohibited. I can't say why we were prohibited. People are always asking me now why we were prohibited, and I can never give them an honest answer. I have to make things up. I say, 'It's because we sang songs that weren't about the Soviet Union or Communism, and people couldn't understand the words, and so on. But I really don't know why. It just happened.'"

As Pokrovsky's experience showed, the ranks of unofficial artists were not limited to the dissident writers who achieved fame in the West for having their books suppressed or the painters whose exhibitions were bulldozed. Every artistic field, folk music revivalism included, had its stylistic norms and internal boundaries that distinguished the canonically official from the aggressively unofficial, but that also included a large gray area in which artists played out a game of "chicken" with the cultural censors. Perhaps it was the passionate anti-Sovietism of a handful of well-known unofficial artists that led Western observers of Soviet culture to view the categories of official and unofficial art as inviolably disjunctive — divided by a Berlin Wall of artistic taste and social choice. But at least in the 1970s and 1980s, it was common enough for artists to probe the cultural no-man's-land between official and unofficial art, and to move back and forth between official and unofficial work, official and unofficial artistic life. Even leaving aside examples like Shostakovich, who maintained a profile of officiality while claiming inner defiance, there are many cases of artists who, either out of principle or economic necessity, led double artistic lives. One of the best known was the singer-songwriter Vladimir Vysotsky, who developed a large cult following in the 1970s and whose appearances at singer-songwriter festivals were banned from television at the same time that he was officially employed as an actor at Moscow's prestigious Taganka Theater.

The official–unofficial relationship could also work the other way, as, for example, in the case of Pokrovsky: while officially an unofficial artist, he seems unwittingly for a time to have enjoyed the covert patronage of the KGB. Pokrovsky recalled how it happened. "Someone came to me — he was just some person without any profession who wanted to help — and offered to work with us. He said that he'd make us a huge success and that we'd have lots of money. He said, 'I'll make an absolutely unofficial performance for you in the center of Moscow. There won't be any tickets or posters, but everyone will come.' That performance took place in April 1975 in the October Hall of the House of Unions. There was a huge crowd, and they went crazy when we came on stage. We had invited singers from villages to perform with us, and people loved it. After the show, this person who had organized it asked me, "Okay, did you like it?' I said, 'Yes.' And he said, 'Well, then let's do it again.' The next time, it was in a huge hall in the Polytechnic Museum. Again, there were no tickets, no posters. He said, 'Don't worry; the hall will be full.' We walked on stage, and the hall was packed. This ad hoc administrator started proposing more and more engagements. I began to wonder, who's paying for all of this? Who's behind it? I started to investigate, and I found out that the man who had been helping us was from the 'organs' [as the KGB was called].

"I still don't understand why, but the KGB did a lot of things like this in the 1970s. They supported avant-garde art. Maybe because they needed to provide a way for people to let off steam; they needed for the intelligentsia to feel that there was an unofficial place where they could go. After we stopped working with the KGB man, we didn't have any performances for a long time. Suddenly, it looked as if no one was interested in us. We had two choices: either stop or find work for the group. Some friends arranged a meeting with the head of RosKonsert — the Russian Concert Agency. He invited us to work as an opening act for Valentina Tolkunova. She was popular among middle-aged concertgoers. She's still singing — she performs Soviet songs, a kind of suburban 'easy listening' music. I said no. So we were invited to work as a separate group in RosKonsert. One of the Deputy Ministers of Culture liked us, and we became a government, state group.

"RosKonsert didn't have any theaters in Moscow. We had to travel. It was very hard. Mostly, we went to Siberia. We'd have five or six people in the audience. Why did RosKonsert need us? Because they had the philharmonia system, and the philharmonias had a plan to fulfill [the philharmonias were urban-based organizations that worked both with local and imported artists, combining the functions of artist management, booking, and presenting]. They made their money mostly from popular music (*estrada*) and Gypsies. There were a lot of Gypsy groups, and they all had black money [i.e., money earned not through an official salary, but by direct, and illegal, payments to the musicians]. It was a crazy system. But the philharmonias had to send reports that they had presented three folk groups, four pianists, one symphony orchestra, and so on. Later I realized why they liked us. The folk groups that had come before us — the Piatnitsky Choir, the Omsk Choir — they had a hundred singers, a hundred twenty singers. We were six people. We were cheap."

Some philharmonias took a literal approach to fulfilling their bureaucratic plan. As Pokrovsky recounted, his ensemble would sometimes arrive in a city where they were scheduled to perform for a week, only to be told that they wouldn't have to give any of those performances. The philharmonia would simply sign off on the ensemble's appearance for the benefit of the central administration in Moscow. "They'd tell us that we were free to do as we liked but that we had to stay in the region for the duration of the engagement. Mostly that kind of thing happened in Siberia. It was great for us. We got a salary. We could support ourselves — barely; we earned 70 or 80 rubles each a month. And during all that free time, we'd go to villages; we'd record and we'd sing, and then we'd go back to Moscow. We got to places where we never would have had the money to go. No one wanted to go to such places. We wanted to. We were happy to go there. Sometimes we gave performances right in the villages. For probably three years, we worked that way. It was terrible for our pride, but we got fantastic material, and we worked together."

When the philharmonias did actually put on a concert, they cared little whether or not there was an audience. "We'd have an official performance and no one would come. But the next day, we'd arrange a performance for students in a conservatory or university or college. Students knew about us already. We had discussions, and we started to use the time that we spent in towns to teach students how to work with folksingers. We had expeditions with local students; we started to create groups like our group. Everyone wanted to sing like us. There might have been only five or six people in the audience at our performances, but those five or six people always loved it. Usually one or two would say, 'Okay, teach me how to do it. We've never heard anything like this.' "

"By 1980 there were already a lot of groups like ours throughout Russia. Even in Moscow and Leningrad. Then we started to notice that if we came a second time to the same town, we'd have a full house. We started to become famous without the image of being a prohibited group. We worked hard to teach in those years. We created folk groups. A lot of people came to us. If we had two days, we'd spend two days teaching them. We didn't teach them to sing just the way we sang; we taught them some basic things; how to find material in their own particular region. We created a new kind of person: a singing folklorist. That's how the youth folklore movement started at that time. By the early 1980s, there were thousands of groups who sang their own material based on our principles. It was the best time for us as a concert group. We were on television almost every week. We recorded our first disc. We were known not only in Russia, but throughout the Soviet Union. Georgian groups, Lithuanian groups, Estonian groups, Moldavian groups took after us — it wasn't just Russians. We performed for Brezhnev. Once, the Politburo invited us. Everybody knew about us."

Why was it, I asked Pokrovsky, that audiences responded so strongly to his performances? After all, there was no lack of smartly costumed, precisely choreographed, musically polished folk song and dance troupes on the Russian touring circuit.

"At that time, we were the only professional group that introduced our own culture to the audience as serious culture. It wasn't just folk culture that people were reacting to. It was the fact that we were presenting the culture of this country. Before, what was supported and what was put on the stage as serious culture was something that looked or sounded Russian, but was really just a Russian variant of Western culture. Shostakovich, Prokofiev, Tchaikovsky, and Rachmaninov were European composers who worked in Russia and of course used the material of Russia. But they worked according to the rules of academic European music. In their own way, the big state folk song and dance troupes were the same. By contrast, we were showing something that was born in Russia; something that had roots in Russia. And most important — we didn't sing *Russian* folk songs. We sang Smolensk songs, Belgorod songs, Don Cossack songs. The intelligentsia wouldn't have accepted us if we had presented Russian music merely as 'Russian.' We — and our audiences — were very far from being nationalists."

What did Pokrovsky mean by "presenting Russian music merely as 'Russian'?"

" 'Russian' folk song is either an abstraction or an artificial creation.

There are many different types of songs that exist in different local population groups. Some of them might be older than Russia. What's important about these songs is that they're from Arkhangelsk, or Riazan. "Russian" folk songs became a creation of composers, who wrote or adopted melodies to present, as it were, the Russian people to the Russian people. When we started our work, we were surprised that those artificial folk songs — songs like "Stenka Razin" — were the only kind of songs that most people associated with Russian village life. A lot of people told me that they had always hated Russian folk music. Of course they hated it, because the music they knew was all artificial."

Pokrovsky's reimagination of "Russian" folk music as a congeries of regional styles and repertories was indeed a key element in his program of revivalism. But unlike the state-sponsored displays of choreographed musical diversity often seen at public festivals or on state holidays — whose goal was to affirm Soviet-style "Friendship among Peoples" and in which, ironically, regional differences largely melted away before the overwhelming, homogenizing force of a Russian-Soviet national folk style — Pokrovsky's performances evolved from a fascination with musical diversity for its own sake. It was Pokrovsky's disinterested embrace of authentic regionalism that more politically oriented cultural activists, both in the Russian Federation and in the colonized republics, later transformed and enlisted in the service of movements for the recognition of a range of "national" and ethnic cultural identities. Pokrovsky, for his part, kept his politics low-key. If his performances were not exactly an embodiment of "art for art's sake," at least he allowed his art to speak for itself.

On 25 January 1982, however, Pokrovsky's political disinterestedness dissolved, and the parabolic rise of his career came to a sudden halt. It was on that day that Pokrovsky interrupted a concert in the Novosibirsk opera house to speak his mind to the audience, and with that brief, impromptu speech, effectively cast himself back into the ranks of artistic unofficialdom from which he had slowly emerged over the preceding decade. "I had walked around town and seen that the foodstores were empty," Pokrovsky said. "I came for the rehearsal, and the Siberian People's Choir was rehearsing. I found it impossible to watch and listen to their artificial music. I'd just returned from an expedition to the Russian north where, in the name of economic productivity, they were destroying 'economically unproductive' villages. They'd cut off electricity, close the school, and take away the store. And that was it. People had to leave.

"I'll never forget going to the village where [the folklorist] Gippius recorded wonderful material in 1929. He sent me to compare what they were singing there in 1982. It was a rich, huge village in Arkhangelsk Region. We walked there — eight hours or more; there was no transportation. We arrived, and we had a feeling that something was wrong, but we couldn't figure out what. There was a strange sound. You know how an empty house sounds when the wind blows through it. There were huge new buildings, and they were all dark. We saw just one light in one window in one house. We went and looked in the window. Two old women were sitting at the table with a bottle of *samaogonka* [moonshine], drinking and talking. We knocked and went inside. 'What are you doing here?' they asked. 'Why did you come?' 'We came from Moscow to record songs,' I replied. One woman fell down on the floor and cried; she got absolutely hysterical. She started swearing. She calmed down after some time, and we talked, and she explained that the two of them were the only residents of that village. It was a destroyed village; everyone had left. It was autumn already, and one of the women was going to go soon to Arkhangelsk to be with her son. The other woman didn't have any relatives, so she had to stay. And she said, 'I will die this winter. There's no store. The closest village is eight hours.' So it was farewell night for them. That's what I saw; and not once.

"At our concert in Novosibirsk, there were four thousand or more people in the audience. It was at the height of our popularity. In the middle of the concert, I gave a speech from the stage. I said that we had to start to fight the Soviet power, or this country would be dead. Before, there had been the question, would culture die in the USSR; and I said, now we had the question, would the country die? Because culture had already died. And I said, there's only one question: will we destroy them, or will they destroy us? The next day, the ensemble was prohibited, I was immediately fired from Ros-Konsert, and for the first time in many years, I met with the KGB again.

"They called me. The man I met with wasn't terrible. He talked to me, and I told him, 'I'm not an enemy of the government; I just travel a lot and I see things. You're killing people. It has to stop.' He said, 'Okay, just write an explanation; say that you were angry; write that you didn't want to say what you said; that you wanted to say something different, but suddenly, it just came out.' I wasn't a hero. I wrote that paper. My friends advised me that the best thing one can do in such circumstances is to get sick. While you are sick, no one can touch you, especially if you're in the hospital. So a doctor whom I knew put me in the hospital. Again, I don't understand. The Deputy Minister of Culture yelled at me. The RosKonsert people yelled at me. But the KGB man didn't yell at me. He just said, 'You were stupid. You shouldn't do such things. We know your record. You didn't do these kinds of things before.'

"After that, we stopped performing. Some of the musicians left, because we didn't have any income. I tried to get a job in one of the houses of folk arts where I'd been invited to organize a folklore club. But when I showed up there, they said, 'You know, we checked, and you don't have the right education. You're not a folklorist. So you can't work here.' But we were invited to work in the movie *Farewell to Matyora* [a dramatization of Valentin Rasputin's short story by the same name, about a Siberian village that is evacuated and flooded to make way for a hydroelectric project]. I was invited to work with the Malii Theater in Leningrad. A lot of artists supported the ensemble and gave us some opportunity to have work and earn money. The Central Committee discussed our case and ordered that all recordings made by the ensemble on television and radio had to be erased. You won't find any television film of our ensemble made before 1982. But when the order came to the radio, a friend there took all our tapes and secretly copied them.

"The prohibition against my performances didn't continue for long — maybe a year, or less. They allowed me to go to Siberia, or to Central Asia. We couldn't perform in Moscow, but we didn't care about that. We started our Academy of Folklore. It was like it was back at the beginning with RosKonsert. We went to small towns and we'd sit around for six days in a small-town hotel without any money, and we couldn't leave, and couldn't have performances; still, the philharmonias needed us for their reports.

I asked, "Even though you were prohibited, you went on tour?"

"The Ensemble wasn't exactly prohibited. Our recordings were erased. You couldn't find our LP in stores; you couldn't see us on television. But we could go to Buryatia [an autonomous republic in southern Siberia, east of

Lake Baikal] and perform in some village, or maybe even in Ulan-Ude [Buryatia's capital]. What was officially necessary was that I no longer be an employee of RosKonsert.

"Little by little, we came back from the edge toward the center. RosKonsert took us in again, and we started to sing in larger cities. But we were prohibited from going abroad, and even as late as 1987 we caused a scandal by singing religious music on the stage. Officially we were supposed to be a folk ensemble, but we gave a concert of sacred music in the museum at the Andronikov Monastery [in Moscow]. When we left the hall, it had been surrounded by KGB men. The director of the museum was reprimanded for inviting us to perform.

"Our rehabilitation was complete by 1988. That's the year that I won the State Prize [formerly the Stalin Prize, the USSR's second-most prestigious state award for achievement in the arts and sciences] for my work with the ensemble and our efforts to preserve Russia's folk culture. It was a kind of victory over the souvenir ensembles that presented Potemkin village folk culture. They said that we sing with this awful sound; that we try to bring onto the stage something that isn't culture — something that's appropriate in a kitchen or in a forest, but not on a stage. For those people, it was a scandal that I won the State Prize."

In the factious social world of glasnost-era Russia, Pokrovsky's award and the official approval it conveyed for his brand of cultural preservation and revival made him a lightning rod for fulminating nativist and nationalist political sentiments. Pokrovsky recalled one of the first jarring episodes: "It was in Moscow, at the House of Artists. We were performing a mixed program of folk and sacred music that included a spiritual song composed for us by Schnittke on a text of Pushkin. When we began the Schnittke, there was loud foot-stomping in the audience. And then a note was passed up to the stage: 'How come you aren't ashamed to sing this music; it's twice not Russian.' What the note-writer meant was that Schnittke is of German and Jewish descent and Pushkin was part black. I got angry and said from the stage that it was a shame to talk like this and write these notes, and we had a fight. It turned out that those people — there probably weren't more than ten of them who stomped their feet — were from Pamiat' ["Memory" — one of the most visible ultranationalist and anti-Semitic organizations of the late 1980s].

"That kind of thing has made me feel uncomfortable about performing here [in Russia], and in fact, I mostly stopped performing here for some time. What it meant was, okay, the Pamiat' people didn't accept our performing Schnittke, but they accepted everything else. They accepted us as their own. It's true that I trained a lot of singers, and some of them became part of the nationalist movement, and they sing our songs. There are folk groups who are members of Pamiat'. There are Orthodox music groups and Don Cossack groups that are extremely nationalistic. I don't want to be part of it, but people associate me with that movement. I'm in a hard position, because if I say, 'I'm singing wonderful Russian folk songs; our culture lost them, and we are trying to get them back; and some people are guilty and I fought these people for a long time before perestroika, and we won, and now Russia can sing these songs freely; you know, about seventy percent would take that as an anti-Semitic remark. You have to be really careful to explain your position to people, or they'll understand it wrong, and that's why I stopped performing here as much. It was a lot easier in the time when we were just thinking about freedom of expression, about being able to sing, about being able to go abroad. Ironically, the more freedom people got, the more nationalistic they became."

I pressed Pokrovsky on what distinguished his group's performance of Cossack songs from a nationalist group's performance. "When your ensemble performs Cossack songs, you dress in Cossack uniforms and your actors carry swords," I said.[3]

"You have to look at the context of our Cossack songs, the swords, the uniforms. We sing Cossack songs along with other kinds of songs. For us, the uniforms are simply costumes that we use to represent Cossacks. We don't wear the uniforms for an entire performance; sometimes just one singer wears a uniform and carries a sword. In dressing up like Cossacks and singing their songs, we're not trying to suggest that we're part of their independence movement. By contrast, the Cossack groups tend to have a small repertory; they sing only Cossack songs, and only songs that represent what they call "simple people." Their music is mostly *khorovod*s — dance music with swords. We have one piece like that in our repertory."

The one Cossack *khorovod* that Pokrovsky had in mind had served as a kind of theme song in the early years of his ensemble. It is called "Open the Door of My Prison," and a translation of the text goes as follows:

Open the door of my prison
Give me the brightness of the day
Give me a grey horse and a girl with black eyebrows
The horse runs in the open field
The girl with the black eyebrows sits in the tower
But in the jail the window is high
And the iron door is locked
Around it are stone walls
Beyond the high walls
Nothing is visible
Beyond the walls, I only hear
Through even steps
The quiet pacing of the guard

"It's a powerful song and a wonderful melody," said Pokrovsky. "They [the Cossack groups] sing it because it's an energetic, militaristic dance. They can show their aggression and their energy. They don't care about the feelings of the hero who is sitting in prison. They don't care about the ideas of freedom for everyone, which led us to perform it. This is the song I sang at the opera theater in Novosibirsk after my spontaneous speech. I told the audience that we were going to sing a song that expressed all of my feelings and all of their feelings. We still sing 'Open the Door of My Prison.' It would be wrong to stop singing it just because nationalists also sing it. And besides, it works against the nationalists if I perform it. We perform it in the context of other music where you can hear that it's part of a broader cultural tradition."

Switching to Russian, Pokrovsky tried to clarify the difference between his own folk music revivalism and that of the nationalist groups to which he is opposed. "I'm not one of these people who is carrying the banner of *narodnost'* [nationalism]," he said. "I identify myself not with *narodnost'*, but with *narodnichestvo* [populism]."

For Russians, to speak about *narodnost'* or *narodnichestvo* is to enter a semantic minefield. Both terms share the polysemous root *narod* (people, common people, folk, ethnic group, ethnic nation), and both have long served rulers and revolutionaries alike as key words in the formulation of social ideas and political ideologies. The particular connotations that Pokrovsky had in mind stem from the use of the terms in the middle third of the nineteenth century. *Narodnost'* was the third element of the trinitarian credo proclaimed in 1833 by Czar Nicholas I's minister of education, Count Uvarov, as the basis of official state ideology: *pravoslavie, samoderzhavie, narodnost'* (Orthodoxy, autocracy, nationality) — later known as the doctrine of Official Nationality.[4] Viewed through the filter of democratic ideas, Uvarov's *narodnost'* was reactionary: it defended serfdom, stressed obedience to the czar, and condoned mass illiteracy as a means of preventing social unrest. And while Uvarov's was not the only mid-nineteenth-century gloss on *narodnost'*,[5] his adoption of the term left it irrevocably tainted — at least in the minds of liberal thinkers — by its association with feudal monarchism and anti-Semitism.

Narodnichestvo, by contrast, is most strongly associated with the democratic, populist spirit of the 1860s, the age of Alexander II. Pokrovsky finds the roots of his own musical *narodnichestvo* in that of the iconoclastic composers known as the "mighty handful" (*moguchaya kuchka*) — Mussorgsky, Borodin, Balakirev, Cui, Rimsky-Korsakov — whose legacy as populists (*narodniki*) remains strong in Russia even as Western music historians have begun to expose a darker side of some of that populism.[6] "These composers — plus Glinka and Tchaikovsky — are often called Russian nationalist composers because they used folk melodies in their compositions," Pokrovsky said. "But melodies of what nationality? They used folk melodies of different nations.[7] They were influenced by the artistic values of Romanticism, so of course they drew on folklore, folk songs, and history. But official *narodnost'* and *narodnichestvo* were enemies. *Narodniki* went to prison because they were against Orthodoxy, autocracy, and nationality. Now we're seeing the restoration of at least some elements of the imperial system. And that creates the same kind of opposition between nationalists who support the imperial system and populists who are against it."

The distinction between *narodnost'* and *narodnichestvo* — nationalism and populism — does not, however, fully convey the spectrum of political sentiments with which folk music revivalists in contemporary Russia have allied themselves. And in a conversation with Pokrovsky that took place in late 1994, several months after our first lengthy discussions about music and nationalism, Pokrovsky emphasized that he was beginning to feel crowded in his self-professed *narodnichestvo* by Russian populism's darker side. "At present, there's not only an opposition between groups like mine and the Potemkin village ensembles that try to present the image of happy and strong Russians singing and dancing in the healthy and wealthy Russian state. There are also ensembles doing authentic folk music that represent what is essentially a fascist position. They claim to represent musically what they call 'simple people,' the real *narod*. They say that the music I do is too sophisticated; that the *narod* doesn't understand it. It's true that my idea all along has been to present the art of what you could call the village intelligentsia. We sing a lot of traditional polyphony, like the *protiazhnie pesni* [long songs], which are quite subtle and complex.

"The fascist groups don't try to use sophisticated genres. For example, for a nationalist, epic is a natural genre. It deals with larger-than-life heroes who move in huge spaces and fight ugly enemies. St. George, the dragon slayer, is one of those heroes. And if you put together St. George, people carrying icons, and Glinka's chorus from *A Life for the Czar,* the way they did in the televised Independence Day celebration, you get a kind of epic. But it's fake epic. It's just as fake as the politicized epics that were created during Stalin's time. Russian music has a great tradition of epic songs, but they're structurally sophisticated and complex, and the nationalist groups avoid them in favor of simpler forms, like the Don Cossack *khorovod:* dance music with swords."

Notwithstanding the diversity of their political messages, the raft of ensembles currently reviving some version of Russian folk music shares one salient characteristic: their performances are about more than music; in fact, in many cases, they seem first and foremost to express political values and only secondarily aesthetic ones. Furthermore, those political values are encoded not so much in music itself—that is, in a musical text—as in its context. For example, if it is true, as Pokrovsky claims, that the performance of one and the same song—for example, "Open the Door of My Prison"—can be "nationalist" in one case but not in another, then this nationalism would seem to be not in the song, but in what, broadly speaking, comprises the song's performance, in all of the various cues that performers provide to guide their listeners' interpretation: where and with whom they perform, their choice of repertory, costuming, staging, and so on. Nationalism "in" folk music is a gloss, not an essential musical attribute.

Could one imagine a Russia in which folk music were free just to be itself? To be reconnected to the land and to the village life from which it sprang? Traditional village music gives no heed to nationality and takes no interest in hypostatizing through music concepts like *narodnost'* or democracy. Anyone who has worked with folk music and folk music texts knows that the imagery, the toponyms, the dramatis personae tend to be either highly localized or highly universalized; the latter occurs, for example, in much Russian folk music in the hagiolatry of the major Orthodox saints. Authentic folk singers don't sing songs of the People, but rather, of the people.

Folk music becomes ethnocentric and nationalistic only when it is removed from its traditional context or used within that context as an instrument of culture policy. For example, in the geographical region known as Poles'e (Полесье in Russian and Belorussian spelling) or Polissia (Полисся in Ukrainian spelling) — a territory that extends over the intersection of present-day Russia, Belarus, and Ukraine — village musicians have long performed a largely unitary repertory of traditional songs and dances. In the local traditional consciousness, this body of music is unmarked by national identity: musicians do not differentiate between items that are "Russian," "Belorussian," or "Ukrainian." During the Soviet era, however, when folk music, like other aspects of culture (most notably, language — witness the different spellings of Poles'e/Polissia), became an artifact of nationalities policies, musicians suddenly learned that they were performing not simply calendar songs or wedding songs, but "Russian" wedding songs, "Belorussian" calendar songs, and so on. The former Soviet Union is full of examples of such musical territorializations and reterritorializations.[8] Thus, the transformation of traditional music into national music can occur both in the form of state culture policy handed down from above, as was standard in the Soviet Union, and under the wing of populist movements that emerge from below.

In his own way, Dmitri Pokrovsky has also transformed traditional Russian music. During an era when the politically mandated demand for easily accessible popular musical forms made bowdlerized and composed folklore — or fakelore, as it is has come to be called by American folklorists — into a Soviet institution (not that the music was all bad; talented composers and arrangers turned out some indisputably first-rate songs), Pokrovsky pointed the way back to the more complex and demanding musical language that is the true legacy of Russia's folk heritage. Perhaps only a revivalist musician could have accomplished this, for Pokrovsky, like the Soviet bureaucrats and the nationalists whose cultural visions he has opposed, is at root an outsider to Russia's village culture. His efforts to revive and reconstruct the authentic performance traditions of Russia's villages are in themselves the product of an ideology that has as much to do with the values of contemporary transnational urban culture as it does with the intrinsic interest of village art and music. What distinguishes Pokrovsky, however, from some other revivalists is that his revivalist efforts have never seemed a response to political opportunism or cultural chic. He has stayed a course that has brought him both fame and opprobrium, and Pokrovsky, for his part, has remained rather oblivious to both.

In our last conversation, Dmitri Pokrovsky expressed guarded hope for the future of his musical work in Russia. "I'm a professional musician and a folklorist, not a social worker or a politician," Pokrovsky said. "The folk music revival has been until now largely social and political. People felt that if we organized a lot of folk groups to perform authentic village music in towns, we would save this culture. My position has been that such groups wouldn't change anything. They wouldn't help. If you want to get this culture back, you have to support authentic singing in the places where it existed: in the villages." There, no less than in the cities of Russia, tradition is no longer ineluctably "passed down." Rather, it is, broadly speaking, a choice. Village people may choose to learn and sing folk songs just as they may choose to learn and sing many other kinds of music accessible on radio, television, and cassette. It is that choice, Pokrovsky thinks, that may ultimately save the culture of the village. "Being able to choose a tradition puts it in a much stronger position than when there is no choice, because when people don't have a choice, or when they feel that tradition is holding them back, they try to leave it. That's what happened in the 1930s. But these days, village people don't tend to see traditional culture and technological culture as competing. They see them as two essential parts of their lives, and many of them want both.

"At the same time that you support authentic singing in villages, you have to develop an audience in the towns that hears folk music as music, as art, not as a statement about politics. Even within the last several months (of 1994), that has started to happen for us. We have a corporate patron—a

Moscow bank, that supports our performances. At first, they wanted to know each time we sang, 'What's in it for us?' They'd ask, 'How many times will you mention us during the concert? How big will our name be on the publicity posters?' Now, they're more relaxed. It's more like American corporate philanthropy. They're aware that you can't look for immediate results. It's more about image."

"We're beginning to perform more and more again in Russia. Our concerts are in big halls, and they're always sold out. The big, government-supported, imperial groups like the Piatnitsky Choir are still performing, but we don't feel that we're competing with them. There's an open cultural marketplace now. We have our own audience, our own field of activity, our own connections. More and more, we're being viewed not as a Russian nationalist group but as a group that's presenting Russian music. There's a world of difference there. Russian audiences are also becoming more mature, more like audiences in the West. And what's strange for Russia, they are beginning to judge music as music, art as art."

Epilogue

Dimitri Pokrovsky died suddenly on 29 June 1996 in Moscow. He was fifty-two years old. As this book goes to press, the fate of his ensemble is uncertain, but Pokrovsky's loss has made only too clear the extent to which his performances of "folk" music represented an artistic vision as personal as it was powerful.

Notes

1. Richard Taruskin, in his important article "Stravinsky and the Painters" (1986) has shown that folk art and folk music were central influences in the development of Russian modernism.

2. The *dom narodnogo tvorchestva* system and the parallel *dom khudozhestvennoi samo-deiatel'nosti* (house of amateur arts — literally, house of artistic do-it-yourselfism) run by the trade union organization both belong to the domain of *kultprosvet,* as it is known in the lexicon of Soviet-era acronyms (short for *kul'turnoe prosveshenie,* cultural enlightenment). Cultural enlightenment in the form of amateur arts activities both for workers (the

function of the Union of Trade Unions' houses of amateur arts) and for peasants (the function of the Ministry of Culture's houses of folk art) remains a potent vestige of the early communists' vision of a society oriented toward the interests of workers and peasants. Both varieties of *kultprosvet* continue in post-Soviet Russia (as well as in other parts of the CIS), supported in many cases by local government or, in the case of the trade union houses, by individual business enterprises. For a useful discussion of *samodeiatel'nost'*, see Mark Slobin's *Subcultural Sounds: Micromusics of the West* (Slobin 1993: 57–60).

3. In prerevolutionary Russia, Cossacks comprised a semiautonomous military estate that served the czar in return for the granting of lands and other privileges. Cossack men served in the military for twenty years, and were renowned for their fighting skills. After the Revolution, several different hosts of Cossacks, including the Don Cossacks, were granted their own autonomous regions within Russia.

4. In Benedict Anderson's important study of the "imagined community" of nationality, *Imagined Communities: Reflections on the Origin and Spread of Nationalism*, the original Russian term for Uvarov's "nationality" is misidentified as *natsionalnost* (1991: 87). This error unfortunately skews the discussion that follows, in which Anderson points out that the concept of "nationality" was "quite novel" in mid-nineteenth-century Russia. In fact, the peculiarly Russian concept of *narodnost'* means something quite different to a Russian than *natsionalnost'*, and has much older roots.

5. In *The Icon and the Axe*, James Billington notes that both Slavophiles and Westernizers idealized *narodnost'* as a "regenerative life force in history": "*Narodnost'* for all of these visionary reformers meant neither nationality as it did for Uvarov nor popularity in the Western electoral sense. It meant the unspoiled wisdom of the noble savage as revealed in the newly collected popular proverbs of Vladimir Dal or the folk songs and poems of Alexis Kol'tsov" (1966: 324). At the same time, however, romantic nationalists had a more visionary and reformist gloss on *narodnost'* in the notion of an unspoiled "spirit of the people" that could serve as a regenerative life force in history (324).

6. See, for example, section 8 in Richard Taruskin's chapter "Sorochintsï Fair Revisited," in *Musorgsky: Eight Essays and an Epilogue* (Taruskin 1993).

7. Richard Taruskin discusses the multinational nationalism of nineteenth-century Russian composers at some length in an article entitled "Some Thoughts on the History and Historiography of Russian Music" (Taruskin 1984).

8. For an example from Central Asia, see my article "The Reterritorialization of Culture in the New Central Asian States: A Report from Uzbekistan" (Levin 1993). See also a kindred article that discusses folk music and national consciousness in Poland by William Noll (Noll 1991).

MICHAEL BECKERMAN

Kundera's Musical Joke *and "Folk" Music in*

Czechoslovakia, 1948–?

In his novel *Nesnesitelna lehkost byti* (*The Unbearable Lightness of Being,* 1967), Milan Kundera writes about Tereza's love for the country:

Why was the word "idyll" so important for Tereza? Raised as we are on the mythology of the Old Testament we might say that an idyll is an image that has remained with us like a memory of Paradise: life in Paradise was not like following a straight line to the unknown; it was not an adventure. It moved in a circle among known objects. Its monotony bred happiness, not boredom.

As long as people lived in the country, in nature, surrounded by domestic animals, in the bosom of regularly recurring seasons, they retained at least a glimmer of that paradisiac idyll. That is why Tereza, when she met the chairman of the collective farm at the spa, conjured up an image of the countryside (a countryside she had never lived in or known) that she found enchanting. It was her way of looking back, back to Paradise. (295–96)

This passage contains many of the qualities associated with the *pastoral:* the image of time as circular rather than dynamic, the recollection of a Golden Age or Paradise. When seen through the eyes of the hero, Tereza, we realize also that pastorals are largely dreamed up by city folk. This idyll, in Kundera's view, was not only a general category of experience, but had distinctly political ramifications. As he put it:

Life in the country was the only escape open to them, because only in the country was there a constant deficit of people and a surplus of living accommodations. No one bothered to look into the political past of people willing to go off and work in the fields or woods; no one envied them. (281–82)

This attitude toward the countryside is an important subtext in Czech literature where, from the rollicking ironies of *Good Soldier Švejk* to Vaculík's Kafkaesque *The Guinea Pigs,* it serves as a place of escape, refuge, and physical and mental health, in stark opposition to the corrupt, venal, and filthy city.

If the countryside itself was considered, almost unequivocally, a place of refuge from the pressures of the totalitarian state, the musical products of those country people — what has been called folk song and folk music until recent deconstructions — had a richly ambiguous role in Czech society under communism.[1] Indeed, the relationship might almost seem a metaphor for the manner in which the state and the people enveloped each other in their strange dance over almost a half century. For, in brief, the State supported folk music and folk festivals in an attempt to show, quite simply, that in this "people's paradise" the folk, at least, were alive and well. Yet in a weird, almost parasitic twist, many people came to use the sounds and symbols of folk music as a means to escape from the State, in much the same manner as Tereza fled to the countryside. This does not imply that folk music, like jazz or hard rock, had a revolutionary quality; it was both more and less than that. It served for many as a kind of spiritual sustenance, a healthy place to turn to and, as I shall argue, a substance of remarkable purity.

Anyone exploring the relationship between folk music and the State is extremely fortunate that one of the finest novels written in Czechoslovakia in the 1960s has the issue at its core. In his novel *Žert, (The Joke)*, Milan Kundera, himself the son of a prominent Brno musicologist, deals with the subject with impressive breadth and depth.[2] After citing and discussing pertinent passages from the novel, we shall seek to open our lens and introduce several "case studies," in an attempt to illuminate the context of music in Czechoslovakia from 1948 to just after the "Velvet" revolution of 1989.

First published in 1967, just at the time of the Prague Spring thaw, the narrative in *The Joke* is sustained by Ludvik, the primary protagonist, and three other characters (like Ludvik, they are identified only by a single name), each of whom tells part of the story in their own words. The "joke" of the title involves a humorous postcard Ludvik sends to his girlfriend. Despite his ardent faith in the Communist Party, he is nonetheless drummed out of it in a particularly humiliating way for this action, resulting in a chain of events and relationships. Less humorous, of course, is the fact that Ludvik has returned to his native village to seduce and humiliate the wife of the man who had him expelled.[3]

Ludvik is a Moravian — that is, a citizen of the central province of the Czechoslovak state — something that has symbolic value in Czech culture. If the countryside in general, and folk songs in particular, represented a kind of safe haven, the Moravian countryside had an even more explicit and powerful identity. Both its physical position in the middle of the country and its profusion of small and colorful villages gave it a special niche in the Czech consciousness. It is no coincidence, for example, that Dvořák titled his first commercially successful work *Moravian Duets,* something that would seem piquant and exotic not only to the Germans but to the residents of Prague as well. Perhaps the most telling manifestation of Moravia's role is a kind of throwaway line by the poet Skacel, suggesting that the (nonexistent) Moravian national anthem was simply the pause between the Czech and the Slovak anthems, a comment framing Moravia forever as a mythical and forgotten land. With all these associations, it followed that Moravian folk songs were considered particularly pure, springing from the soil.

In Kundera's novel, it is the character of Jaroslav, an amateur ethnographer and director of a folk song ensemble, who most effectively articulates the nationalist/ethnographer's vision of Czech folk music:

During the seventeenth and eighteenth centuries the Czech nation almost ceased to exist. In the nineteenth century it was virtually reborn. Among the old European nations it was a child. True, it also had its own great past, but it was cut off from that past by a gap of two hundred years, when the Czech language retreated to the countryside, the exclusive property of the illiterate. But even in their midst it never ceased to create its own culture. A modest culture, completely hidden from the eyes of Europe. A culture of songs, fairy tales, ancient rites and customs, proverbs and sayings. The only narrow footbridge across the two-hundred-year gap. (128)

Moravian folk culture was not only different from the dominant German one, but it was quite unlike Bohemian culture to the West.

There is one passage in the novel that brilliantly describes a prevalent attitude toward Moravian music. I would like to look at this closely because it is unique in any novel for at least two reasons: it mounts a serious musical argument, quoting such composer-ethnographers as Bartók and Janáček, and it uses musical notation.

It is a kind of speech made by Jaroslav in response to Ludvik's seeming indifference to the songs. It both frames the quintessential advocacy of Moravian folk songs and cements their pastoral quality:

Prague musicologists have long claimed that the European folk song originated in the Baroque. Village musicians who played and sang in the orchestras of the great houses brought the musical culture of the nobility into the life of the people. From this they concluded that the folk song is not an original artistic form. It is merely a derivative of formal music.

Now that may have been the case in Bohemia, but the songs we sing in Moravia can't be explained in this way. Look at their tonality. Baroque music was written in major and minor keys. Our songs are sung in modes that court orchestras never dreamed of!

For example, the Lydian. The scale with the raised fourth. It always evokes in me nostalgia for the pastoral idylls of antiquity. I see the pagan Pan and hear his pipes. [musical example]

Baroque and Classical music paid fanatical homage to the orderliness of the major seventh. It knew no other path to the tonic than through the discipline of the *leading tone*. It was frightened of the minor seventh that stepped up to the tonic from a major second below. And it is precisely this minor seventh that I love in our folk songs, whether it belongs to the Aeolian, Dorian, or Mixolydian. For its melancholy and pensiveness. And because it abjures the foolish scamper toward the key note with which everything ends, both song and life: [musical example]

But there are songs in tonalities so curious that it is impossible to designate them by any of the so-called ecclesiastical modes. They take my breath away: [musical example]

Moravian songs are, in terms of tonality, unimaginably varied. Their musical thought is mysterious. They'll begin in minor, and in major, hesitate among different keys. Often when I have to harmonize them, I just do not know how I am to understand the key.

And they are similarly ambiguous when it comes to rhythm. Especially the long-drawn-out ones that are not used for dancing. Bartók called them *parlando* songs. Their rhythm cannot be written down in our notation system. Or let me put it differently. From the vantage point of our notation, all folk singers sing their songs in a rhythm that is imprecise and wrong. (130–131)

We may note all the verbal codes that qualify the music. The Lydian fourth evokes "nostalgia for the pastoral idylls of antiquity." While the major and minor systems are seen in terms of "discipline," and the leading tone ends "both song and life," the lowered seventh is notable for its "melancholy and pensiveness" and is, by implication, immortal. The terms used to describe "classical" music are negative — it is "fanatical," "frightened," and even "foolish" — while the words used to describe the Moravian songs are positive and richly textured: "curious," "unimaginably varied," "mysterious," "ambiguous," "complex."

As Michael Heim notes, there was a great enthusiasm for folk music just after the revolution: "Stalin called for art that was socialist in content and national in form, and folk music — with new, propaganda-inspired lyrics — flourished" (1972: 48). The character in *The Joke* who illustrates this point of view is Zemanek, also the man responsible for throwing Ludvik out of the party. Unlike Jaroslav, who is deeply in love with the Moravian village music and culture, Zemanek appears to us as an actor playing a role inspired by his love affair with the Communist Party, standing for all the party faithful who lent their support to village music when it appeared to be part of Communist experience. Ludvik, whose attitude toward folk music lies between Jaroslav's passion and Zemanek's posturing is deeply critical of the latter:

For Zemanek loved singing Moravian folk songs; at the time it was very fashionable to sing folk songs, and to do so not like schoolchildren but in a rough voice with arm thrust upwards, that is, in the guise of a *man of the people* whose mother had brought him into the world under a cimbalom during a village dance. Being the only genuine Moravian in the Natural Sciences Division had won me certain privileges: on every special occasion, at meetings, celebrations, on the First of May, I was always asked to take up my clarinet and join two or three other amateurs from among my fellow students in a makeshift Moravian band. So we had marched (clarinet, fiddle, and bass) in the May Day parade for the past two years, . . . (40)

The larger question of folklore, and the eventual ambivalence it aroused in the Czech lands in the 1960s is captured in the relationship between Ludvik and Jaroslav. Ludvik remembers Jaroslav's wedding, and with some

irony reveals the hypocrisy of those who kept the "authentic" folk movement alive, though without the church:

On top of it all, Jaroslav was a dyed-in-the-wool Moravian patriot and a folklore
expert, and he availed himself of his own wedding to satisfy his ethnographic pas-
sions by arranging the festivities around a structure of old popular customs: regional
dress, a cimbalom band, a "Patriarch" and his flowery speeches, the rite of carrying
the bride over the threshold, songs, and any number of details to fill up the day, all
reconstructed more from textbooks of ethnography than from living memory. But
one curious thing caught my attention: friend Jaroslav, the new head of a flourishing
song and dance ensemble, clung to all the old customs but (presumably mindful of
his career and obedient to atheist slogans) gave the church a wide berth, even though
a traditional wedding was unthinkable without a priest and God's blessing; he had the
"patriarch" give all the ritual speeches, but purged them of all biblical motifs, even
though it was precisely on these motifs that the imagery of the old nuptial speeches
was based. (47)

Jaroslav's wedding occurs directly after Ludvik's expulsion from the
Communist Party, and his attitude mirrors that of many intellectuals ap-
palled by the way folk music had been seized by the Party for its own
purposes. Ludvik's refusal to play at the wedding haunts Jaroslav until the
very end of the novel.

The sorrow that kept me from joining the drunken wedding party had sensitized me
to the chloroform seeping into the clear waters of these folk rituals, and when
Jaroslav asked me (as a sentimental reminder of the days when I had played in the
band with him) to grab a clarinet and sit in with the other players, I refused. I suddenly saw myself playing the last two May Day parades with Prague-born Zemanek
at my side singing and dancing and waving his arms. I was unable to take the clarinet
and all this folkloric din filled me with disgust, disgust, disgust . . . (47)

This disgust was felt by many intellectuals who had originally embraced
village music. Even though the Party continued to support folk festivals
throughout the 1950s and early 1960s, there was a significant erosion of
support by the 1960s, especially around the time of the Prague Spring. The
despair felt by many in the folk song movement is articulated by Jaroslav.
Jaroslav is deeply involved with the presentation of an ancient Moravian
folk ritual known as the Ride of Kings, but local monies have dried up.

The meeting was devoted to last-minute preparations for the Ride of the Kings. The whole thing was a mess. The District National Committee was starting to cut back on our budget. Only a few years ago it had provided lavish subsidies for folk events. Now we had to support the District Committee. If the Youth League had no way of attracting members anymore, why not let it take over the Ride of the Kings? That would boost its prestige. (126)

It is not merely that there is diminishing State support for folk music, but in addition that folk music, because of the manner in which the Party co-opted it, is becoming a subject for the most vicious public ridicule. Jaroslav is humiliated by an experience in Prague:

I went to one of those little theaters, the kind that started springing up in the early sixties and quickly became the rage owing to the student humor of the young players. The show wasn't very interesting, but the songs were clever and the jazz quite good. All of a sudden the musicians donned feathered hats like the ones we wear with our folk costumes and did a takeoff on a cimbalom ensemble. They screeched and wailed, mimicking our dance steps and the way we throw our arms up in the air. . . . It went on for no more than a few minutes, but it had the audience rolling in the aisles. I couldn't believe my eyes. Five years ago no one would have dared make clowns of us like that. And no one would have cracked a smile. Now we're a laughingstock. How is it we're suddenly a laughingstock? (126)

Jaroslav begins to suspect that the Ride of Kings will be a disaster. He is interviewed by a woman from the radio and asked to talk about how successful the Ride will be. Jaroslav is suddenly himself filled with disgust, especially when he comments on the artificiality that has infected the music he loves:

I had an impulse to tell her exactly what I thought. That the Ride would be worse than in past years. That every year folk art loses more supporters. That the authorities had lost interest as well. That it was nearly dead. The fact that something like folk music was constantly on the radio should not delude us. What all those folk instrument bands and folk song and dance ensembles play is more like opera or operetta or light music, not folk music. A folk instrument band with a conductor, a score, and music stands! Almost symphonic orchestration! What bastardization! The music that serves you, those bands and ensembles, my dear radio reporter, is just old-style romanticism with borrowed folk melodies! Real folk art is dead, dear lady, dead. (254)

Almost as the fulfillment of Jaroslav's worst fears, the Ride of Kings turns into a complete debacle and Jaroslav is forced to acknowledge its failure:

Ear and eye alike were assaulted by confusion, everything clashed: the folklore from the loudspeakers with the folklore on horseback; the colors of the costumes and horses with the ugly browns and grays of the badly cut clothes of the spectators; the laborious spontaneity of the costumed riders with the laborious officiousness of the organizers, running around in their red armbands among the horses and people, trying to keep the chaos within bounds . . . (258)

He concludes by saying he had expected some kind of disaster but not "this sad, almost moving *forlornness* . . ." (259).

For Jaroslav, the final blow is struck when his son, who is supposed to be the King in the Ride sneaks away to "ride" in a motorcycle race in the provincial capital of Brno, leaving a friend in disguise to participate in the ceremony. When Jaroslav finds that this has been done with the complicity of his wife, he smashes the china in his house and runs out:

I left the house. The calls could still be heard across the village roofs. We have a pauper king, a righteous one. Where could I go? The streets belonged to the Ride of Kings, home belonged to Vlasta, the taverns belonged to the drunks. Where do I belong? I am the old king, abandoned and banished. A righteous pauper king without heirs. The last king.

Luckily there are fields beyond the village. A road. And ten minutes away the river Morava. I lay down on the bank. I put the violin case under my head. I lay there for a long time. (308)

Once again, the countryside, populated simply by a man and a violin, serves as a place of refuge and health. Ironically, just as Jaroslav's hopes are at their lowest ebb Ludvik rediscovers his original sense of village music. His attitude toward the Ride of Kings is antithetical to Jaroslav's:

And so, to my astonishment, the initial mistrust with which I watched the straggly departure of the Ride soon vanished and all at once I was completely enthralled by the colorful cavalcade as it slowly moved from house to house; the loudspeakers had at last fallen silent, and all I could hear . . . was the strange music of the heralds' rhymed calls.

I wanted to stand there, to close my eyes and just listen: I realized that here, in the middle of a Moravian village, I was hearing *verse,* verse in the primeval meaning of the word, verse unlike any I could ever hear on the radio or on television or on the stage, verse like a ceremonial rhythmic call on the border between speech and song . . . It was music sublime and *polyphonic:* each of the heralds declaimed in the monotone, on the same note throughout, but each on a different pitch . . . like a canon for several voices. (262–63)

A final harmony is achieved when Ludvik, under the influence of this reassessment, finally decides to sit in with Jaroslav's band. Kundera's writing at this point is particularly beautiful and focuses on the relationship between the educated awareness of the intellectual and village music:

"If the mountains were paper and the oceans ink, / If the stars were scribes, and all the world could think, / Not all their words upon words, in the event / Could come to the end of my love's testament," sang Jaroslav with the violin still at his chest, and I felt happy inside these songs . . . where sorrow is not lightness, laughter is not grimace, love is not laughable, and hatred is not timid, where people love with body and soul . . . where love is still love and pain is pain, where values are not yet devastated; and it seemed to me that inside these songs I was at home. (315–16)

In *The Joke,* Kundera captures the paradoxes and problems of maintaining folk music traditions in the modern world, particularly a world in which ideology plays such an outsized role. As we have suggested, his characters and their attitudes mirror the shifting attitudes toward folk music in Czechoslovakia from 1948 until the late sixties. Even though a good deal of folk music had been kept alive for propaganda purposes, many people like Ludvik eventually discovered its power on their own terms.

Especially compelling is Kundera's preoccupation with the pastoral and idyllic in connection with folk music. Kundera's willingness to grapple with a whole range of musical issues is impressive, but there is one interesting question that remains to be explored: what was the effect of all these issues, events, and policy shifts on the music itself? Did the music begin to show any effects from its contact with the State? While it is easy to create facile answers, it is almost impossible to be definitive without a control group. We have no idea how this music would have fared under a different system of government, but what seems to have happened fits in well with Kundera's notion of the Idyll. For the Moravian folk song, and folk song in general, became idealized and changed, and other methods of engaging idyllic worlds came into play.

I would like to pursue this question with the aid of several field studies that deal with the issue of State and music. As an outsider to the field of ethnomusicology, I might begin by expressing some caution about the "scientific" nature of these brief case studies. As with all nonrecorded descriptive encounters, they are largely undocumentable. My observations are based on notes and subsequent reflection on those notes. If the reader wishes to view them as fiction, it will in no way disturb me.

The Detva Folk Festival

One of the largest folk festivals in Czechoslovakia was held in Detva, a small village in west-central Slovakia. We attended the festival in 1977. It featured ensembles not only from the Czech Lands and Slovakia but also other Slavic countries. There are actually two Detvas, a newer town in the valley and the old village about a mile up the hill. The new town was dominated by dormitories housing many Vietnamese students who were studying welding.

We arrived before the festival began in order to talk to musicians and hear ensembles play informally. We noticed that, with much fanfare, a group of villagers were building a wooden structure over the stage. They had placed regional designs on a series of posts, which were bridged by a beribboned arch. We asked about its purpose but were only told that "it was for the festival."

When we arrived for the festival proper, we immediately saw the purpose of the structure, although we didn't yet know how it was to be used. It was the support for a huge movie screen. It remained dark until a Bulgarian women's choir appeared to sing shepherd songs. The screen lit up and suddenly we were looking at flocks of sheep on a Bulgarian hillside, sometimes with close-ups of sheep chewing, drool and all. Of course, in this case the attempt to be realistic was disastrous. Instead of producing a sense of "being there," the effect of the film was to make the wowen's choir look "false," or rather like a sound track for a film rather than the event itself.

The "staged" folk festivals held in Czechoslovakia tended to have this quality. It was not in any sense "folk music" but rather a series of performances "about folk music" or about some concept of folk music that fit the picture of it held by urbanites. We noticed that when a group of musicians remained backstage after the conclusion of the evening's "entertainment," their style of performing was considerably different.

The Deleterious Effect of Large Russian Army Ensembles

In 1990 I brought a group of students to Prague to attend the Prague Spring Music Festival and participate in a conference devoted to the works of Bohuslav Martinu. This was just after the revolution, and musicians were playing regularly on the Charles Bridge. We watched a Moravian ensemble play for a while. When they packed up, a young violist stayed behind. By chance he met a friend with a violin case. In a short while they were playing a range of South Bohemian melodies in a style I had not yet heard, simple and stark, with large numbers of open intervals. Their names were Martin and Pepik, and both of them had studied at the Prague Conservatory. Their approach to playing was an attempt to offset, as they put it, "the deleterious influence of large Russian army ensembles" on Czech folk music. They explained, as does the character Jaroslav in Kundera's novel, that choreographed folk art had almost totally replaced "real" folk art. Further, they felt that the dozens of dancers and performers stamping and screeching distracted from the music. For this reason, they have dedicated themselves to trying to revive the improvised folk art of the eighteenth century in its directness and simplicity.

"Co budeme robit brat' a" versus "Na horách na dolách"

One possible argument to be made is that the process of political and personal interaction in Czechoslovakia between 1948 and the present affected the manner in which the songs were presented: in other words, their performance style. In brief, many artists gradually created an ever more idealized sound; for all the reasons we have outlined, the folk song itself became richly pastoralized over time. A version of the song "Co budeme robit brat'a" ("What Work Shall We Do, Brothers?") recorded in 1955, a mere seven years after the Communist takeover shows a style of singing featuring harsh attacks, almost violent rhythms, and an instrumental accompaniment rich in microtones. A modern version of the South Moravian folksong "Na horách na dolách" ("In the Mountains, in the Valleys") performed by a group of musician-ethnographers from Brno shows a completely different aesthetic. The violins and clarinets have been replaced with a flute. The percussive sound of the cimbalom is now harplike, and the voice of Jožka Cerny is mellow rather than sharp.

It is, of course, not profitable to argue about which performance traditions are (more) "authentic." I think in both cases we can assume that performers and audiences felt they were playing or hearing "the real thing." We might instead label a hypothetical (no longer existent) "original" as the first tradition, and label subsequent evolutions as second, third, fourth, etc. For example, it is clear that "Na horách" is at least a kind of fourth-tradition piece. The sound has been subjected to a radical reformulation. It has become nostalgic, creamy and dreamy; there are drones where there were none before, and the flute creates a quasi-gallant series of gestures, while the oboe weaves an exotic line. It is not an insignificant fact that the drones have been added here, since they are the quintessential pastoral symbol, increasing the sense of stasis and helping to create an illusion of the circular motion of time to which Kundera refers in his novel. Thus "Na horách" is not simply a song, it is the evocation of a place and the quality of life at that place.

After the *Ples* Was Over

Like many places in Europe, the *ples* or "ball" season stretches from Shrovetide to Lent. Each year Brno University, led by the Socialist Union of Youth, sponsored a ball for all the faculty called the "Representační ples filozofické fakulty Univerzity J. E. Purkyně" (Grand Ball of the J. E. Purkyne University Faculty of Philosophy). It was a formal affair, with dance band music and great fanfare. One by one the leading figures of the faculty were led out with their partners and introduced: "And now, introducing Prof. Dr. Jaroslav Novák, Dr. Sc. and spouse."[4]

We took part in the *ples* of 1980. After several hours of dancing, the event broke up. With no signal or any acknowledgment, many people remained behind, sitting at tables in one of the darkened rooms, and sang a wide range of Moravian songs a capella for more than an hour.

Among those who remained behind there were many whom I knew to be deeply tormented. The university, supposedly a place of enlightenment, was in reality a nest of people writing reports about each other. Many of the department chairs were apparatchiks, and there was nothing even resembling intellectual freedom. The temptation to give in to morally ambiguous stands and postures was almost irresistible. However, before we judge them harshly, we may remember that American universities have known moral cowardice in their time, and there still can be places where intellectual fashion triumphs over both courage and common sense.

The large number of people involved in the singing, the way the activity seemed to unfold naturally, as well as the long time spent singing, leads to the conclusion that these songs have a special value to many of the people at the university, a shared value that has no analog in American society. I would argue that in a public sphere rendered barren and impure by the intrusive nature of the regime, the songs functioned as a repository for that great unacknowledged human longing: the need for purity. For this reason the style and selection of works performed was affected by the role it played, that of a deeply nostalgic search for a better world.

Music Bohemica and the Search for Purity

The same kind of search may be found in the sound of Musica Bohemica, one of the most successful recording groups in the Czech Republic outside of pop music. The desire to escape from the public pressures and private emptiness of the totalitarian state led to several related phenomena, in areas not nearly as dear to the regime as the activities of the folk. For example, despite the advocacy of scientific atheism for over forty years, Czechoslovakia produced an enormous number of Christmas records, tapes, and CDs.

The tradition advocated is not, like American Christmas music, a compendium of different styles and types — from "Come Emmanuel" and "Greensleeves" to "Jingle Bells," "Rudolph the Red-Nosed Reindeer," and "Jingle Bell Rock" — but a more homogenous collection from the Renaissance to the last century, richly pastoral in tone and intent. Bohemia and to a certain extent Northern Austria have always been lands of the Christmas pastoral, but this has become ever stronger in Bohemia and Moravia. If we may consider Christmas a kind of chronological parallel to the countryside — not a protected place but a protected *time* — we can articulate analogous phenomena: a *time* to escape to and a *place* to run to. Thus nothing is more perfect than an old-fashioned Christmas in the country. These musical symbols address a range of real problems. They reveal a people looking for a place to hide.

I believe that the effect of this process on music can be heard in the music of a group that has been among the most popular in the country: Musica Bohemica. Under their leader, Jaroslav Krček, Musica Bohemica has virtually rewritten Renaissance and Medieval Czech music, recasting it as a synthesis of folk and art music, and presenting it in the prettiest possible garb, a world of sopranino recorders and finger symbols, gentle pipes and sweet voices. This is particularly true for the group's Christmas CD, which is a compendium of pastoral devices: the beautiful, the idyllic, and the childlike coexist in complete harmony. Krček, who has dozens of recordings to his credit, has purposely created a sound world of archaic brilliance, folklike innocence, and childlike sonorities.

For some, all this music might be discardable, showing as it does the "ill effects" of state control, contaminated by the regime. But as Ivan Klíma remarked in his insightful lecture "The Unexpected Benefits of Oppression" (1990), the question is not so black and white. There are reasons why we might be a bit sympathetic to our Czech friends.

Let us turn to the nonlinear model for change, which is now so prevalent in publications dealing with mathematics, biology, meteorology, and even clinical medicine — sometimes given the trendy appellation chaos theory. Using this model we might argue that a given musical substance, let us say a folk song, will either disappear or evolve in some way; it is almost impossible for it to remain the same. There is no way to prove that the tendency of the Moravian folk song to move in the direction of idealization for at least a few decades is automatically a dishonest thing or an inappropriate outcome. How would such a substance have fared in our own society? Would the result be more healthy? More artistically satisfying? This last bit of field-work suggests the opposite.

Postscript: Moravian Cimbal Music for Tourists, 1990–93

For many years Czechoslovakia was a country practically without Western tourists. Beginning in 1989, though, increasing numbers of travelers from Western Europe, the United States, and Japan visited the country, especially Prague. One of the reliable spots in which to hear *cimbalová hudba* (cimbal music) was a *vinarna* (wine bar) at a place in Letna we used to call the Hotel Stalin. Here, in 1989 we had heard an excellent cimbal player. She had been featured on several recordings and played beautifully. By 1991 her public style had changed drastically, and her playing had deteriorated to the point of caricature. She had learned dozens of new songs from every country likely to contain a tourist, and we heard her regale a large group of Japanese tourists with several songs that they evidently knew well.

In addition to the type of playing, we found that the choice of repertoire had also been conditioned by new performance conditions. With the infusion of foreign currency and still low salaries, many Czech folk musicians found that they could make significantly more money playing in the streets. I encountered a group of Moravian village musicians ranging in age from 35 to 70 playing *cimbalová hudba* in the Old Town Square in Prague. They informed me that they played there almost every day. As I listened to them play, I missed hearing several well-known and especially beautiful songs from the region. I was informed that these songs are too "soft," in volume, that they don't contain enough "rhythm" for the tourists. In short, they don't "sell."

Perhaps the attempt to characterize something as vast as "Musical Life In Communist Czechoslovakia" is misplaced. Whatever the case, we must realize that our evaluation of musical life in Communist Czechoslovakia or anywhere else depends almost entirely on what we think of our own musical life. The extent to which we think that the incursions of the radical right into government funding of the arts are either normal, acceptable behavior or nothing to worry about, we will be condescending and dismissive when we talk about things like the South Bohemian Amateur Paper Factory Symphony Orchestra. On the other hand, if we admit that the U.S. government does not spend substantially more on the arts than Frankfurt spends on its opera house, we might be somewhat more sympathetic to a society where an enormous amount of money is spent on serious music and where factory workers form a string orchestra instead of a bowling team. We might at least be able to articulate the fact that although the recent revolution was undoubtedly a good thing for most Czech people, it wasn't necessarily a good thing for Czech string players.

Many of us looked with horror at the brutality, idiocy, and damnable ineffectiveness of the old regime in Czechoslovakia. Yet we cannot and should not make generalizations about "life under the communists in Eastern Europe and the Soviet Union," any more than we can compare "under American capitalism" the lifestyles of a Chicano rancher, a homeless woman in New York, and a bartender in Pittsburgh. In the musical life of the time, as in almost all arenas, it was a time of ambiguity, something richly evident in Kundera's *Joke*. Some things were very good for music and musicians, and some things were very bad, and the paradoxes involved were rich — in short, just like our own lot. There is no reason we should discard the sound or the musical experience because the bagpiper may have been writing reports about the fiddle player.

As Kundera's Ludvik reflects during one of his last fateful bits of musing:

Yes, suddenly I saw it clearly: most people deceive themselves with a pair of faiths: they believe in *eternal memory* (of people, things, deeds, nations) and in *redressability* (of deeds, mistakes, sins, wrongs). Both are false faiths. In reality the opposite is true: everything will be forgotten and nothing will be redressed. (294)

Notes

1. I am going ahead, at my peril, and using the terms "folk music" and "folk song." As long as we keep invisible quotation marks around the words, it will do no damage, and whatever term I choose will eventually be replaced anyway.

2. All quotes from Kundera's *The Joke* are taken from the so-called "Definitive Version — Fully Revised by the Author," published by HarperCollins in 1992. The translation

of the work has a bizarre history, recounted in the preface. This subject has been briefly treated by the scholar and translator Michael Heim in an article in the *Journal of the Folklore Institute,* titled "Moravian Folk Music: A Czechoslovak Novelist's View" (Heim 1972). Although Heim quotes several of the same passages as I do, his aim is quite different; in his words: "The main purpose of this article is to release the missing section of *The Joke* and place it in its proper context." The final four pages of Heim's article consist entirely of Kundera's text.

3. In his most recent book, *Testaments Betrayed,* Kundera reflects on the creation of the novel: "I think back to the time when I was beginning to write *The Joke:* from the start, and very spontaneously, I knew that through the character Jaroslav the novel would cast its gaze into the depths of the past (the past of folk art) and that the "i" of my character would be revealed in and by this gaze. In fact, all four protagonists are created that way: four personal communist universes grafted onto four European pasts: Ludvik: the communism that springs from the caustic Voltairean spirit; Jaroslav: communism as the desire to reconstruct the patriarchal past that is preserved in folklore . . . Each of these personal universes is caught at the moment of its dissolution" (Kundera, 1995: 13).

4. I am grateful to Don Sparling of the English Department of Masaryk University (formerly Purkyne University) for background details about the ball, which I attended in 1980.

The Aesthetic of the Hungarian Revival Movement

The Hungarian revival movement is a unique development in the modernization and revitalization of folk music. Its uniqueness lies not only in the fact that folk revival became very popular in Hungary, producing a whole range of new social contexts for this music — for example, its use in avant-garde theater, for modern poetry, and in the urban dance-house movement. More important, the movement created a category of music entirely unlike those previously existing in Hungary. Most of its creators and its public come from the urban intelligentsia, and thus the musical tradition that previously belonged exclusively to the peasantry has become also the music of the educated middle class.

This is, of course, not an entirely new situation: peasant music had long been enjoyed by various social strata besides the peasantry. As far as it is possible to know, the educated segments of European societies have always used elements of folk art in their culture, transforming them according to their tastes, and similarly, peasant art borrowed elements of art music. Moreover, since the Romantic era, peasant music was looked upon as the music of the "folk," that is, the music of the entire nation, and thus was regarded somewhat as a common cultural heritage. However, the Hungarian revival movement belongs to neither of the above categories of musical interchanges. In this case, there is no question of the use or the integration of the peasant tradition into some essentially different cultural product. In the Hungarian revival movement, genres of peasant music have been taken over in their entirety, preserving the traditional framework of forms and performing styles and much of the context as well.

Hence a new category of music has been created. This "folk music of the intelligentsia" is not really peasant music, but it is not art music or popular music either. Nor can it be regarded as a form of national music; it is not the music of the "folk," at least not in the way the word "folk" is traditionally used.

What is important here is not simply that the creators and performers of the revival movement and most of its audience came from the educated segments of the society. In fact, such a claim would be not entirely true. Parallel to the emergence of the revival movement in the 1970s and 1980s (and to some extent already before this time) a gradual modernization of traditional music took place in the villages too. This could be regarded as a kind of organic revival movement, initiated partly as a response to outside influences but also generated from within the village (as is the case of the citera orchestras and the somewhat modernized instrumentation of performances designed for cassette distribution). This circumstance facilitated the rapprochment between the urban revival movement and village music: in some cases, the revival groups merged entirely with the traditional village ensemble.

All this being said, however, what we may call today the core of the Hungarian revival movement is undoubtedly the creation of the intelligentsia. This is important not so much for its social implications, especially since — although class distinctions do exist in Hungary — there is a great overlap among the circles of blue-collar workers, white-collar workers, well-to-do peasants, lower and upper middle classes. Recognition that the movement belongs to the educated classes is important rather for its aesthetic implications: the musical and cultural "rules" of revival music are determined more by the aesthetic awareness of the educated middle class than by the taste of today's Hungarian peasantry or by any kind of state ideology. This aesthetic consciousness is apparent in decisions directly relevant to musical practice, like the choice of performing style and repertoire. But it signifies also a cultural awareness, a special attention on the part of its creators with regard to its function in a broader social and cultural context.

The revival movement brought something new to Hungarian cultural life that was difficult to interpret in terms of existing musical categories.[1] Some considered it a kind of light popular music, a type of dance-café music which in Hungary is called *diszkó* (from the word disc, referring to the fact that the music for dancing came from records in these cafés). Others saw in the revival movement the great opportunity to reestablish a Hungarian popular music and expel from the market foreign popular musics like rock'n'roll. This hope was the more naive because several of the revival groups experimented at some point with the inclusion of rock and various other foreign popular styles (Muzsikás 1986). Others believed the movement to be an attack on the academic school of folk song arrangement (which it was, although not intentionally); yet others thought it to be in opposition to avant-garde composition (which it clearly was not). Many hoped to exploit the movement for nationalist aims, interpreting its orientation toward Transylvanian Hungarian music as a sign of Hungarian right-wing nationalist revival on the whole, the creators of the movement had no nationalist agenda. Some groups take utmost care to emphasize their nonnationalist attitude; Muzsikás, for instance, regularly include Romanian and Jewish pieces in its programs. But certainly not all revival events are devoid of nationalist overtones, and although the musicians rarely encourage nationalist expressions, they sometimes allow them. In the dance houses one often finds a map of greater Hungary evoking the period before World War I. Many of the intelligentsia turned away from the movement because they feared that it would be used for political aims.

At the same time, the supporters of the movement did not regard it as more than a new kind of light music whose importance for national culture was essentially secondary. Somfai expressed this opinion when he wrote:

I cannot regard the movement as a whole to be anything but the flourishing of "functional (entertaining) genre" whose life will be very short (in a historical sense), but in this short period it will have a tremendous impact on society. [For all its positive effect, this movement] should not be protected as some "cultural treasure" . . . After all, this folk music of the intelligentsia, which they learned from the violinists and singers of a peasant art that is about to die out, could be only a secondary artistic phenomenon, even though we can see its reverberations in a kind of re-folklorization. Nevertheless, this culture does not belong to the ancient-original phenomena of Hungarian folk art for the preservation of which we would have to cry out. (Somfai 1981: 32)

The Concept of Art in Hungary

Before evaluating these widely diverse attitudes toward the movement, and explaining what they really represented, it is necessary to provide a brief explanation of the character of Hungarian cultural life in general. As will be seen, the revival movement had a cultural significance far greater than could be expected in the case of most new developments within the world of musical entertainment. At first sight, it may seem almost absurd that a seemingly insignificant cultural movement could stir up such passionate feelings in Hungary. But, paradoxically, it is precisely because the music of the revival was considered "art" (both by its creators and receptive public) that it was judged not only for its "artistic" value but also became a national and political issue. It would be tempting to suggest that such a politicized attitude toward art is the result of Communist ideology and shows the attempt of the leadership to control all spheres of life, including entertainment and art.

The truth, however, is that in Hungary there had never been "free" and "noncommitted" art in the way it exists, for instance, in the United States. Since the sixteenth century, and even more obviously since Romanticism, Hungarian art has always been considered a crucial part of national life, or even more: the embodiment of a national desire in the social sense, the manifestation of communal thinking. This was not a question of official ideology, although it is true that the political establishment was always ready to exploit art for its own purposes. This happened not only in the Communist era but also much earlier: in the course of the nineteenth century, for the cause of the Revolution of 1848; at the end of the nineteenth century, for the sake of chauvinist propaganda; and from the 1920s until the end of the Second World War, for the promotion of right-wing and fascist ideologies (Frigyesi 1994). In fact, the abuse of a national cultural tradition was by no means as extreme during the Communist period as it was during these other eras.

The historical reasons for this development are too complex to be discussed here. Several historians, sociologists, and artists view this inseparable connection of art and social life as a great problem, which has paralyzed both of these spheres in the modern period of Hungarian history (Heller

1992). But however much certain intellectuals would like to see what they regard as a healthy separation of culture and politics, such separation has not yet happened in Hungary and there is no sign that it will occur in the near future. Moreover, in Hungary, artists traditionally have accepted this integral role. They have refused to retreat into an aesthetic of *l'art pour l'art;* they have believed in art's and the artist's commitment to public life. At this point, such commitment has a historical tradition, which looks back to models like the reform generation of the 1930s, the Romantic movement of literature in the middle of the nineteenth century, and the emergence of artistic modernism at turn of the twentieth century (Frigyesi 1989; Horváth 1961). This tradition has continued in our era with the underground movement of the Communist period, which, similar to its counterparts in preceding eras, was an opposition led by artists and other intellectuals (sociologists, philosophers). As we shall see, the musicians of the revival movement on the whole accepted this role, the most obvious expression of such social-cultural commitment being their devotion to teaching.

Indeed, the novelty and significance of the revival movement cannot be understood only in terms of musical innovations. It forced the public to reevaluate conservative opinions with regard to basic cultural issues like the question of "national," "folk," "popular," and "high" art. The movement helped develop a new cultural sensitivity toward tradition, particularly in three domains:

1. It claimed and proved that social and performing context of music could be expanded — that is, that traditional peasant music is not necessarily only the music of a specific social segment and that it is not the music of the past but can find context in the modern city; its authentic form and context have meaning in modern life.

2. It insisted on a new attitude toward the peasantry and folk music by regarding the peasant musicians to be colleagues and peasant music to be art similar to high art.

3. It made possible a real rapprochment between musical life (performance) and scholarship, by merging practical aspects of performance with those of research and carrying out scholarly work (fieldwork, documentation, analysis and historical reconstruction) alongside performance activities.

The History of the Revival Movement and
Its Contribution to Cultural Life

The Hungarian revival movement started with the activities of a few persons: Sándor Timár, the choreographer of the Bartók Dance Ensemble; the instrumental duo of Béla Halmos and Ferenc Sebő; and the scholar of folk dance, the late György Martin. The Halmos-Sebő duo formally became the "Sebő Ensemble in 1973, when they were joined by Péter Éri, Gergely Koltay, Albert Nagy, and Márta Sebestyén.[2] Another group, the Muzsikás ensemble, was formed almost at the same time (1972) with four members: Mihály Sipos, Dániel Hamar, Sándor Csoóri, and Péter Éri; they were joined later by Márta Sebestyén.[3] In its early phase the movement was inspired and encouraged by several ethnomusicologists, most importantly Zoltán Kallós, Bálint Sárosi, Imre Olsvai, and László Vikár. By the late 1970s there were dozens of revival groups in Budapest and the countryside (including the Jánosi, the Vujicsics, the Téka, the Vízöntő ensembles), and several dance houses were operating, where authentic folk dances were taught by members of the revival groups, who also provided the music.

The "dance-house movement," as the revival is called in Hungary, created a new context for folk music and folk art. In Hungary, as elsewhere in Europe and in several countries of the Middle East, folk music and folk dance had been assigned a "national" role during the preceding decades; they were elevated to the rank of representative national art. Elements of folk dance were used to create grandiose stage productions that competed with the splendor of classical ballet. The small ensembles originally used for folk dancing were replaced by large orchestras, solo singers by choruses, and the communal event of spontaneous folk dance gave way to stage performance. In all instances (not only in the case of the Communist states), this modernized form of folk art was ideologically the property of the state; it was the symbol of national unity and greatness.

In Hungary, there were several attempts to break out of this framework. In the 1970s, Sándor Tímár, the choreographer of the Bartók Dance Ensemble, tried to introduce a new style in his stage performances. He envisioned something that was more spontaneous and simple than the ballet-like choreography, but it was difficult to find the music for such performances. In that era, a director who wished to use live music had only two options: to use either the Gypsy orchestras of the city restaurants or musicians trained in the Conservatory. Tímár did not consider either of these options appropriate for his ideas: he did not find the performing style and the repertoire of the Gypsy bands original or appealing, but the conservatory-trained musicians could perform only composed music, without improvisation. Finally, he decided that spontaneity and common work were more important· than technical quality, and he hired for his rehearsals the Halmos-Sebő duo, who were perhaps not on the technical level of professional musicians but were willing to improvise for the group (M. Sági 1981: 14).

Actually, for Sebő and Halmos, the initial impetus to play folk music did not come from an interest in folklore. Like many other young intellectuals in the 1960s, Sebő was looking for avant-garde expressions in art. He had great admiration for the poetry of Attila József, and at gatherings with his school-mates he sang poems of Attila József set to his own melodies with guitar accompaniment. Similar sorts of performances were common at the time among the youth — even though few did it with such invention as Sebő. After his Attila József songs became popular,[4] thanks to a theater performance with Kati Berek, he was commissioned to compose incidental music for a production of the avant-garde theater, called Huszonötödik Színház (Twenty-Fifth Theater). This piece, based on the text of an old Chinese opera, became a centerpiece of avant-garde theater at the time. I remember this production; it appeared strikingly new and powerful, primarily for its theatrical virtues but also for the music. With this, the group began its career. Berek, Halmos, and Sebő toured the country with their programs of poetry reading, continued to work with the Bartók Dance Ensemble, and were broadcast on the public television.

Thus the impetus for the folk-music revival did not come from the Romantic idea of return to the past, nor from a search for ethnic or national identity. Rather it was part of the avant-garde movement of the 1970s. Hungarian sociologists usually regard the years beginning with the 1960s as a period that saw several waves of spontaneous cultural developments coming from the younger generations. The first was the Hungarian reception of the music of the Beatles, the second was the emergence of a series of experiments in amateur avant-garde theater and poetry reading. The third wave, the dance-house movement, began in the 1970s and has continued up to the present. As can be seen in the case of Sebő, the involvement with avant-garde theater and folk music virtually overlapped. Characteristically, Sebő "discovered" for himself the sonority of peasant music while experimenting with new musical sounds for the theater:

I was commissioned by the Twenty-fifth Theater [Huszonötödik Színház] to compose incidental music for the text of an old Chinese opera for a one-person ensemble. To achieve an exotic quality, I had chosen a real folk instrument, the citera, and used it together with drums and gongs. I tried to use these instruments in as many different ways as possible; for instance, I hit the strings with a stick. When the ethnomusicologist, László Vikár heard this, he asked whether I knew of the instrument *gardon* from Gyimes whose playing technique was very similar.[5] When he saw my surprised expression as I answered "no," he said that it was a waste of time to discover things that have existed already for centuries. I realized that he was right and began to find a way to know "real" folk music. (M. Sági 1981: 17)

But at the time, it was not easy to find real folk music. Halmos described this period of searching with the following words:

First we were trying to sing the folk songs from the published collections, with the accompaniment of guitar. Later we found László Lajtha's transcription of his collection of instrumental folk music from Szék. I had already played Bach at that time, I had seen difficult music, but I had no idea how to read this music [it had so many ornaments in Lajtha's transcription] — it was awful. We played it somehow, but one cannot learn something like this without the knowledge of style. First we played the accompaniment on the guitar or on the piano, but later we tried it with viola. . . . And then finally, in 1971, we had access to Lajtha's sound recording on the basis of which he made the transcriptions. Then, we put out the score and listened to the music and finally understood what the notation meant. After hearing the music, we could start to learn somehow, but this was not easy either. . . .

Then, in 1972, we started to play for the dance house. At that time we knew only a few melodies for each dance. . . . But this experience forced us to understand what it means to play for dance. . . .

We visited Szék in 1972, for the first time. We were quite a sight there — three hooligans with long hair visited István Ádám's dance house. We asked the musicians to let us play with them and they agreed gladly. It turned out that they had already been playing for four days without stop. It was possible to dance to our playing too, they did not beat us up. . . . Since 1974, I have been returning to Szék, to study from István Ádám, *prímás* [first violinist of the ensemble]; I continued this until his death in 1980. (M. Sági 1981: 19–20)

This account may sound astonishing to those familiar with the so-called Kodály Movement and who have heard of the prestige that folk music enjoyed in Hungary thanks to the activities of Bartók and Kodály. How was it possible that the young generation of the 1960s had to "discover" folk music in a country where it was part of the curriculum of public schools and of the Academy of Music? How was it possible that Lajtha's collection of the instrumental music from Szék was virtually inaccessible to the public — that is, the transcriptions were published, but the sound material was not?

It is said sometimes that the suppression of "real folk music" was part of a Communist propaganda. But it does not follow from Communist ideology that authentic folk music performances be excluded from public circulation. I believe that the Communists followed — or, better to say, misinterpreted — an earlier ideology when coming to this decision. The attitude of the institutional network can be understood only if we look at the status of folk and popular music in its broader historical development.

In Hungary the second half of the nineteenth century witnessed a real peak of popular folk musics.[6] This era brought the climax in the development and spread of *verbunkos* (a nationally known style of instrumental dance music) and a new wave of popular urban song composition, the so-called *magyar nóta* (Hungarian song), which spread quickly in both the towns and the villages. These two developments coincided with the spread of the instrumental string ensembles and the professional Gypsy musicians. By the end of the century, these aspects of a more modern popular instrumental music were inseparably connected with each other: (1) the primary musicians of string ensembles were mainly Gypsies, (2) these string ensembles were most commonly employed for dance music, and (3) this dance music used, in addition to an older dance repertoire that included elements of *verbunkos,* melodies of *magyar nóta.* Although there were stylistic connections, neither the repertoire nor the performing style of these string bands were unified: the Gypsy ensembles of small villages played often very differently from the Gypsy orchestras of the urban centers.

Within these many varieties, the urban branch of Gypsy music became somewhat more homogeneous, and from it developed the popular style that has been known as "Hungarian Gypsy music." This "Hungarian Gypsy music," which hence was not the music of all Hungarians, nevertheless gradually was elevated to the rank of Hungarian national musical style. By the end of the nineteenth century, its main patron was the middle nobility, the so-called gentry. The gentry was among the most conservative segments of the society, with little economic but great political power. The conservative politics of the turn of the century exploited the historical image of the Hungarian gentry-noble for the sake of a conservative propaganda, and the gentry of the period was willing to play this role, promoting itself as the "core" of the Hungarian race. Consequently, Gypsy music, the music par excellence of the gentry, began to be viewed as the most real expression of Hungarianness. It became the tool in the hands of the leading right-wing politicians to gain the sympathy of the population for conservative and racist ideologies during the 1930s and 1940s (Frigyesi 1994).

Reaction to this ideology had a major role in the government's policy after World War II. What happened was a gross simplification of the real situation of popular and folk musics: virtually all string ensemble music was suspect because it had some relation with this urban Gypsy style. Even Bartók could not see entirely clearly in this matter. It is true that he noticed the difference between the performing styles of the village and urban Gypsy ensembles, and regarded the village style as part of the folk tradition. Nevertheless, even he could not rid himself entirely from the idea that this music was somewhat secondary to the core of the "pure" Hungarian peasant repertoire. There was a myth created that real Hungarian music was purely vocal and that instrumental music was only the rendition of vocal tunes.[7]

Another false belief further aggravated the problematic situation of folk music in Hungary. Folk music was thought of as something more primitive than high art. "Primitive" should not be understood pejoratively, it meant that folk music was considered more pure, natural, and original than art music, and in this way it ranked higher. Unfortunately, this status did not help in understanding its real qualities. It was thought that folk music was so elemental and basic that those who had not been in contact with it could not understand it, that it needed the insight of artists to transmit its essence. For instance, Bartók and Kodály insisted that the folklorist had to listen to the peasant song in its original performance and environment, for they firmly believed that only through the real experience can one grasp the essence of this art. But they spoke only about the artist whose aim was to create national music and did not think it necessary for the population at large to hear this music. It was thought to be the task of great masters to listen to and understand the voice of the folk and then integrate it into their musical style — in order to transmit, in this way, the "message" of original folk art to the people. It is not possible to explain why this standpoint was necessary at the beginning of the twentieth century and why it was, indeed, the most honest attitude toward folk art at the time. What matters here is that by the 1950s such ideology was conservative and useless, and it became the main obstacle in the dissemination of authentic folk tradition.

To this thinking, folk song was not a self-contained work of art, rather folk culture as a whole was looked upon as one great natural-artistic man-ifestation. Its importance for modern life was thought to be embedded in the rules of its form, tonality, and rhythm — it was the totality of these rules that was respected rather than the individual pieces in their incidental, living forms. This was the ideology behind the educational plan that taught pupils only the "melodic essence" of folk songs (and, of course, only of "pure" folk song and not of instrumental music). In the textbooks of elementary school, folk songs were reduced to basic melodic lines, to a sort of *Ur-melodie*. At the same time, there was an emphasis on teaching pieces of great composers, which were thought to give these melodies a form in which they could be understood outside of their original context.

It cannot be denied that such arrangements had a certain influence on young children and helped them realize the beauty of peasant art, which might have seemed alien and almost ridiculous to them otherwise. At the same time, the teaching of simplified folk melodies as an obligatory part of the curriculum had a damaging effect, especially since it was used also at higher levels of the educational system. It is true that the generations raised before the Second World War learned no peasant music whatsoever in the school system. But the situation after the war was not much better. Students, including those in the Academy of Music, had to memorize dozens of folk songs and attend folk song classes for years, but most of them have never heard a single, authentic folk music performance.[8] Ironically, during this period urban Gypsy music was broadcast regularly on the radio and televi-sion and issued on records; indeed it was the only folk repertoire that circulated broadly in its original performing style. From the official point of view, Gypsy music belonged to the category of "light music" (popular music) and was supported as such. "Pure folk music" entered the institutional system through different channels: it was art music in the case of folk song arrangement, and it was an educational material in the case of the skeletal melodies taught at school. Authentic folk performance, however, had no place in this establishment; it lacked the ideological support and also the appropriate department in the institutional system. It is characteristic that when some ethnomusicologists approached the state-supported record company in 1964 with the idea of publishing original field recordings on commercial records, the company categorically refused the proposition. The idea was to bring out something original for the Conference of the International Folk Music Council, which was going to be held at Budapest that year (Szász, 1981: 103). Finally, the company produced 1,000 copies of one record, which sold so well that it had to be reissued a few years later. (It should be noted, however, that once the company realized that the record was a success, it produced a series of albums, each containing four records, of high scholarly quality. It is also remarkable that several records of such seemingly unattractive, monotonous, unaccompanied peasant singing — which probably would be turned down by any recording company in the West — proved to have a market in Hungary, and ultimately received official support.)

This is how the absurd situation developed that the intelligentsia of the 1950s and 1960s had known only a purified pseudo folk song on the one hand and an entirely popularized Gypsy performing style on the other. This latter style was not appealing to the young urban intelligentsia, not because it was not in line with official politics but rather because the generation after the war found both the political overtones of this music and its excessive sentimentalism disgusting. At the same time, folk song was known only in its skeletal form — it was dead and boring material.

Against this background, the revival movement of the 1970s constituted a real revolution. It was motivated by two cultural desires: an avant-garde opposition of young people against the conception of art in general and against the intellectual's attitude toward folk art in particular. As part of a cultural avant-garde, the folklore revival was not opposing the idea of art. On the contrary, its aim was rather to show the artistic quality in products that were considered still somewhat secondary to Classical art. This art-centered ideal was nothing essentially new; in its spirit, it was not different from the aesthetic that purged folk music of its "Gypsy music excesses." Most of the performers as well as the listeners and participants of the movement did not turn away from the idea of artistic expression, rather they wanted to find this expression in forms that were free from the control of the establishment and also from a conservative artistic expectation and context. It could be said that the youth hoped to discover avant-garde music in the playing techniques of authentic folk music and to create an avant-garde context for art in the dance-house movement.

For this reason, because they searched for "new" sounds, members of the revival movement turned toward authentic performance. They were not motivated by nostalgia for the past, nor was preservation their primary aim. Simply, they found this music to be most interesting in its original form. It is not an accident that many of the performers came to the revival movement from Classical music, that is, they began to play folk music after they had already played Bach and Mozart. Their "discovery" of peasant music was, in its function and effect, something similar to the reinterpretation of the Baroque style by the early music movement: they looked for something else in folk music than their predecessors had. Compared to the spiritless, academic folklore arrangements (a basic requirement at the composition curriculum of the Academy of Music) and to the purified Hungarian folk songs taught at school, and in opposition to the popular version of urban Gypsy music, these original peasant performances seemed indeed something like avant-garde music. It turned out that the most authentic performing style sounded the most modern; it was "stronger" and more attractive even than modernized versions that included electric instruments. The rhythmic quality, the strange accents, the exuberant ornamentation but restrained dynamics, the unusual combination of art and service in dance music was something new. The musicologist László Somfai recalls that at a concert where the Jánosi ensemble performed the "authentic" folk version side by side with the Bartók arrangements, the audience felt, or it seemed to Somfai, that the original folk songs sounded more modern, more avant-garde even than Bartók's arrangements (Somfai 1981: 37).

This aesthetics was the motivation of the young musicians in their turning toward the traditional performing style. Nowadays, the quasi definition of a real revival group is that it has an authentic peasant repertoire — that is, a series of pieces that they learned directly from a peasant ensemble or at least learned from recordings and with the help of other revival groups who had a direct contact with peasant musicians. This was the criterion of a 1981 collection of essays on the revival movement, which contained a partial list and discography of revival orchestras defined as such (Széll 1981: 11). This collection describes about 92 ensembles in Hungary that played authentic folk music at the time.[9] This number does not include the modernized village ensembles, which emerged somewhat internally from the old village bands, but only those groups that started out in towns with the aim to "recreate" and "relearn" traditional folk music. None of these groups plays only such "authentic" repertoire and, obviously, the aim is never an exact reproduction — this would not be possible, since the peasant ensembles themselves play in a variety of styles and differently at different occasions. In general, performances are considered "authentic" if they can function in the original context — that is, if the peasant dances could be danced to them without much change and if the peasants of the villages from which these pieces originate recognize these performances as appropriate.

One important consequence of this "tradition-oriented" attitude was that it regarded instrumental folk music as it really was — that is, as functional music, as entertainment. This was not primarily an ideological decision but something that came from practice: the musicians of the movement learned this style in function and found the best context for it also in its original function — that is, as an accompaniment to dance. Even today, in spite of the fact that the revival ensembles often perform on stage, the primary context of this music is in the dance clubs. The fact that the context of this music was not the concert but the dance house meant again an opposition to the traditional view of folk music. For the older generation and many of the younger people too, folk music is something to be respected but only from some distance; it is something that a serious person does not get involved with too much. This self-imposed alienation resulted, partly from an honest admittance that the music of the peasantry was not their music and that it would be tasteless to try to imitate the peasants. At the same time this generation no longer believed, as Bartók did, that folk music could be merged with art music; they had seen too many unsuccessful attempts during the Communist period of the 1950s. Thus folk music was considered "high art" that had no relevance to modern life. As the more austere defenders of the concept of "high art" could not find a place for the new movement in ideology, the musical establishment was similarly confused. The revival performing groups could not be categorized; what they performed was not really pop music, not really entertainment, but not really folk or art music either (Héra 1981: 126–30).

But the supporters of the dance-house movement saw the questions of function, art, and context differently. Of course, they also knew that the context of the peasant village could not be recreated, but they did not regard the dance music of the folk repertoire as out of place in the city. In their view, this was a natural expansion of the original context: one part of the context was lost — that is, the village community, the wedding, and other traditional occasions — but the most important aspect of the context, that is, communal dance, could be preserved. In fact, there was an emphasis on preserving as much of the context as possible — again, not simply for the sake of preservation but because of a general trust in the traditional forms. The principle of the directors of the dance houses was that there had to be a reason for those dance cycles as they existed in villages and one should at least try out whether they work in the modern context. In fact, they often worked. In the teaching of the authentic dance cycles, the Muzsikás ensemble was in the forefront. Since 1973, they had planned various integral dance series for each year: in 1973, they taught a shortened version of the Szék dance cycles; later they added dances from Szatmár (1974), from Palatka and Gyimes (1975), from Méhkerék (1976), and Marosszék (1982). In certain years, they taught full cycles of certain regions (Szék, 1976; Dunántúl 1978; Mezőség 1979, 1981; Gyimes 1980). The members of the dance house could learn, within ten years, most of the Hungarian (and also some of the Romanian) cycles and the styles of the main regions (Both 1981: 25).

The musicians of the dance house did not find it problematic that this new style was at the same time both entertainment and art. As Halmos described it:

We have learned that the spirit of this music is playing and service at the same time. It is dance music, so that its function is to serve the dance. Every individual effect is born from the service to the dance; it has to match the movement. If I listen to [the recording of such performances] just as music, I will perhaps hear notes out of tune, cracking sounds and some other mistakes, but I will not hear an ambiguity in the tempo. All this is so that the accents could be heard, that the rhythm be perfect, so that the musician would help the dancer, that he would be a partner. This part is the service. But the joy, the game in it is that musically I shape it as I want. How I actually improvize the melody, that is my business, it is the game of the ensemble. (M. Sági 1981: 20)

This performance-oriented attitude, however, is not in opposition to a scholarly, approach. Most groups also carry out fieldwork in the traditional sense; they not only learn from musicians but also record them and analyze these recordings. Several among them publish articles (Virgávölgyi), and some have become ethnomusicologists (Halmos, Sebő). Such research often goes beyond what would be necessary for performing purposes. Among the most notable examples is a recording by the Jánosi ensemble of original folk tunes arranged by Bartók. (Jánosi 1985).[10] On this record, the Jánosi ensemble recreated a series of folk dances on the basis of Bartók's phonograph recordings and of their experience with modern peasant performers. In essence, they brought to life a music that could not be heard otherwise by the public, since the early phonograph recordings have deteriorated to such a degree that one can no longer enjoy the music on them. Another similarly original recreation is *Máramaros, The Lost Jewish Music of Transylvania* by the Muzsikás ensemble. This recording was the fruit of several years of preparatory work, in the course of which the ensemble interviewed Gherghe Covaci, a Gypsy musician from Transylvania who used to play for Jews. He still remembered the music, although he could no longer perform it because he had neither the proper accompanying ensemble anymore nor a public that would have wanted to hear these tunes. The members of the Muzsikás formed an ensemble together with him and asked him to teach them these pieces as much as he could remember. They recorded (and partly videotaped) these teaching sessions and produced a CD as a result of this experiment. (Muzsikás 1993).[11] There were several similar recordings made by members of revival ensembles.[12] It should be noted that not only the Muzsikás but many other ensembles include musics from other local ethnicities. The Vujicsics ensemble specializes in Serbian music and plays often for Serbian villages (Szász 1981a: 55).

Today, the musicians of the revival groups take for granted what Sebő and Halmos discovered only after much searching, namely, that this music can be learned only in practice and only from the musicians who still play it. To them, these musicians are not informants whom one may record and then store the material in an archive; rather, they regard them as partners and masters. They approach them in a manner that young musicians always would have approached great musicians: with respect and with a desire to learn. With this, the revival movement realized the dream of the ethnomusicologists of an earlier generation, who hoped for a folklore movement that not only exploits the tradition of the village but helps it maintain its own culture (see Olsvai's remembrances of László Lajtha's opinion about the potential of spontaneous folk dance, Szász 1981b: 106).

Such an attitude would not have been possible at the first half of the twentieth century. There were many personal, cultural, social, and scholarly reasons why Bartók and Kodály did not collect in this manner, but even if they had wanted to carry out such a project, it would have been impossible (Ortutay 1972). At that time, the chasm between the gentleman of the city and the peasant of the village was unbridgeable. We know from travelogues and other accounts (including those by Bartók and Kodály) that the folklorist — or for that matter, anyone from the higher classes — was received by the peasants with deep suspicion; someone coming from the city was a potential enemy. In our days, the relationship is very different. As Halmos recounts, the musicians of Szék accepted the young, long-haired, hooligan-looking students from Budapest without any problem. It is common today that members of the revival groups play together with village musicians or are hired to play just as the village ensemble had been before. In Esther Rónai's recent documentary film, one can see Halmos playing the part of the *prímás* together with the group at a village festivity (Rónai, 1992).

The revival movement also helped to destroy the myth about the differing capacities of Gypsy and Hungarian musicians. It was a commonly held opinion that Hungarian instrumental music can be played only by Gypsies, but, paradoxically, it was also believed that the best and most authentic performers of Hungarian dance music are, nevertheless, the peasants who had been forced out from the profession by the Gypsy bands. Both notions are, of course, entirely wrong; for instance, the musicians on Lajtha's recording from Szék, the supposedly most original Hungarian music, are all Gypsies. The revival movement showed that Hungarian instrumental folk music can be learned by anyone who is devoted to learning and understanding it. This music can be played even by violinists trained in Classical music.

The relationship between the young intelligentsia and the peasants involved issues beyond music as well. As Halmos explained:

I perhaps do not exaggerate if I say that the youth of the movement, including ourselves, were looking for a "wholeness" of life in these songs and dances. These old people have inherited a human dignity, not only beautiful dances. They learned how to work, how to celebrate. This is what we wanted to learn while we were learning from them and playing with them, and perhaps we succeeded somewhat. (M. Sági 1981: 20)

In this manner, the performers of the revival movement regard their attitude toward this art as similar to that of those who perform Classical music. To the revival ensembles, peasant music is not some original, spontaneous creation of nature through the peasants, as Bartók had attempted to explain it. It is both less and more: it is simply art that manifests itself continuously in always unique, individual creations and contexts. As Sebő wrote:

I consider it essentially anti-cultural to pose the question that is often asked: "Why should we keep alive or bring to new life the pieces of peasant folklore?" We could ask, for the same token, "Why do we have to keep alive a piece by Bach or Mozart?" or why should we cultivate any product that is not a contemporary creation, or take an interest in and transmit anything that belongs to the past? . . . I consider any form in which we can face the past absolutely right and necessary — be it even nostalgic or ironic. (Sebő, unpublished manuscript)

It would be exaggeration to say that the revival movement has ever been officially suppressed by the government. But it is certain that these young musicians were at least suspect in the eyes of the establishment, whose members were often afraid to openly support them. This is how it could happen, for instance, that several cultural centers "allowed" the organization of dance house evenings in their building but refused to pay them or provide the usual services. In one of the cultural centers, for instance, the participants of the dance house had to organize a cleaning team among themselves and also reconstruct part of the building so that they could perform (Széll 1981: 10).

Similarly, it could not be said that the movement developed entirely apart from, or in opposition to, the institutional channels for cultivation of folk music. Although it is true that the new groups often met with hostility on the part of the cultural establishment, they were helped and inspired by several other institutions, often from within the same framework. For several groups, the folklore festivals and national folklore competitions provided such support. In Mohács, for instance, there has been an annual folk song competition for young people since 1970 (Szász 1981b: 95). By the 1980s there were four counties represented at this competition, and similar competitions were held in Kaposvár, Zalaegerszeg, and Szombathely. About the same time, folk music competitions were instituted on a national level: the folk song competition called "Röpülj páva . . ." ("Fly, peacock . . . ," named after the beginning line of a well-known Hungarian folk song in the old style) and the folk music category of the art performance competition for youth, called "Ki mit tud?" ("Who knows what?"). These competitions were not without problems, but they had a positive effect in giving live performance of folk music a rank in cultural life. Also, they brought together traditional peasant performers from the villages with young performers from the cities. Olsvai recalls that at one of these competitions, young peasant boys performed bagpipe tunes in a traditional style that had been thought of as virtually nonexistent (Szász 1981b: 95). Among the first impetuses for the formation of the Sebő-Halmos duo was their participation at the "Röpülj páva . . ." competition in 1969.

Many initiatives came also from the public school system. Mrs. László Bencze (aka Judit Mező) organized collection and performance of folk music even before the revival movement had actually began. She encouraged her students to learn from village musicians, and soon the music teachers of Debrecen created the Délibáb ensemble under the direction of Árpád Joó (1970) (Bencze 1981: 42). Like most other revival groups, these musicians also collected, used old folk recordings, played at concerts, and taught young musicians.

Parallel to the revival movement, there was a gradual change of village music within the villages themselves. In some regions, the traditional music disappeared almost entirely and has been replaced by modern popular music. At other places, the music was radically changed by employing, for instance, the instrumentation and style of rock music. But alongside these changes, there are more organic developments too. The new fashion of citera orchestras, a widespread practice, is only a few decades old; this is neither a real revival nor an entirely organic continuation of the old styles. These orchestras use traditional melodies and continue an older performing style but with a new sonority: homogeneous instrumental ensembles like these were previously unknown to Hungarian music. In general, a much more varied and ad hoc use of instrumentation has developed in the village, aiming at new sonorities. It should be also realized that the aesthetic ideal behind many of these performances is different even when they "sound traditional." Today they often create their style having in mind a broader audience than just their village, knowing that they may play at national competitions and festivals and that their performances may be distributed on cassettes or records.[13]

The revival movement thus is part of a general tendency in Hungary that aims at modernizing and continuing peasant music. Looking at it from the point of view of the educated segments of the population, it could be said that the revival movement is part of a historical development; it represents the most recent stage in the intellectuals' approach toward folklore. Within this development, there were three waves during the twentieth century: the first was the so-called "village movement" of the 1920s and 1930s, which attempted a more objective description of the social life of the village in literature and sociological studies. This was contemporaneous with the choral movement launched by Kodály and supported partly by Bartók, which aimed at a musical education of the broader public based on folk music material. The second was a folk song and dance movement launched by the Communist state and integrated into a Communist ideology during the 1950s. This was followed by various state-supported institutions, such as the national folk competitions, which represented a departure from the previous Communist ideology but were not in direct opposition to it. The third wave, prepared somewhat by the latter developments, was the dance-house movement of the 1970s. Undoubtedly, this has been the most significant folklore movement in this century. I think it is not an exaggeration to say that, since the activities of Bartók and Kodály, the revival movement has had the greatest impact on the Hungarian population in terms of transmitting authentic peasant repertoire to a broader public.

Notes

Unless otherwise noted, all translations from Hungarian sources are the author's.

1. Although there have been a number of newspaper articles published about the revival movement, the style and practice of the music and its social and cultural implications have not been treated in a scholarly manner. This brief summary of the various opinions regarding the movement is based partly on conversations I have had with a number of persons in Hungary in the past ten years and partly on newspaper articles. A good introductory summary to this subject is Széll (1981: 5–13).

2. Ferenc Sebő, the ensemble's director, sang and played *kontra* (second violin), hurdy gurdy, citera, gardon, koboz, guitar, Jew's harp. Halmos stayed with the ensemble till 1983 and played violin, guitar, bass, citera, koboz, drum, and also sang. Péter Éri stayed with the group till 1979 and played bass, kontra, and tambura and sang. Gergely Koltay stayed till 1975 and played flute and bagpipe, Albert Nagy joined in 1975 and played bass and guitar, Márta Sebestyén sang with the group between 1975 and 1979. In 1983, the group dissolved, and Sebő and Nagy formed a new group with Levente Székely as *prímás* (first violin). That group no longer exists; some of its members joined other revival groups. Sebő and Halmos both have become ethnomusicologists (M. Sági 1981: 14–22; Széll 1981: 181).

3. The Muzsikás ensemble had the following members in 1973: Mihály Sipos (violin, citera), Dániel Hamar (cimbalom, bass), and Sándor Csoóri Jr. (bagpipe, hurdy-gurdy, koboz, viola). Their first singer was Zsuzsanna Vincze. They were joined in 1979 by Péter Éri (tambura, viola, bagpipe, bass) and Márta Sebestyén (voice, flute). The group ensemble accompanied the Bartók Dance Ensemble in 1973–74 and has led its own dance house from 1974 to the present (Both 1981: 23–30; Széll 1981: 175–76).

4. Sebő composed songs for the poetry of several other Hungarian poets. One of his recordings, made in 1980, contains poems by Sebestyén Tinódi, Vitéz Mihály Csokonai, Miklós Radnóti, Attila József, László Nagy, and Sándor Weöres (Sebő, 1980).

5. The *gardon* is a cello-like instrument known from the Gyimes region of East Transylvania, used exclusively for a percussive effect by hitting the strings with a stick.

6. I have summarized these developments in my entry "Hungarian Folk Music" for the *Garland Encyclopaedia of World Music* (in progress). See also Dobszay (1984), Frigyesi (1994), Sárosi (1970), Szabolcsi (1951, 1964).

7. This is true to some extent in the case of several peasant instruments that are not normally played for dancing but are used essentially by amateur musicians (that is, musicians who do not play for remuneration). Although elaborations on these instruments may be extremely artistic and complex, their melodic and structural basis do follow the model of a vocal melody. This structural constraint, however, is not present in dance music. The structural difference is paralleled by the difference in social status and function: dance music is played by professional musicians, usually by string ensembles, and the per-

formers are mostly Gypsies. Thus there is a considerable difference between amateur and professional music-making, both in terms of the character and function of these performances (Sárosi 1981).

8. My description of the situation of folk music in the Communist period is based on my own experience. During this period, I was a student in the public school system and later at the Academy of Music. See also Sebő's account in M. Sági (1981: 16).

9. It is difficult to determine exactly how many groups existed at a given time because the members of different ensembles often joined together or split up and joined other groups. Some musicians regularly played in several groups.

10. On this recording, the Jánosi ensemble reconstructed the folk-music original of the following arrangements/compositions by Béla Bartók: Rhapsody No. 1 (1928), Sonatina (1915), Rhapsody No. 2 (1928), Three Folk Songs from the Csík District (1907), and Rumanian Folk Dances (1915).

11. The members of the Muzsikás ensemble — Mihály Sipos (violin), Péter Éri (viola, buzuki), Sándor Csoóri Jr. (violin, viola, guitar), and Dániel Hamar (contrabass, small hammer dulcimer) — are joined on this recording by Márta Sebestyén (vocals), Csaba Ökrös (violin), Gheorghe Covaci (violin), Árpád Toni (cimbalom), Gheorghe Florea (zongura), and Ian Florea (drum).

12. For instance, the record *Kalotaszegi népzene,* introduces the famous village fiddle-player Sándor Fodor ("Netti"). On this record, he is the *prímás* of a band formed of musicians of revival groups (some from the Muzsikás ensemble). The *kontra* is played alternately by Sándor Csoóri Jr. and László Kelemen, the cello alternately by Pál Havasréti and Gyula Kozma, the bass by Péter Éri. The producer of the record was Béla Halmos (Hungaroton SLPX 18122).

13. One of the most notable of such folklore groups is the ensemble of the famous primitive painter, Juli Dudás of Galgamácsa. Based on local folk rituals, her group created a stage production with which they toured Hungary and had considerable success in other European countries too (Moldován 1976). There were various local attempts to create records or cassettes with the best singers of a region. Among these, some of the Hungarians from Romanian territories were especially successful (for instance, Petrás n.d. and Tóth n.d.).

Lakodalmas *Rock and the Rejection of Popular*

Culture in Post-Socialist Hungary

During the late 1980s, a type of music called "*lakodalmas* rock" became immensely popular in Hungary and northeast Yugoslavia. Intellectuals who were the authorities in the media and record industry excluded *lakodalmas* rock from established channels, not because it was overtly dissident but because they considered it to be in bad taste. As a result, *lakodalmas* rock flourished in the newly forming private sector and became the basis of a cassette industry, which emerged as the Socialist system dissolved in Hungary. Fans and opponents interpreted *lakodalmas* rock in contrasting ways. For its devotees, the music was a commentary upon real conditions of existence. At the same time, it violated a belief, deeply held by intellectuals, that folk music should be the idiom of choice for Hungarians. The understandings of *lakodalmas* rock were informed by a previous history of conflict over indigenous popular music in Hungary. The 1980s controversy was a phenomenon of Hungary's transition out of Socialism, when citizens utilized late-twentieth-century media vehicles to assert values that had existed prior to Socialism.

As a cassette industry, *lakodalmas* rock is part of a trend that has been identified in many regions of the world. Cassette industries thrive in nations as diverse as India, Indonesia, Turkey, and Egypt (Manuel 1993; el-Shawan 1987; Stokes 1992a; Sutton 1985). Music directed from above and disseminated through the dominant media of radio, television, and film is susceptible to the ideological stamp of governing elites or to monolithic commercial visions. By contrast, cassettes bear the ethos of the marginalized. Often disseminated through piracy and gray market economies, they are a vehicle for the expressions of people with few financial and political resources. Peter Manuel observes that in India, dominant film music tends to promote an "amorphous, homogeneous, rootless sense of identity" (Manuel 1993: 54), while music on cassettes expresses specific local, political, and religious viewpoints. Martin Stokes argues that in Turkey, intellectuals who have power in government institutions promote a perfectionist view of the nation with classical and folk music. The popular genre *arabesk* expresses a pessimism associated rhetorically with the periphery, although in fact this ethos permeates Turkish society (Stokes 1992a: 124–27; 225–27). In Hungary, as in Turkey, intellectuals believe that folk music embodies national ideals. But the popular genre *lakodalmas* rock is not pessimistic; it bears an ethos of pragmatism.

In Socialist Hungary, deep divisions of social rank persisted despite the efforts of Socialism toward equalization; at the end of this period, "Hungarian Socialist society was no more open than capitalist societies at a similar level of economic development" (Szelényi and Szelényi 1991: 8). People of different social ranks in Hungary thus judged *lakodalmas* rock in opposing ways; these interpretations issued from the contrasting relationships of the classes to artistic and material resources in Hungary. Pierre Bourdieu has argued in his study of French society that contrasts of taste between classes are a manifestation of the difference in access to several types of resources or "capital" (Bourdieu 1984). Bourdieu's theory, with modifications, has relevance for Eastern European societies. Several studies of the intelligentsia under Socialism apply his basic approach. Katherine Verdery argues that in Romania, because access to material wealth was restricted, cultural authority and political status played a far greater role in the constitution of intellectuals' power (Verdery 1991a: 92–94).

A further aspect of Bourdieu's argument applies to the present essay: that specific aesthetics attach to different classes. Iván and Szonja Szelényi believe that whereas in France material capital was primary, in Hungarian society cultural assets determined power in the social sphere (Szelényi and Szelényi 1991: 10). This reversal of factors makes the modified Bourdieu model particularly relevant to the subject of the present essay. Lacking the material resources to assert elite status, Hungarian intellectuals were doubly invested in the sphere of the arts.

Intellectuals accorded high value to some of the music of ordinary Hungarians. They documented it in villages from the mid-eighteenth century on, defined it as folk music, and attributed to it the character of "true national poetry" (Manga 1969: 6). Starting in 1896, they researched village music intensively through phonographic recording. With their methods of detailed stylistic classification of Hungarian folk music, Béla Bartók and Zoltán Kodály influenced the directions of European folk music study in the early twentieth century (Bartók 1981; Kodály 1960). But ordinary Hungarians had patronized a far broader stylistic spectrum of music than that which researchers selected for study. This contrast produced the central tensions over *lakodalmas* rock in the 1980s; ordinary people, supposedly the bearers of Hungarian national character, expressed themselves with *lakodalmas* rock in a manner that repulsed nationalist intellectuals.

The Emergence of *Lakodalmas* Rock

Lakodalmas rock is the rendition on electronic instruments of rural Hungarian popular music. It takes its name, "wedding" rock, from the event at which it was most often performed prior to becoming a genre of recorded music. The music is played at concerts, for casual listening at village bars, and for dancing at large celebrations like weddings and saint's day festivals. Its repertoire is derived from the nineteenth- and early-twentieth-century Hungarian theater and dance songs known as *magyar nóta*. Besides rendering the classics of this repertoire on electric instruments, *lakodalmas* rock groups have made some of their biggest hits with newly composed texts and songs that include stylistic elements from *nóta*.[1]

Utilizing the established venues of restaurants, arena concerts, and radio where possible, but also the "second economy" system of flea markets, *lakodalmas* rock gained huge popularity with Hungarian speakers, first in the Voivodina area of Yugoslavia and then in Hungary proper. It was Yugoslavia's somewhat flexible market system and local radio programming policies that provided the means for *lakodalmas* rock to become a full-blown commercial genre. The first band to exploit these commercial possibilities, outside of playing at local inns and weddings, was the 3+2 ensemble. Originally a rock band that played for youth dances near its hometown of Ürményhaza, 3+2 netted an enthusiastic response by switching to the *nóta* repertoire, which until then had been played by Gypsy string orchestras. The group made a master recording of its music in 1985 at a private studio. Initially, 3+2 was unable to convince producers at Jugoton, the Yugoslavian state record company, to publish or distribute the recording. The group managed, however, to persuade the local radio station in the Yugoslavian town of Temerin to play cuts from the recording on the air.[2] Then 3+2 quickly became so popular in the Temerin listening area that the station's request program started receiving 80 to 100 requests per individual number.[3] Fans, assuming these cuts were from an actual record, tried to purchase it at local music stores. Exasperated store managers finally got the ear of the producers at Jugoton, and 3+2's album *Faded Fall Rose* was pressed in 1986. The initial pressing of 15,000 sold out in two days (Csorba 1988: parts 3–5).

In a prime illustration of the transnational character of mass-mediated culture (Appadurai 1991: 147–49, 208–9), citizens in Hungary near the southern border who could catch the Yugoslav radio signal also became fans of 3+2. That Hungarian citizens embraced a genre from outside the country's existing borders illustrates the persistence of a concept of the Hungarian nation dating from before World War I. As part of the defeated Austro-Hungarian empire, Hungary lost two-thirds of its territory under the Treaty of Trianon (Lázár 1989: 179). Significant numbers of ethnic Hungarians now live in peripheries outside the country; the Voivodina is one such area. Hungarians express a wide spectrum of affinity with these minorities, ranging from irredentism to universal human rights advocacy. Starting in the 1970s, young Hungarians had adopted a unique style of peasant music from another ethnic minority area, Transylvania in Romania. Hungarians thought of Transylvanian music and culture as endangered and in crisis because of human rights violations committed in the region under the Ceauşescu regime (Kürti 1989: 33–40). Hungarians had a far different picture, however, of the Voivodina area in Yugoslavia. Due to Tito's somewhat flexible economic practices and ethnically pluralist policies, for much of the Socialist period Hungarians in the Voivodina enjoyed linguistic autonomy, accumulated relative wealth, and developed a more commercialized culture than that of citizens in Hungary proper. Hungarians recreated Transylvanian music as a symbol of survival; they imported *lakodalmas* rock as a commodity.

Hungarian media authorities tried to ignore the success of 3+2, initially refusing to either distribute their record or give 3+2 permission to perform live concerts in Hungary. Rather than keeping 3+2's music out of circulation, this decision by Hungarian authorities actually threw 3+2 into what has been termed the gray market, the private commercial sector that was partly proscribed in Hungary but which local police often did little to regulate. Because Hungarian authorities chose to ignore 3+2's record, gray market entrepreneurs had a clear avenue for commerce in it; it is estimated that at least 180,000 pirate cassette copies of 3+2's first recording were sold inside Hungary (Fodor 1987). A report from a Yugoslav newspaper describing 3+2's rise to popularity explained the details of this cross-border activity.

The 3+2 ensemble's record or cassette (often just a cassette recorded from the record) became the most profitable article for smuggling. It was possible to multiply its price with our northern neighbors, and [sell it] in unlimited quantities. The more ingenious earned considerable profits with 3+2 [recordings], until our northern neighbors' record distributors came around to the idea that they should import 3+2 by the legal route. (Csorba 1988: part 6)

When Hungary's laws on private enterprise were liberalized after 1988, legally organized cassette companies came into existence, capitalizing on 3+2's success with new *lakodalmas* rock recordings by copycat bands. The money from *lakodalmas* rock sales, according to Sándor Beck, the owner of the Kembeck cassette company, financed subsequent recording ventures like Vlach Gypsy music or Hungarian-language covers of Western rock hits (Beck 1991; Valkó 1992). As of 1992, there were some seventy cassette companies in Hungary, taking a wide variety of commercial and aesthetic approaches. With *lakodalmas* rock as its foundation, this industry constituted a "cassette culture" (Manuel 1993). Both small entrepreneurs and larger firms were involved; there were varied genres, production resources, and qualities of recording.

Lakodalmas Rock and a Popular Aesthetic

Lakodalmas rock was successful because, as vernacular musical culture, it expressed the values of ordinary Hungarians in multiple ways (by "ordinary Hungarians" I mean those who were villagers before World War II and then formed an urban "working class" under Socialism).[4] *Lakodalmas* rock had continuity with ordinary Hungarians' past as villagers. It interpreted the changes after Socialism from an ordinary person's viewpoint, and it conformed to a working-class aesthetic, which Pierre Bourdieu has called the "taste of necessity" (Bourdieu 1984: 379).

Ferenc Csók, a village disk jockey, *lakodalmas* rock fan, collector of the music, and one of my interlocutors, attributes the music's broad popularity to two factors. He says that older people enjoyed the melodies, and young people enjoyed the music because it was *gépzene* — literally, "mechanical music" (Csók 1992). His comment makes clear that although the music used electronic instruments and many newly composed texts, fans understood the *lakodalmas* rock style to represent the continuation of a tradition of popular music in Hungary.

The repertoire performed in Hungary's rural areas during the twentieth century includes folk songs, the *magyar nóta* songs originally composed for Hungarian theater, European popular dances, and Hungarian *csárdás* dance tunes. Several of these genres had begun to enter the villages in the nineteenth century when Hungarian-language theater was started and when young villagers increased their contacts with urban culture through military and domestic service. The Hungarian ethnomusicologist Pál Járdányi stated as much in his 1943 monograph about a Transylvanian Hungarian village, observing: "the song material is decidedly of an urban character . . . many new songs are continuously absorbed into the village" (Járdányi 1943: 87). With their appearance as a type of recorded music in the 1980s, these varied kinds of music were then dubbed *lakodalmas* rock.

The use of electric guitar, synthesizer, and drums by *lakodalmas* groups demonstrates a pattern of updating instrumentation that local bands had followed at least from the early part of the twentieth century. *Magyar nóta* was originally sung to the accompaniment of so-called "Gypsy bands," small string ensembles (Sárosi 1978). In local practice, however, accordion, tambura, or brass instruments were often added. Snare drums and the saxophone may also have made an appearance in these bands before the Second World War, reflecting the taste for European dance orchestras that prevailed in the country's capital, Budapest (Szeverényi 1988). The use of electric guitar, synthesizer, and drum set simply updated *nóta* performance to the late twentieth century, by which time a demographic shift had taken place and most ordinary Hungarians worked at factory jobs in urban areas rather than in the agricultural sector.

Pierre Bourdieu posits that working people in France have a "popular aesthetic" that applies an ethos of the ordinary conditions of existence to works of art. Bourdieu observes that gratification is one manifestation or praxis of the popular aesthetic; another is a "taste of necessity." This type of taste manifests itself in ways that the upper classes perceive as vulgar and excessive, but which to the non-elite is a truthful interpretation of its own social conditions (Bourdieu 1984: 4). For the ordinary, non-elite Hungarian, *lakodalmas* rock offered a localized interpretation of post-Socialist economic conditions, openly acknowledged sexual gratification as a condition of contemporary existence, and in its musical sound manifested a special "taste of necessity," which has historical roots in Hungarian peasant culture.

A significant number of *lakodalmas* rock songs rework the motifs of *nóta* lyrics to make implied sexual references more explicit than they were in the nineteenth-century genre. For example, 3+2's hit arrangement of "The Lace Slip" utilizes the convention from *nóta* of a rendezvous at a well-known Hungarian landmark. The song's narrator meets a girl at the Margaret Bridge, a Budapest fixture dating from the days of the Roman Empire. But the narrator of 3+2's song not only meets the girl, he seduces her there. The realism of the song is enhanced by the fact that the Margaret Bridge actually is a common place for sexual encounters in Budapest.[5]

> Slip, slip, the lace slip
> Tonight I'm going to lift it up.
> Bridge, bridge, under the Margaret Bridge
> We stared at the girls there.
> Don't be afraid, little girl,
> The sheet will cover you up.
> (Majorossy, Szenes, and Darvas 1986)

Other *lakodalmas* songs mix erotic allusions with comments on the illicit commercial activities in flea markets or on the influx of computerized technology.

Bourdieu, maintaining that working-class taste is pragmatic, observes that the decor chosen by working-class people accords with established conventions. Because of the working class's limited relation to economic

resources, a "taste of necessity" prevails, "inspired by an intention unknown to economists . . . that of obtaining maximum 'effect' . . . at minimum cost" (Bourdieu 1984: 379).

Ordinary Hungarians cultivate a "taste of necessity" both in their physical surroundings and with music. Just as certain rooms in their houses are
filled with brightly colored embroidery, paintings, and pottery, so their music is florid and thickly textured. All over Eastern Europe, the propensity for
elaborate ornamentation was a manifestation of the peasant mentality in the
nineteenth century, which converted the potential for monetary wealth into
spectacular, homemade artistic display and ritual extravaganzas (Foster
1965: 305–6; Hofer 1984: 117–18). Tamás Hofer observes that in the context of present-day Hungary, the preference for elaborate decoration has
been "compartmentalized" and may be evident, for example, in the decor of
only one room in a dwelling (Hofer 1984: 125). Although its roots may be
uniquely Eastern European and although it is not as pervasive as it was in the
nineteenth century, this orientation of taste parallels the "maximum effect"
aesthetic of the Western European working class.

In *lakodalmas* rock instrumentations, as in those of its nineteenth-
century predecessor *magyar nóta,* effect dominates. The texture of traditional *magyar nóta* arrangements is very thick. The melody may be hetero-
phonically rendered by a singer, the violinist bandleader, a second violinist,
and/or a wind instrument, particularly the clarinet (Sárosi 1986: 148–52).
The melody is accompanied by at least one and sometimes more chord
instruments, and a separate bass line. In slow songs, the bass moves by
glissando, and the chords are played portamento, so that there are few
"gaps" in the texture. Pauses in the singing are filled in with what musicians
call *cifrázás* or decoration, a standard repertoire of motives that can be
transferred between pieces. Tunes at fast tempo are accompanied by chords
in an offbeat pattern.

Lakodalmas groups balance *nóta* and electronic arrangement techniques,
utilizing options on keyboard synthesizers and amplification techniques like
reverb to thicken musical texture. In accompaniment to a solo singer, two
synthesizers with contrasting timbre options may be used simultaneously.
Instruments like the clarinet or the violin from traditional *nóta* bands may be
added. Heterophonic texture is common, and conventional melodic motifs
from the *magyar nóta* genre may be interjected.

Many of the musical elements used in *lakodalmas* rock might not be considered on the surface traditional or locally conventional, as they are lifted from Western rock music and from the sound options available on drum machines and synthesizers. However, although these may initially sound like ordinary Western uses or untutored experimentation, they still serve to thicken the musical texture and they conform to a Magyar preference for thick and raspy sound. From an economic standpoint, the synthesizer in *lakodalmas* rock also obtains multiple effects at minimum expense; because it can produce percussion, melody, and harmony, it eliminates the need for many band members.[6]

Lakodalmas rock, like its string band predecessors, exhibits a "taste of necessity" by seeking maximum effect at minimum cost. In addition to its details of musical sound, *lakodalmas* rock texts express a vernacular orientation of taste as well. Song lyrics reflect everyday life, with sexual gratification and socioeconomic conditions as major themes. Like the propensity for profuse, homemade decoration in Magyar homes, *lakodalmas* rock expresses the aesthetic of ordinary Hungarians.

The Rejection of *Lakodalmas* Rock by Intellectuals

Lakodalmas rock was vehemently rejected by intellectuals and the media in Hungary. Because they considered *lakodalmas* rock in bad taste and of inferior quality, media authorities excluded *lakodalmas* rock from the airwaves and, for a period of two years, from record stores and formal concert venues (Décsi 1987).[7] When 3+2 finally made its first tour of Hungary in 1987, newspaper reviewers all over the country attacked the group fiercely. One review, titled "Blődli dal" ("Idiotic song"), dubbed *lakodalmas* rock

overly modern electronic kitsch, dumped on the audience, reviving a lacy, pink, brandied, beribboned village art-song romanticism which . . . we thought had finally passed away. (Blődli dal 1987)

This passage, like most other reviews of *lakodalmas* rock, is full of charged metaphoric language. The writer is objecting to the fact that *lakodalmas* rock sounds like nineteenth-century *magyar nóta* rendered on electronic instruments. By calling the music idiotic, he implies that its fans are stupid.

The term "dumped" equates the music with commercial wares that are flooded on markets to lower their value. The reviewer also calls up an image of almost indigestible sweetness, equating it with the "art-song" of villages — that is, with popular music and not folk genres.[8]

Those who attacked *lakodalmas* rock were not state authorities per se but conservative intellectuals with a nationalist bent, who were well integrated into the authority structure of the media in Hungary. That the reaction was widespread is evident not only from the expressions of distaste by many intellectuals with whom I spoke personally about the genre but also by the broad variety of newspapers in which negative reviews appeared. The newspapers that published essays on the subject ranged from those filled with Communist rhetoric, like the *Szolnok Megyei Néplap,* to *Magyar Nemzet,* the most liberal paper of the time.

The liberal or so-called "urbanist" intellectuals and dissidents in the Socialist countries usually had an outward-looking orientation, toward the West, and were indifferent about *lakodalmas* rock. Unlike them, conservative or "populist" intellectuals were oriented inward, toward their own countries. The state often gave them the authority to define and control the day-to-day operations of cultural policy.[9] Under a Socialist cultural policy for the region, which had its origin in Stalin's 1930s reconciliation with non-Communist intellectuals, they assumed the privilege and duty of guiding the tastes of nonintellectuals (Fitzpatrick 1976). Many of the intellectuals were not wholeheartedly complicit; they followed a strategy of "para-opposition," whereby they paid lip service to the state in order to gain partial autonomy (Fehér, Heller, and Márkus 1983: 196; Schöpflin 1979: 142). Ferenc Fehér, Agnes Heller, and György Márkus note that because of this compromise, this group "seeks for a piece of firm ground untouched and unsoiled by the doctrine" (Fehér et al. 1983: 196). In Hungary, folk music and nationalism served as this grounding force.

Nationalist intellectuals reacted so vehemently to *lakodalmas* rock because it violated their deeply held belief that folk music should be the idiom of ordinary Hungarians, as former villagers. Hungarian intellectuals had specific standards of appropriate behavior for "the folk" because, following the romantic ideals of Central and Eastern European nationalism, the folk were a basis upon which to define national character and identity. This intellectual nationalist ethos emphasized and redefined the purity of the

Hungarian people, while at the same time it reinforced intellectuals' aesthetics as members of an elite.

Magyar nóta had been the first nineteenth-century product of Hungarian nationalist enthusiasm. The musical standards of the day required some compositional treatment of folk music, whether it was harmonization of melodies or wholesale composition in folk style. In the twentieth-century interwar period, Bartók and Kodály became proponents of the student *népi mozgalom* or folk movement, which aimed at Hungarian autonomy in the shadow of German dominance. Bartók and Kodály introduced the idea that artistic perfection and purity lay in actual folk music and not in *magyar nóta*. Village culture (not staged musical plays about peasants) was the ideal national model. Its perfection lay in its natural purity; folk music was

the outcome of changes wrought by a natural force whose operation is unconscious . . . it is as much a natural product as are the various forms of animal and vegetable life. For this reason, the individuals of which it consists — the single tunes — are so many examples of high artistic perfection. (Bartók 1981: 3)

Magyar nóta was then considered artificial. Composed only in the *style* of folk music, it was considered a shallow, sentimental, and therefore false expression of Hungarianness (Losonczi 1968: 41).

Realizing that in most of Hungary, *nóta* really was the music of choice for villagers, Kodály designed a plan to reintroduce folk music. Even after the Socialist system was instituted, which promoted internationalist ideals and the drawing of folklore into centrally organized institutions, Kodály had the power to apply his ideas at the local level because of his fame and prestige. He implemented his musical education method containing exclusively Hungarian folk music materials (Dobszay 1993: 180–83, 202–4). Village teachers and other local intelligentsia started clubs for folk singing in the 1960s. These moves to reestablish folk song as the musical literature of all Hungarians, but particularly of villagers, appeared to be successful when young villagers and workers participated along with intellectuals in the 1970s *táncház mozgalom* or dance-house movement revival of Transylvanian Hungarian music and dance (Siklós 1977). Meanwhile, conservative intellectuals ignored Ágnes Losonczi's study (1969), which discovered that working-class and rural people continued to prefer *magyar nóta* to folk and classical music. *Lakodalmas* rock's appearance in the 1980s thus shocked many intellectuals. One reviewer essentially admitted failure for the programs of reinstituting folk music, observing "it seems that *magyar nóta* has a thousand heads" (Jurkovics 1987).

One obvious reason why intellectuals reacted so vehemently against this music was that *lakodalmas* rock used electronic instruments, which violated the naturalness that country people's art was supposed to embody. But intellectuals did not object to electric instrumentation if it was used in a high art context; for example, the rock opera *Steven the King* gained critical acclaim for its blend of pop instrumentation with classical music and folk song (Markos 1983). Critics were primarily disgusted at *lakodalmas* rock lyrics. The song texts obliterated rustic ideals by referring to elements of modern life, like hard currency and computers. *Lakodalmas* rock lyrics were sentimental and had sexual references. Even the enthusiastic response of audiences was objectionable. One reviewer criticized what he saw as a lack of control, observing that "at the concerts of the 3+2 ensemble, the audience gets drunk on musical champagne dinners" (Hajba 1987). The words of this reviewer and the horrified reaction of other intellectuals indicate a complex operation, combining what Bourdieu called the "dominant class" aesthetic with Hungarian national consciousness.

According to Bourdieu, intellectuals in France belong sometimes to the dominant class and sometimes to the petite bourgeoisie. The dominant-class aesthetic emphasizes restraint and inaccessibility and manifests itself in what Bourdieu, following Kant, terms "pure taste" (Bourdieu 1984: 86). When, as in the popular aesthetic, the subject is lost in the object, those who hold the dominant aesthetic experience horror and disgust.

The whole language of aesthetics is contained in a fundamental refusal of the *facile* . . . "pure taste," purely negative in its essence, is based on the disgust that is often called "visceral" . . . for everything that is "facile." . . . Disgust is the paradoxical experience of enjoyment extorted by violence, an enjoyment which arouses horror. This horror [is] unknown to those who surrender to sensation. (Bourdieu 1984: 486, 488).

That *lakodalmas* rock texts were sentimental and that the music's fans exhibited direct enjoyment of the music is a violation of pure taste as set forth by Bourdieu. Sexual purity is also tied in with the idea of the nation, so that when *lakodalmas* rock texts referred in a comparatively direct manner to sex, this was a grievous violation against intellectual aesthetics. George Mosse argues that from its inception, nationalism in Europe was intertwined with the concept of sexual respectability. It was this interrelationship that upheld the social order for various European nations in the nineteenth and twentieth centuries (Mosse 1985: 1–20, 181–85). Therefore, when 3+2's song "The Lace Slip" implied that the narrator had sex underneath a national landmark, the Margaret Bridge, intellectuals may have reacted to it not just as a violation of "pure taste" but also as a violation of the respect and respectability due the nation.

The gratification experienced by *lakodalmas* rock fans actually threatened to destroy Hungarianness. Ordinary Hungarians indulging in their own enjoyment of *lakodalmas* rock's sexually explicit lyrics, sentimental melodies, and electronic instrumentation forced intellectuals out of an idealized, pure realm into the visceral. Because *lakodalmas* rock sullied or even eliminated the idealized Other, the villagers by which intellectuals constituted themselves as a class and a nation, it threw intellectuals' concept of themselves as human beings into jeopardy.

Reinterpretations

The fans of many popular culture idioms suffer the predicament of subalterns, effaced by the opinions that others voice about them (Spivak 1988). They act through consumption, listening to music, attending concerts, and buying recordings. Martin Stokes observes that in Turkey, negative rhetoric so dominates the discourse on *arabesk* that its advocates lack the ability to articulate their views (Stokes 1992a: 129–30). This was not the case for *lakodalmas* rock in Hungary. Fans of the music found venues to express their opinions as Socialism dissolved; the transition to a capitalist system also caused some intellectuals to rethink their positions on *lakodalmas* rock.

Provincial newspapers were one forum for the interchange of views. Socialists exercised a policy of pragmatic press control in Hungary. This policy focused censorship on the national press and allowed localized publications some degree of editorial flexibility (Schöpflin 1979: 144). A few local newspapers published letters to the editor that *lakodalmas* rock fans sent in reaction to negative reviews; these letters often alluded to broad social dissatisfactions.

It's my position that people demand music for enjoyment. It may be kitsch, but we people who are tired out from too many educational texts and from daily work are in need of relaxation. (Kozma 1986)

This writer makes clear his exasperation with intellectuals' attempts to edify him on the musical front; with his comment on work fatigue, he also manages to get in a subtle jab about the general negative effects of an overly regulated Socialist society. Another response to intellectual condemnations came in the tabloid publications that mushroomed in the early 1990s, when Hungary had officially given up its Socialist system in favor of capitalism. In these pages, *lakodalmas* rock stars were depicted as heroes — extremely rich from their earnings but terminally saddened because of exclusion from the upper class. "I don't have a single friend" was the title for one of the many tabloid feature articles on the star Lagzi Lajsci. He reported there and in several other interviews that his donations to artistic foundations were refused (Lagzi 1991; Zoltán 1991).

Many intellectuals continued to condemn and exclude *lakodalmas* rock, although their authority in the media began to erode as capitalism became a more dominant force in Hungarian society. When the programming of Hungarian state radio was revised to become "listener friendly" and less education oriented at the beginning of 1992, one of its program directors asserted that *lakodalmas* rock would still be kept from the airwaves (Varsányi 1991). But other intellectuals broadened their view on the *lakodalmas* rock controversy to go beyond questions of quality. One Hungarian essayist, utilizing the title of 3+2's hit song in synecdoche, asserted that *lakodalmas* rock had transmuted Western elements into a native Hungarian idiom.

"Slip" music promises a kind of violin-like, native realism in the shadow of the foreign magic of computerized entertainment music trends. . . . Of course, this realism is not the realism of the ballrooms of select hotels, not the strobe light truth of urban discotheques, and not the purple radicalism of high culture or its sallow pickiness. No refinement, no selectivity, no alienation. This music has the smell of sweat. . . . It is the custom to shout this music out at dawn after weddings, drunkenly and with bared souls. It mirrors a kind of general need, regardless of age group. (D. Szabó 1986)

This writer does not express disgust at the facile. Eliminating the question of taste, he sees *lakodalmas* rock as expressing a general national need. The issue of "refinement" is reconstituted as a question of foreign versus native. This is a new point of interpretation, addressing the late and post-Socialist influx of Western capitalism and all its glitter. *Lakodalmas* rock, at least for this essayist, could be a genuine expression of Hungarianness for all.

Conclusion

Lakodalmas rock resulted from the transition of Socialism to capitalism. The music recalled conflicting visions of Hungarianness from the pre-Socialist period. The political message of *lakodalmas* rock was not particularly important; it was rather the music's pragmatism, which contradicted the high aesthetic constructions of intellectuals. *Lakodalmas* rock was grounded in the musical tastes of ordinary Hungarians. Members of the intellectual elite who had tried to manipulate these tastes were shocked that the Other upon whom they depended to mirror the nation had violated their cherished ideal of pure Hungarianness.

That the nationalist intelligentsia could not reform the musical preferences of ordinary people supports Bourdieu's contention that artistic taste is rooted in broad structural differences. The intellectuals utilized a cultural capital that they gained as a partially compromised opposition under the Socialist system. Ordinary people resisted their reform efforts both as alien state and elite direction, while the intellectuals held to folk music as a subject unsullied by Socialist planning and rhetoric. *Lakodalmas* rock is part of a worldwide, postmodern clash of center with periphery over cassette musics. But in Hungary, the marginal confronted the dominant at a unique historical moment. *Lakodalmas* rock was one of the first subjects upon which Hungarians reflexively engaged their own internal differences.

Notes

This essay is based on research performed in 1990–92 under the auspices of a U.S. Fulbright grant for graduate research and a research grant from the International Resource and Exchanges (IREX) Board. The funds of the IREX grant were provided by the National Endowment for the Humanities and the United States Information Agency. None of these organizations is responsible for the views expressed. The help of Tamás Hofer, Erzsébet Szeverényi, Júlia Lévai, Alice Egyed, and my principal field colleague Ferenc Csók is gratefully acknowledged. I thank Judit Frigyesi and Henry Glassie for their comments on this article in its written and lecture forms.

1. Both fans and critics refer to this music in a variety of ways; "*lakodalmas* rock," as the most prevalent expression, is adopted here with the understanding that it is a reductive term.

2. The playing of records not in public distribution was a pattern for Hungarian state radio as well, particularly if authorities decided after the fact of publication to censor specific cuts on a record (Lévai 1992). See also Szemere (1992: 102).

3. It would have been impossible to have generated popularity by this means in Hungary, because the request programs were faked on Hungarian radio (Szeverényi 1992).

4. In my opinion, Peter Burke's terms "non-elite" or "ordinary people" (Burke 1978: 1–2), although formulated for an earlier historical period, are more accurate than the term "working class." An industrially based working class in Hungary existed only after World War II, and then dissolved along with Socialism.

5. One effect of the realism in these songs, where sex is concerned, is that it departs from the formal conventions of lyric song. Many *lakodalmas* rock texts generate a narrative sequence through slight changes in textual phrases, which indicate that a sexual encounter was initiated and then took place.

6. The actual cost of investing in an instrument does not seem to be relevant. My interlocutors rarely complained about financial or even tactical inability to get an instrument. Many successful club and wedding musicians earn from tips much more money than the average salaried Hungarian (Lakodalmak 1987).

7. The first concert of *lakodalmas* rock in Hungary's capital city drew more than ten thousand fans at the Budapest Sports Stadium, without formal advertising (Fodor 1987).

8. In Hungarian parlance, the term "art song" does not always refer to Western art music. It also means music that falls outside the formal stylistic boundaries of folk song.

9. Urbanist-populist debates took place in Hungary before and during World War II; discussions on the topic were revived at the end of the Socialist period (Nagy 1990; Gyurgyák 1990).

ANNA CZEKANOWSKA

Continuity and Change in Eastern and Central

European Traditional Music

There has been an intense reevaluation of the nature of folk culture and folk art since the 1950s. Their future is often seen as uncertain. Even when the predictions for the future of traditional forms are optimistic, they include statements about change of function. Current theories of folk culture and art are numerous and diverse, ranging from the concrete results of empirical studies to very general and highly abstract formulations. Theorizing tends to apply itself both to European and non-European cultures, covering very distinct, incommensurate societies. Two approaches seem to predominate. The first is the concept of "revival," while the second refers to "invented traditions." Both date back to the mid-twentieth century. The former may be related to Walter Wiora's term *Das zweite Dasein* ("second life"; Wiora 1958), and the latter to the even older approaches of Robert Redfield (1941, 1947, 1968) and the more recent work of Hobsbawm and Ranger (1983), among others. Over the last century, of course, folk culture has undergone serious transformation as a result of social, political, and economic changes, which have caused migration of populations as well as internal shifts in social structure. It is impossible to analyze recent change according to assumptions of nineteenth-century European folklore studies or approaches largely related to non-European contexts.

The relatively conservative culture of the peasant communities of Eastern and Central Europe is quite specific and in no way homogeneous. The present essay seeks only to clarify the picture of this region, suggesting the scope of possible studies in continuity and change. For many of the scholars researching the traditional communities, the concepts of "revival" and "invention" seem somewhat misplaced (see Mozeyko 1991; Shchurov 1994). These scholars remain convinced that the vividness of the "nature" or "essence" of folk music and folk culture are holding firm and that current changes, although observed and taken into account, are too weak to break the paradigm of tradition. Polish researchers, however, are more cautious in their judgments, since the position of traditional culture is quite different in Poland.

Polish folk culture, while undergoing change, still shows considerable signs of continuity. Indications of "revival" and "invention" are marginal, if they are understood as the reconstruction of musical instruments or songs that nobody now remembers and that are known only from the literature. Yet in many cases it is difficult to imagine an ongoing "natural" functioning of folk transmission. It goes without saying that in order to continue, folk culture would need to be supported by cultural policy and new programs such as festivals, whose importance is now crucial. However, answering questions about the transformed "nature" or "essence" of tradition is very difficult in the Polish case. The issues concern the admissibility and range of intervention. The new "myths" that are being created around folk culture should neither divorce tradition from its natural breeding ground nor alter the present motivation for its survival. However, one must also consider the very nature of the new communities that are springing up, in terms of their permanence and their ability to assume the functions of the older traditional groupings. For example, despite the great popularity of folk ensembles, it is difficult to regard these as alternatives to the communities formed by ritual and customary norms.

Indeed, the paradigm of traditional culture has undoubtedly changed in Poland. People no longer live their lives according to the calendar, and family customs that relied heavily on traditional music are no longer observed. Significant changes have taken place in this respect. Even the Church allows people to rehearse singing and dancing for a festival during Lent. As far as family celebrations are concerned, one notices the evident decline of traditional repertoire. Changes also concern normative gender roles and the differentiation of repertoire with regard to age group. Often women are now instrumentalists and dominate the management of festival activity (Czekanowska 1996b), and the creation of so-called children's groups and songs is a totally unprecedented phenomenon. Finally, references to occupation — for example, shepherds and farmers — are no longer important. None of these changes could have been observed even twenty years ago.

The transformation is now so advanced that it calls into question the factors that preserve the "nature" or "essence of folk culture. The most significant of these are psychological, possibly relating to an innate sensitivity and openness to nature as well as maintenance of traditional beliefs on an intuitive basis. Of course, this varies considerably by region, even within Poland — as, for example, the obvious difference between the more rationally motivated and rather humorous songs of Central and Western Poland compared to those lyrical and nostalgic songs of the East and the Northeast in particular. One way to focus in on some of the most salient issues affecting change and continuity is to address the issue of "ethnicity," to which I now turn.

In assessing this factor, it is critical to differentiate between cultural programs imposed by higher authorities (which are usually politically motivated) and local conventions conditioned by local sensibilities. "Ethnic" programs are vulnerable to nationalist programs. There is no doubt that many well-developed folklore projects and initiatives to "revive" and/or "reinvent" tradition are in fact nationalistically inspired. This can be seen in both Western European countries (e.g., Ireland) and Eastern European countries (e.g., the Baltic nations) in which the fight for cultural/national identity is still of crucial importance, as it is in the post-Soviet states such as Kazakhstan, since the population has been dominated by other nations and cultures. Drawing a line of demarcation between nationalist motivation and the inner need for self-identity is a highly essential task. In brief, it is important to differentiate between the need to confirm one's self and values and the incitement of prejudice and discrimination against others. This is why neither the concept of a seemingly universal, in fact unicultural, music nor new categories of globally understood spirituality — proposed by such modern composers and thinkers as Stockhausen (*Telemusik,* 1966; *Stimmung,* 1968), Schnebel (*Denkbare Musik,* 1972), and Zender (*Happy New Ears,* 1991; see Ruf 1994) — seem to have had great success in Eastern and Central Europe.

Although the literature on ethnic sensitivity has been growing rapidly, the issue is still not fully understood and needs further research. Changes currently observed in the area of consciousness often lead to misunderstanding. Here we have to keep in mind the discrepancy between what exists in the artifacts of study (musical structure), revealed by scholars only after strenuous research (although they may not realize or even wish to realize this), and what is actually expressed in the discourse about music and the opinions of the "subjects" of investigation (performers and listeners). It is only through deep insight into these two realities and their proper juxtaposition that we can approach the situation (see Herndon 1993).

"Ethnicity" is based on existing myths that are not always the result of historical events but are rather the result of programs imposed by dominant authorities that also refer to history. The reality under examination is often more complicated than the available mythology, and performers as well as listeners may not always be aware of this, since they are the targets of manipulation. As research shows, the preservation of tradition is often influenced by myths that refer to an idealized past, especially when this past was lost involuntarily — for example, as the result of enforced displacement or the imposition of new political borders. The mythologizing of the past, resulting in a cherishing of a particular traditional repertoire, can be observed among Polish communities outside Poland, especially those that remained on their native soil after having been cut off when new borders were drawn — for example, the Poles from the Grodno region after 1939 (Frasunkiewicz 1996). This can also be seen among the Ukrainian, Ruthenian, and Łemke communities in Poland, which were subjected to enforced resettlement in 1946–47 (Tarasiewicz 1996). In both cases, the past — lost involuntarily and irretrievably — becomes a mythic sphere referred to and idealized, and the preservation of cultural elements with which people wish to identify becomes a primary imperative.

These examples appear to confirm what is known from the literature and supports one perspective on "ethnicity." National cultural programs that refer to historical events, seen locally as crucial in arousing integrative feelings, offer corroborating evidence. These programs include commemorations of historical facts such as uprisings and battles — for example, the idealization of the Chmielnicki and Cossack revolts in Ukrainian projects. This type of reinterpreted history contributes to the creation of myths that become extremely vital under new social conditions. Far more difficult to understand is the mythologizing of Bosnia as the lost homeland by émigrés who returned to Poland in 1945 after living in Bosnia only seventy years. Their carefully preserved culture is an extremely interesting example of an interethnic phenomenon. People are fully aware of reciprocal cultural infiltration and preserve it, carefully privileging what was irretrievably lost (Dahlig 1996). The results of interviews clearly indicate the dominance of psychological factors that seem even more important than history.

The conventionality of borders is another helpful perspective. Not only does this pertain to situations in which a border has been imposed but also to contexts in which borders have not changed over long periods of time. One of the most interesting cases is the conventionality of Polish borders in the south, where reside communities of different nationalities who used to live on opposite sides of the border. Often these communities have more that unites them than divides them, and here cultural ties are clearly stronger than national ones (Czekanowska 1996b). Much the same applies to the southeastern Polish-Ukrainian border established in 1945, where apparently different national groups preserve essentially the same culture. These results seem to confirm the sociological research on the awareness of neighboring communities that points to Poles having closer ties to their eastern rather than their western neighbors (cf. Illasiewicz-Skotnicka 1996). This fact appears to be not a relic of the past but a current, ongoing process.

The opening up of borders in Eastern and Central Europe, which is so characteristic of our times, seems to be accelerating this process, but further study is needed to clarify the situation. It is difficult to say definitively whether a growing interest in the approval of a neighbor's music in fact results from closer acquaintance and greater consciousness based on an understanding for the need of tolerance, which is characteristic of communities with experience and perspective that reach beyond the local community. Alternately, this interest could be seen as a recognition of a deeply rooted kinship that is in fact ethnically or even pre-ethnically motivated. In other words, our aim should be to decide whether interest and approval of the neighboring Other reflects a realization of long-standing ties that can now be made apparent or whether it represents the formation of a new post-ethnic society. Regional contexts make a difference in this determination. Without a doubt, the awareness of people in eastern Poland is best interpreted in ethnic or pre-ethnic terms, as is the case in many regions of Belarus and western Russia, where national borders do not divide people clearly. The most interesting, however, is the phenomenon of local identity, which takes priority over ethnicity. It is to be found in northeastern Poland, as well as in Belarus and eastern Lithuania (Djukya). People identify themselves simply as *tutejsi,* "from here," and their language as *po prostu,* "speaking simply."

In the Carpathians, the situation is different. Evident understanding of the music of one's neighbor — for example, a Slovak or Hutsul song highly appreciated by Poles — has changed from past understandings. This seems to be the result of current shifts in awareness that are motivated partly by economic factors. Indeed, it can be explained by the spectacular effect of a neighboring music that serves as a better product for marketing.

Yet another approach takes into account the correlation between a sense of identity and the degree of traditional ethnic heterogeneity. Today's conservative homogeneous communities are located in areas that were historically quite mixed, as in Poland, where formerly Ruthenians, Lithuanians, Poles, Belorussians, Jews, Tatars, and Karaites lived side by side for long periods of time. Overall, there is a tendency toward a higher degree of conservatism in rural and relatively isolated communities. The conscious preservation of tradition in Poland is particularly distinct in regions known to be ethnically homogeneous (Carpathian highlanders) or having self-conscious, elaborate national programs (Ukrainians, Lithuanians), whereas some heteroethnic regions continue to be conditioned by long experience to cultural coexistence. Yet the situation is fluid and unpredictable despite some apparent patterns. For example, often very small groups may take a stand for identity more strongly than larger groups (e.g., see Sowińska 1994 on the Lusatians in Germany).

It is difficult to project a vision for the future, especially for the younger generations, whose needs and likes can be so easily manipulated. One of the peculiarities of our times is young people's interest in folk culture, yet it must be stressed that this too is a complex phenomenon that may have many roots. In the Polish case, it is basically an activity of the youth of the musical elite, usually representative of the "third generation," grandchildren of former folk performers and listeners. But we must also acknowledge the Western — e.g., Irish — sources of this Polish activity; one may speak even about fashion in regard to Irish music. By contrast, in Russia or Belarus these movements have indigenous roots and a more extensive social resonance. A closer look at these folklore movements helps to answer some questions about the autonomy and "rooting" of these activities by referencing the needs and predispositions of the younger generation. Close observation seems to indicate two types of motivation. One stimulus is a desire to get to know the world and other cultures, typical for young people and related to a need to oppose the accepted model of consumer culture. This may evoke unrealistic desires to return to the past, to patterns known from mythologized stories. However, one should not neglect an apparent contradiction: the purely economic motivations behind many folklore activities, even among the youth. This is especially clear in the culture of highlanders concentrated on tourism and economically motivated international travel and on the presentation at mass media in particular.

There are additional factors at work as well as these "signs of the times." The "Green Front" program that is very popular among Russian and Belorussian scholars (Mozeyko 1991), which aligns folk culture with the natural environment, seems to hit home and to prosper better than other attitudes. One can expect that traditional culture will be long preserved in these regions and nations. Indeed, the culture of the eastern areas does not seem to need quite so much revival and is not basically motivated by the economy. This "green" ideology has a natural background, being created by people still deeply rooted in local culture, and often also does not require the instruments of political or economic manipulation that are, sadly, common elsewhere.

Overall, the heritage of a common past seems to be the most important factor, along with common aims and objectives. A wide range of motivations tip the scales toward the basic character of today's changing folk culture. It is not easy to assign the role and need for folk art for contemporary societies. It is even more difficult to identify their "nature" or "essence" — that is, to draw a boundary between what is still more or less natural and seems to be long-lasting and what seems to be an ephemeral phenomenon that is artificially implanted. We continue to simply identify the creative power of traditional or newly reinterpreted activities. Let us hope that artistic sensitivity will be preserved and that a psychophysiologically motivated openness to nature will not disappear as societies continue to change.

LJERKA VIDIĆ RASMUSSEN

The Southern Wind of Change: Style and the Politics

of Identity in Prewar Yugoslavia

In the mid-1980s, a group of musicians called Južni Vetar (Southern Wind) set a stylistic model, referred to as "the oriental," within the largest folk-based music market in the former Yugoslavia — "newly composed folk music" (henceforth NCFM). The group, organized around its recording studio in Belgrade, was made up of a three-member production team/performing band, and five individual singers from Bosnia and Serbia. Južni Vetar emerged as a self-created attraction that generated a large audience, substantial music influence, and a boycott of their music by the media.

This discussion examines the controversy prompted by critics' imputation of the Eastern/Islamic origin of the oriental. The political underpinning of this imputation — the media exclusion and marginalization by the industry on one hand and the music's great popularity with the audience on the other — suggest the oppositional dynamics of the oriental surge. Even so, the controversy cannot be reduced to a single issue of opposition within the structure of domination. The ascending line of Južni Vetar's popularity throughout the 1980s coincided with the NCFM market climax and this market's dramatic downfall in the mid-1980s. Viewed against the background of the general economic decline and ambiguity of political direction in this period, the oriental controversy was no more than the surface manifestation of what was euphemistically and hopefully called "the political crisis." We will see, however, how the ideologically indexed aesthetic judgment of oriental music was pursued within an increasingly politicized public discourse, with its empowering nationalist effect on (de)legitimization of cultural practices. It is in this last period of federal Yugoslavia that the commercial breakthrough of the oriental became a point of controversy.

The Setting: Newly Composed Folk Music

Definitions of NCFM set forth by Yugoslav authors, which illustrate the precedence of sociological argumentation over musical analysis, can be summarized by two key points: (1) NCFM is a by-product of the migration of rural population to the cities and the rapid process of urbanization after World War II; (2) it is a hybrid genre drawn from local folk music sources (rural nostalgia) and commercial pop patterns (aspirations to progress), thus reflecting the conflicts inherent in migrants' adaptation to institutions of urban culture. In other words, it is a psychological statement of living in two worlds.

Far from remaining an evanescent phenomenon of post-1945 social transition, the cultural impact of NCFM, which continues unabated today, has led to an agreement that this indeed is a uniquely Yugoslav product of mass culture (Bošnjaković 1984: 101). Underscoring the "mass culture" qualification are the related factors of this music's enormous popularity and its negative aesthetic evaluation, expressed in recognition of its subversive effects on tradition, culture, and good taste. The controversy around NCFM has crystallized internally divisive issues: the homogenization of ethnic and regional diversity of Yugoslav folk music and the reference to an "eastern cultural model." This model — which accounted for NCFM's greatest consumption and popularity with the audience in southeastern parts of Bosnia-Hercegovina, Serbia, Macedonia, and Montenegro — highlights the contentious issue of its national identity: the internal East/West duality of Yugoslav culture as a projection of the Balkan/Western European distinction. Even though the argument of duality could have been challenged easily by evidence of the strong interregional linkages and the national scope of the NCFM market, the political frictions of the late 1980s only exacerbated it. The Serb-Croat conflict, in particular, has given the folk/pop music divide new political legitimacy in redrawing the East/West cultural frontiers.

NCFM can be described best in terms of a shift in the perception of folk music, fostered by its increasingly market-organized production since the 1960s, rather than as a linear development of a hybrid, acculturated musical prototype. In post-1945 Yugoslavia, the domain of *narodna muzika* (folk or people's music) included a rich variety of village and urban music and their modernized forms — the so-called "music in the folk spirit" (*muzika u*

narodnom duhu), which was created under the patronage of cultural administrators and composer-arrangers affiliated with radio stations. This genre —
which reflected the stylistic standards of Eastern European national models
of "arranged folklore," based on state-supported programs of artistically
"improved" village music performed by enlarged orchestral and choral
ensembles (Rice 1994: 181–83) — grew to represent an important material
and symbolic legacy of the post-war social practice and ideology of progress. However, Yugoslavia's early moves toward a decentralized, consumer-
oriented economy impacted expressive culture in ways that were atypical
for the state-managed cultural systems of its ideological neighbors. Record
companies, built in the 1950s as state-founded and market-operated institutions, allowed Yugoslavia to develop an industrial base of music production
that gave rise to, arguably, the strongest popular music market in Eastern
Europe. Its development was marked by waves of imported sounds beyond
the dominant Anglo-American shares; at various stages, Italian, French,
Hungarian, Greek, and Mexican influences, among others, competed for
momentum on the national music scene. This orientation toward foreign
music, in interaction with local traditions, created resources for the unprecedented growth and direction of commercial folk music, which prompted
moving away from the official-arrangement canon. As recording companies
and folk music festivals became the main promotional avenues for folk song
writers and singers, the broadcasters' monopoly over folk music production
and dissemination was gradually relegated to a formal rather than an oper-
ative function of music authority. This pattern of administrative control
over music broadcast (selective inclusion by popular demand) and a semiautonomous system of music production describes what, in stern political
jargon, represented the Yugoslav model of a socialist market.

The NCFM market provided for continuities of the Eastern (Balkan-
Mediterranean) and Western dimensions in Yugoslav music, adding to the
historical perspective and self-image of Yugoslavia as a cultural crossroad.
By the early 1970s, a rich variety of Bosnian, Serbian, and Macedonian
music grew into the main stylistic pool for "new folk song" composition,
thus setting the broad regional pattern for national consumption. During the
1980s, which saw a new generation of young singers and pop-oriented
production, an even more cohesive system of regional links emerged. Unlike the previous identification of singers with their local backgrounds and

the aesthetic of rural roots, in the 1980s a "classic" NCFM style for musicians represented merely a point of departure. Other musical variables began to play a role in reflecting on and encouraging the diverse demographic and subcultural organization of audiences. To illustrate this national constellation of regionalism, Serbian *dvojka* (double meter), Bosnian melismatic singing style, and Macedonian asymmetric (mixed-meter) rhythms grew into the most prominent stylistic codes of NCFM, valued for their regional appeal as well as national hit-potential. Underscoring this Slavic oriental juncture has been the most distinguishing feature of the performance style — expressed in vocal embellishment of song melodies — which, though frequently inviting the notion of kitsch, has provided an aesthetic distinction and a sensibility unique to this genre. In such a music climate — where local, regional, ethnic, national, and foreign elements intersected, producing a national audience as well as village markets — the notion of ethnic music has been as debatable a construct, as has the notion of national music.

Underlying this seemingly open-ended stream of historical intersections and new directions in Yugoslav music was the central music policy issue — the national identity of the music. Specifically, music variously referred to as southern, oriental, and Eastern has been the focus of recurring controversy. As early as the 1930s, the broadcast of Bosnian *sevdalinka* songs on the newly founded Radio Belgrade presented officials with the issue of the artistic value of "improvised music." Their efforts at stylistic cultivation via orchestra-arranged versions (which reduced improvisation) had produced only more listeners' demands for *sevdalinka*-style singing. We know of the continued popularity of Bosnian music from a commentator in the late 1950s who warned then of its "destructive influence on real *izvorna* [village music or music from the source] and healthy folk music: Its beauty is in simplicity and monumentality, and not in the ballast of the complicated and confused Muslim world, language, expression, and mentality which is not ours" (Zdravković, in Milošević, 1964: 9). These early institutional moves at reshaping the oriental tradition, which culminated with the national project of modernization ("music in the folk spirit"), not only had limited influence on local performances but had effectively helped the transition from the "stylized" to the "newly composed" commercial mode of orientalism.

It is within this musical context — saturated by messages of regionalism, ethnicity, Yugoslavness, and East-West and folk-pop intersections — that the group Južni Vetar set out to succeed in the market in a similar eclectic fashion — by recreating and capitalizing on a syncretic music emblematic of the regional juncture of Balkan oriental tradition: Southern Serbia, Bosnia, Macedonia, and Turkey as a cross-cultural axis.

The Terms of Controversy

If one makes a comparison, one will see that the tune is stolen, only the text is changed. Ornamentation here is something that flashes out at you, but you can't tell if you like what you hear because of that flash. — radio program director

I'm Bosnian, Muslim, but this music doesn't have any basis in our music. Why would I need Arabic music in my Bosnia, my Yugoslavia? — song writer/producer

This music has been under some kind of veto; radio simply wouldn't play it, but it continued to live in its milieu. Naturally, it became superfluous to, like, "prevent" it. — record company official

This commotion suits us fine. In fact, others began stealing from us. — the leader of Južni Vetar

While most commentators in the 1980s did not differentiate within the geocultural fixation — the "East" — or pinpoint the borrowed elements beyond the ubiquitous ornamentation, they did speculate readily about the main channels of music transplantation to Yugoslav soil: tourists and other individual contacts of musicians in Turkey and the Middle East, and the old Bosnian *muhadžer* (emigrant, refugee) network centered in Istanbul.[1] The popular press added a conspiratorial tone to the music transfer by introducing the reference label "Khomeini music," thereby effectively conveying the danger of political manipulation of the mass market. Illustrative is an analysis by a commentator who singled out Južni Vetar as a "striking example of 'exotic' kitsch of the oriental type in national, 'newly-composed song': It's been asserted that the leader of this group . . . 'actually takes ready made pieces directly from contemporary Turkish, Arabic, and Iranian popular music, and that the whole thing is not naive at all, neither from the legal, nor cultural, nor ideological point of view' " (Anastasijević 1988: 154).

Criticism highlighted two related themes of oriental discourse: denationalization of Yugoslav music and the regression of culture. Belgrade commentators raised the issue of the national identity of Yugoslav folk music, premised upon the homogeneity of older layers of Serbian folk music, being subjected to orientalization of a new (Islamic) type, spreading from the South Serbian/Bosnian hotbed. Sarajevo media authorities denounced the music as an act of blatant borrowing and a marketing strategy playing upon the Bosnian audience's predilection for "cafe music," understood as synonymous with the crude, locally cultivated, melismatic vocal style of NCFM. The oriental was, in their view, sharply distinct from the comparable model of *sevdalinka,* associated with the tradition of urban Muslim music in Bosnia-Hercegovina. As a way of probing into deeper layers of the psychodynamics of the style, some industry insiders resorted to determinist concepts of inner "genetic code" and "ethnic program" — that is, the historically conditioned and culturally reinforced preference for oriental sound among a broad section of the audience. In an attempt to evaluate the cultural impact of modern orientalism, the debate recaptured a negatively stereotyped Ottoman legacy in the region — an antithesis of the European conception of progress that shaped modern Yugoslavia.

Yet another perspective on this spectrum of positions came from musicians who pointed to a locally missing link behind the "Khomeini wave" in Yugoslav music: the *gastarbeiter* (guest-worker) communities in Western Europe. A prestigious Serbian singer with vast experience in performing for Yugoslavs in Europe and North America found it natural that "if some common musical language was to be found in the wide open world, then it was Turkish melos" (Predrag Gojković, in Luković 1989: 75). However, it was the Yugoslav variant of the oriental, promoted through NCFM's immigrant markets in German-speaking countries, that had the appeal of a musical lingua franca among diverse audiences, including Turks. Yet, the historical and cultural ties across Southeastern Europe could not always account for the new musical links and validate their contemporary value in the homeland. The critics' stance is echoed in Gojković's opinion that while we can agree that much of the music in southeastern Yugoslavia evolved under the influence of Turkish Anatolia, the new oriental "shouldn't be a cause for our worry as we are still holding on to our tradition" (Luković 1989: 75).

The rise in popularity of this music heightened the issue of ill-defined Radio authorities spoke of the urgent need to "clean" radio programming of the trashy sounds that had accumulated since this music's emergence in the market. The sense of confusion, described in 1989 by a Sarajevo radio music program director as "all boundaries are shifted now and many broken down," was created by what radio officials perceived as simultaneous pressures on the media from the music industry, the NCFM audience becoming the cultural mainstream, and the social meltdown that was feeding on the "anything goes" misconception of democracy. The realization that the music market and, by default, the broadcasting media had reached a critical point prompted broadcasters' calls for a revival of tried values of radio music (e.g., "evergreen" music, old pop standards). Policy makers cried out for some sense of stylistic coherence and integrity of culture, but did not appear to have any real confidence in their own power to control music production, much less the course of its decline. They also articulated the need for a cultural calm amid the political cacophony brought about by the conflicting programs of newly founded national parties and proponents of civil society.

Finally, the orientalism of Južni Vetar rekindled the depreciatory meaning of the notion of "newly composed culture"; Yugoslavs succinctly characterized the protagonists of the political power shifts in 1989 as "newly composed democrats." Two years later, first "newly composed regions" and, soon after, "newly composed heroes" were created by the war. The artifice of musical style became a potent metaphor for political change.

The Južni Vetar Project

The Južni Vetar musicians responded to the controversy from an economically secure and self-consciously alternative position, which the group continued to enjoy in the politically unquiet period of the late 1980s. Keenly aware of the historically determined meanings of oriental music in the South Serbian area of Vranje, Macedonia, and Bosnia, they explained their music as the product of creative freedom and implicitly, a reaction against the issue of origins. Familiar with local music traditions, *gastarbeiter* markets, and the new avenues opened up by the "world music" trend, they found oriental models to be aesthetically more satisfying and, in terms of musical depth of emotion, superior to the Western idioms with which they had begun as struggling rock, and later café, musicians. Their specific models emerged from an admiration of Turkish *arabesk* singers and their own backgrounds in southern Serbia and Bosnia.

The group was propelled into the arena of critical discussion by their remarkable success at a time of general decline of the mainstream NCFM market, largely attributed to the economic turmoil in the country. The industry estimate of this decline was from top sales figures of 600,000–900,000 copies per album in the mid-1980s down to 70,000–100,000 copies in the late 1980s. In the same period, the sales of Južni Vetar recordings continued to be markedly higher than those of many established singers and major regional producers. (The group's own estimate, based on their average annual production of five albums, amounted to well over 10 million records and cassettes sold.) It was at this juncture of the market fall off and the group's commercial rise to prominence that the oriental emerged as an oppositional undercurrent within the "hegemony of periphery," the NCFM market as a whole. When the group's niche became economically defined and the singers' media visibility increased, the friction began to manifest itself in symbolic terms, bringing the issue of identity to the forefront.

That the multinational makeup of Yugoslav culture, a dominant theme of the political program of unity and national experience, was becoming anathema became apparent as outsiders began questioning the musicians' motives on the grounds of their identities. Here the irony and contradictions are apparent; to the extent to which the Bosnian (Muslim) core of the singing team suggested the strategic purpose of ethnic authentication of the alien sound, the all-Serbian (Christian Orthodox) background of the band members undermined critics' arguments of religious intent.[2] For the musicians, who privately expressed uneasiness about the religious implications in the debate, the issue was not an issue, for it was precisely the emblematic power of the musical style and ambiguity of identity by which they transcended the obligation of national allegiances. This seemingly paradoxical claim to pluralistic makeup of the music by a conspicuously ethnic component, becomes clearer when considering how these ideas were articulated in structural terms of the music. As the issue of the disputed identity of the music emerged, the interpretation of a style as an economic category revealed conflicting demands for political rationalization of musical choices.

Recently, we came up with a nice Albanian tune, but there was a dilemma whether to include it on an album or make it so it didn't sound Albanian. This is how daily politics can be influential. We can easily become local: we turn off Turkish music, we turn off Albanian music, we turn off Serbian . . . We are expressly a Yugoslav-oriented group, and this is what is upsetting. (Interview with Miodrag Ilić, the leader of Južni Vetar, July 1989, Belgrade)

Here "Yugoslav orientation" is meant to imply inclusiveness, hence the playful suggestion that should one (preferred) ethnic idiom — Albanian — be eliminated, it follows that the key (national) idiom — Serbian — can also be eliminated from the presumed ethnic sum of a national whole.

This statement puts in sharp focus the problem of defining oriental style, indicating that it was not as homogeneously structured as its critics claimed. The orientalist elements appear marked precisely because they were juxtaposed against and integrated with different "ethnic programs" upon which Južni Vetar music drew. Their music was a repository of melodies and rhythms used in various forms in NCFM, including the most exploited Serbian *dvojka,* the Macedonian dance-based *čoček,* and the elements of pop music incorporated into band instrumentation (accordion/keyboards, electric guitar and bass). The elements most emblematic of the oriental were at the same time the most controversial: flexibility of rhythm, pseudo-modal setting of songs, melismatic improvisation, and nasal timbre of singers' voices — the performance mode that evoked Islamic chant. However, these isolated stylistic components do not indicate their structural position or their significance relative to song contexts. Vocal improvisation, for example, was most often limited to refrain sections and ending phrases of melodic lines. At times, an overtly "Eastern" aura of singing was intended to provoke the sense of unfamiliarity if not Otherness among the audience. Reverberation effect in particular was used consciously in a manner that went, in the words of the Južni Vetar musicians, "beyond the Yugoslav music market norms": the spatial depth simulated by reverb was added to sparse instrumental backgrounds while the voice was foregrounded with long, heavily ornamented stretches of improvisation. While these excesses of ornamentation and reverb may have "frightened" people who perceived them as the sonic agency of the Islamic Orient, in the musicians' discourse this was one way to recreate the "mystique and beauty" of oriental music.

Locating the Oriental in Regional Discourse

It would probably come as a surprise to most Yugoslav protagonists of the oriental debate that similar discussions have been taking place at the very sources of the disputed influence, in the near and middle eastern proximity of Turkey and Israel. According to studies by Stokes (1992b) and Regev (1989), the assumption of inferiority of what is interchangeably defined as "Eastern" and "oriental" music in the national taxonomies of Turkish and Israeli music, respectively, speak strongly of the forces of Eurocentricity at its peripheries. In Turkey, the broadcast ban of the very popular *arabesk* genre is tied to the perception of its being of foreign — that is, Eastern — origin (because of its relation to Egyptian film music); this stands in contrast to European art and popular music, which are privileged by national music broadcasting (Stokes 1992b: 215). Similarly, Regev points out strategies in the marginalization of oriental music by Israeli radio, which is dominated by art, pop, and the national *eretz* repertoire (1989: 148–49). Stokes's account is particularly illuminating, as he dissects the dynamics between ideologies of the Turkish state and of Islam, pointing out their mutually exclusive pronouncements on culture as well as ambiguities and contradictions that are played out in the experience of *arabesk* music (1992b: 225). In *arabesk* discourse, the meanings of music are easily contested by its symbolizing the politically divisive regional, ethnic, and class differences.

Closer to the regional nexus of the Balkan Orient, the popularity of wedding music in Bulgaria and its condemnation by authorities, makes a strong case study of political control of music associated with the Ottoman legacy and Muslim ethnicity. As Timothy Rice points out, the fact that the personnel of wedding ensembles was predominantly ethnic minority (Turkish and Gypsy) and that wedding music asserted a new, improvisatory, "free" performance style, effectively challenged the homogeneous notions of Bulgarian national identity and folk music authenticity (1994: 247–50). Here the "oriental" and "Turkish" appear as universalizing markers of problematic identity, underscored by the political psychology of foreign threat; for Bulgarians, this included Turkish, Greek, and Romanian music played by wedding musicians as well as Macedonian and Serbian sources.

An interesting picture of the spectral positioning of the "East" emerges as oriental music is defined from the different geographic positions (national viewpoints) in question, moving progressively southeastward. For Yugoslav observers, the primary point of reference is Turkey; for Turkish media authorities, it is Egypt; for Israeli commentators, it is the Arabic Middle East and its northwest point, Turkey. What seems to underlie the anxiety shared by cultural arbiters and mainstream audiences in these culturally and politically distinct settings is a familiar anthropological notion of "an exotic and threatening 'other' existing within the cultural or political boundaries of the state" (Stokes 1992b: 214). Devalued musical styles variously associated with the local notions of "Eastern," "Islamic," "ethnic," and "foreign," stand for marginal groups within the national hierarchies of the culturally representative. Their aesthetic inferiority, further denoted by technological qualification — cassette music — and the subcultural notion of "informal" thriving in communal, ritualistic, and club settings, supports the equation between the popular, the socially marginal, and the culturally illegitimate.

But just as the Yugoslav musicians of Južni Vetar conceived of oriental music in universalist terms, they also saw their experience at home as fitting the broader pattern of a deeper cultural friction in Europe. Especially after an episode with potential German producers who responded timidly to their music, they recognized the factor of "fear" regarding the potential penetration of music associated with Muslim identity into Western European markets — that is, beyond the immigrant enclaves within which it is largely contained. For like-minded observers, the 1989 Eurovision Song Contest only reinforced this sense of exclusion. Judging by the comments of the Južni Vetar musicians and some local press reports, the Turkish entry created the most exciting moment of the show. The group's performance contrasted sharply with the agreeable sound of European pop, making an exemplary ethno-pop statement from its eastern periphery, but it was placed last among all the participants. Indeed, the Eurovision Song Contest continues to be the powerful institution of pan-European entertainment, an arena in which national markers of difference are displayed for a moment while at the same time the structure of economic and cultural center and peripheries is disclosed, sometimes painfully for participants. As Stokes notes, Turks perceive the repeated failure of their singers on this stage as a measure of Turkey's subordinate standing in the international economic and cultural order, reflecting the Muslim world's dependency on the Christian West (1992b: 224). Similarly, the national debate on the strategy for success in the contest has continued vigorously in Yugoslavia.

Within the New Frontiers

The charge that the music by Južni Vetar had a subversive impact on the national integrity of Yugoslav culture can be illuminated from two perspectives, which span, respectively, the politically volatile period of the late 1980s and the events of 1991: the political claim to cultural distinction between the Yugoslav east and west, and the nationalist agitation of cultural schism within the eastern part itself.

The intense political debate that preceded the initial east–west partitioning in 1991, following upon the Slovenian and Croatian proclamations of independence, revived the historical legacy of Croatia's cultural orientation toward Western Europe and Serbia's toward the Eastern Slavic complex. The theme of cultural contrast began to be examined retrospectively as the issue of conflict. Against the historical background of the South Slavs' political frictions and claims about the cultural uniqueness of each group, those who argued that the two cultural models were incompatible could easily find supporting evidence in the regional patterns of popular culture consumption. For example, the popular, taste-culture stereotype of Croatians' affinity for pop music and Serbians' affinity for NCFM began to be invoked along with the political effect of cultural schism and overtones of cultured versus barbarian culture-core. The assertions of cultural differences also drew on reciprocal threats along the religious lines of Slavic Orthodox and Roman Catholic irreconcilability.

By 1990 the regional cleavages were manifested openly. The last efforts at a confederalist restructuring of Yugoslavia, which seemingly provided a temporary middle ground for negotiating the centralist position of Serbia and the secessionist plans of Slovenia and Croatia, ceased in the face of nationalists' agitation of interethnic resentments and their promises of salvation by separation. If in 1990 there was a question of salvation "from what," the answer was found soon after in the new ideological key word: "ethnic endangerment." Croats' calls for the defense of their cultural and historical space were countered by a Serbian plan to expand the frontiers of its own lebensraum, a historical occasion provided by the circumstances of the breakup. Bosnia-Hercegovina followed by declaring its own sovereignty in 1992, thus extricating itself from the remaining eastern, Serbia-dominated sphere. Only as an afterthought to the Serbs' unheralded military encroachment on this multinational land "in between" was the threat of Islam brought out to legitimize the Serb insurgents' claim to national self-determination by the conquest.

Although the new "truths" revealed by the war in Bosnia may provide many answers to complex issues from the period preceding it, they cannot be read easily into the prewar ethnography. In other words, the commentators' imputation of the Islamization of Yugoslav music cannot be linked directly to the surge of political divisiveness brought about by Serbian nationalism in the mid-1980s. Despite the subsequent totalizing impact of Serbian nationalist politics, the immediate effects of its rise were not monolithic nor were they readily observable as a legitimate expression of popular sentiments. Specifically, it was in the arena of the Belgrade *estrada* (stage entertainment/industry), the center of Južni Vetar's recording activity, where the momentum of Yugoslav political transition from 1989 to 1991 displayed the conflicting levels of opposition and acquiescence to the nationalist cause.

As one commentator put it in the politically ambiguous terms of Yugoslav culture, *estrada* itself grew into "a matrix of fierce fighting for survival and a veneer of totalitarian manipulation in the disguise of absolute freedom of choice" (Tijanić, in Luković 1989). Within this context of interacting hegemonic forces of market, high ideology, and mass audience, the media boycott of the oriental appears analogous to the moral panic that was prompted by the introduction of capitalist jazz in Yugoslavia in its early post-1945 years. In both cases, the cultural critique that articulated its opposition to music as an aesthetic concern was mobilized as a reaction against a different ideology: the critique was implicitly a critique of free choice. However, the political circumstances of musical changes were dramatically different at the onset of the 1990s.

Within the institutions of culture and *estrada,* the increasing pressure to ethnically separate and align groups brought about artists' expressions of resistance, which vacillated between proclamations of an apolitical stance, belief in a Yugoslav unity, and appeals to a peaceful answer to the crisis. The undercurrent was a collective drifting toward the nationalist solution. As the Yugoslav war entered its first stage in Slovenia in 1991, the political pronouncements of well-known artists and singers were beginning to define a politically mobilizing role for *estrada*. Both pop and folk cultures revealed new alignment with emerging regimes by employing old strategies: capturing popular political ideas and sentiments and packaging them in poetry and songs for the people's market.

It can be argued then that to a society that was drifting away from one of its professed ideals, the Serbian/Bosnian project of Južni Vetar appeared as a statement of unity. By interpreting the experience of interethnic, cross-regional collaboration as the rationale for the invention of a musical style, the group defied ever louder calls by actors of "daily politics" for musicians to align themselves with ethnicity rather than community. Južni Vetar's claim to a Yugoslav identity of their music reflected the value placed on diversity, in terms of the musicians' freedom to affirm a particular choice of ethnicity. The political effect of this orientation highlighted the ongoing ideological shift in Yugoslav culture: political delegitimation of the concept of unity and its subsequent collapse. Finally, the Bosnian authorities' denunciation of the oriental as a culturally alien model only reflected the complex layering of aesthetics, style, and ethnicity within the oriental debate, in which Islam was evoked to serve particular and conflicting interests of national ideology of Yugoslav culture.

Similarly, in 1989 a commentator could say that "NCFM still possesses a utopian element of the 'Yugoslav dream,' " but he asked the lingering question "for how long?," articulating the uncertainty of hope in being able to "look back with a sense of admiration and nostalgia" and the anticipation of fear of "what will happen after waking up?" (Kršić 1989: 607). If one entertains this possibility of admiration by looking back at the celebration of NCFM in the 1970s, the time of "greatest expectations and prosperity," as Dragičević-Šešić put it (1989: 609), then by the end of the 1980s one sees the drastically narrowed space for social optimism (and consumerism) and, soon after, the anxieties of waking up. For many, the NCFM market decline in the mid-1980s symbolically marked the breakdown of Yugoslavia's sociocultural transition from within: the issues of innovation, borrowing, the supremacy of stylistic code and image over structure and substance became aesthetic euphemisms for critiquing the excesses of *estrada*. They in turn afforded insights into the society's political experience of cultural and moral decline.

Into the Culture of War

Even though cultural changes in the former Yugoslav republics are developing in more than one direction, they are evolving in synchrony with regional and national/ethnic reconfigurations of old Yugoslav identities. As the newly independent states move inward — while contesting their territories, economic resources, and expressive means of once shared cultures — the national-populist movements and the first signs of consolidation of the war condition have emerged: their subcultures. The "sub" prefix here indicates both the complicity of subcultures in the symbolic and military performance of nationalist programs as well as a dimension of the original equation of "subculture" with social deviancy. As some Serbian commentators have discerned in the process of the glorification of war, what is particularly sought within the expressive range of folk culture are historical forms that take pride in patriarchical values and are resilient to modernist reconstruction of meaning (e.g., epic narrative). At the same time, the iconographic scope of pop subcultures is as vast and eclectic as it has ever been, reflecting stylistic distinctions in media-shaped perceptions of the warfare: Rambo-styled images of local heroes, fetishes of military dress, discriminating emblems of paramilitary formations and urban guerilla gangs, posters and videos as manifestos of war entertainment. While the subversive intent of the corruption of pop symbols may not be obvious, their appropriation in circumstances of war fragmentation is a commentary on Western culture. As Senjković notes in the context of Croatian culture at present: "[Postmodernism] . . . by its insistence on decentralization . . . has shaped a category of small identities. In that way, the national has also become a trend" (1993: 24).

NCFM itself has come full swing from the people's embrace of diversity to required ethnic legitimacy (now often achieved at the level of explicit political statement), while previous connotative strategies are pushed into the background. A significant portion of music cassette production in Serbia provides insight into a new use of regional codification — depicting military territorial gains as specific Bosnian places and landmarks are sung about in the narrative style of a (condensed) epic in praise of an (expanded) homeland. Muslim singers are solidifying the spirit of connectedness within the community by turning to their tradition of the *sevdalinka* performance which — along with newly produced songs evoking Bosnian places, images of belonging, war, and freedom — make up the main repertoire of popular singers who have joined the emerging Bosnian diaspora in Europe.

To note the militant inflections of triumphant nationalism and ethnic awakenings in the recent NCFM is not to suggest the lack of politically inspired debate related to NCFM during historically happier times of this music's social uses. As this discussion has shown, the oriental is a single issue that brought to light a serious political interpretation of NCFM. However, between entertainment and politics, NCFM has contained and mediated conflicting cultural paradigms while evolving into the grand narrative of the Yugoslav post-1945 experience of integration. In this, it has projected an apolitical nature rather than a critique of the society that condemned it. The NCFM song-form continues to provide an expressive means for musicians and audiences as they redefine their views of themselves and others. The war messages spoken through it reflect these new experiences of national identities but also call for nationalist terror. NCFM's misuse seems only to prove its communicative power: its messages are being redefined in much the same way that pop, video, and posters have smoothly accommodated to war-inspired expressive energies while retaining their media and genre distinctions.

Conclusion

It seems appropriate to close by suggesting points of continuity beneath the drama of separations, using examples from the musical diaspora, where national and ethnic cleavages created by the war reveal varied and unexpected patterns of allegiances.

The leader of Južni Vetar continues to work in Serbia (with new singers) and in the mixed *gastarbeiter* and refugee music market. An example of this is a German reissue of Južni Vetar's first commercially successful recording from 1981 with the singer Šemsa Suljaković. This singer recently issued her own recording made in collaboration with Bosnian and Serbian musicians in Austria. Among the cassettes circulating in this ex-Yugoslav émigré community, one finds a song that praises the leadership virtues of a Bosnian-Serb leader Radovan Karadžić, which is helped by a 7/8 rhythm, an appealing marker of the southern (Macedonian) oriental tradition. At another émigré venue, a Bosnian band engages the audience in singing and dancing a medley of songs featuring *sevdalinkas,* NCFM items in *dvojka* idiom, and the once all-national *kolo* dance.

These examples are perhaps only surface manifestations of continuities or failed separations in the former expressive culture, now thriving in the diaspora, but it seems these can be found as easily as are symbolically overstated practices of separate identities. In between the narrative, which strives to express the ethnically essential, and the musical practice, which continues the mixing of Serbian *dvojka* and oriental sounds, deep reconstruction of musical structures may take longer than the political process — which seems to be coming to a close — suggests. After observing the performance of a former Južni Vetar singer from Bosnia, now a refugee in Austria, a colleague of mine remarked, "Nothing has changed." This is perhaps an overstatement, but it may compete with other temporary answers that attempt to account for the nature and structure of musical changes in the region.

The oriental debate illustrates a particular aspect of political transition impressed upon culture — that music can be at once a reflective statement on the past, express ambiguities of the present, and foreshadow political change. It also highlights the perennial issue of the aesthetic autonomy of music and its ideological signification, articulated in discourses of musicians and critics by conflicting paradigms of music's meaning and value. The repetitious pattern of the oriental controversy — underscored by institutional attempts at its control, co-option, and exclusion from the media — appears as an aesthetic veneer of politicized sensitivity to ethnic expression of Otherness, the issue of identity that continues to be central to the national experience of Eastern European cultures.

Yugoslavia continued its course of exception, as evidenced by its disintegration. The political paths taken by the successor states point to similar features, with other, peaceful, post-communist transitions taking place in an interplay of the old and new — democratic changes, new socialist visions, and discriminatory attitudes inspired by nationalism.

Cultural changes are constructions of the political reality that produces, shapes, and gives meanings to them. New freedoms brought by secessions and the break with communism have had invigorating effects on interpretative revisions of the Yugoslav cultural past. In contrast, extraordinary and currently unexplainable fragments of war ethnography may easily "sink in the known places of old knowledge and texts" (Feldman, Prica, and Senjković 1993: 3) of the peacetime culture. In retrospect then, the oriental controversy appears as a metaphor for Yugoslavia, a casualty of its own strategy: positioning itself politically and culturally between the West and an imagined East, yet failing to reconcile the resulting overlap internally.

Notes

1. The Bosnian Muslim community was established in Turkey through a succession of migrations following the major political upheavals in the region: the Austro-Hungarian occupation of Bosnia-Hercegovina (1878), the establishment of the Yugoslav state (1918), and World War II.
2. The singing team also included a Rom Gypsy singer from Bosnia, a fact that illuminated the important component of Gypsy music in the oriental.

MIRJANA LAUŠEVIĆ

The Ilahiya *as a Symbol of Bosnian Muslim*

National Identity

The late 1980s to early 1990s in the former Yugoslavia are marked by the shift of power and control from the communist superculture[1] to national (ethnic)[2] and religious groups. The rapid and radical changes in the country forced reorganization on all levels of the social structure, moving the boundaries between superculture, subcultures, and intercultures and changing their contents and appearances.[3] In Bosnia and Hercegovina, a republic in the central part of former Yugoslavia (referred to hereafter simply as Bosnia), Muslim subculture took on the role of superculture after the Muslim national party won the elections in the fall of 1990. The process of taking power was not only connected with but was even enabled by the use of music in forging group cohesion among Bosnian Muslims. Although this essay focuses on the prewar period, the most recent use of music for political purposes is also addressed.

The decline of the Yugoslav superculture paved the road toward supercultural status for the Bosnian Muslims.[4] To trace this historical path and provide perspective on the present-day situation, I begin by defining and analyzing superculture–subculture relationships in Yugoslavia before 1990.

The Yugoslav Superculture

Ever since the formation of Yugoslavia in 1918, the so-called "national question" had been the hottest political issue in the country. After World War II the socialist government tried to solve the national question by enforcing the ideology of "brotherhood and equality" among all Yugoslav nations. In light of this ideology, national feelings were perceived as nationalistic (separatist) ones. The cultural expressions of different nations were seen as capable of arousing strong national(istic) feelings that would tear apart the weak, young country and lead toward conflicts among the nations and national (ethnic) groups that had fought on different sides in their recent history.[6]

Since the socialist superculture used its power to discourage identification along the lines of national (ethnic) groups, the young socialist country had to provide a new and common identity for its citizens. In other words, its power and control was directed toward engendering social cohesion among different national (ethnic) groups living "under the same roof." Emphasis was placed on shared values — a common, communist "religion," mixed marriages, blending of ethnic cultural features — and on creating a whole new symbolic world and imagery with which all Yugoslavs could identify. The superculture used all the arts in creating this imagery, but music's unique ability to address and affect large numbers of people gave it an extremely important role in supporting the aforementioned values, and in providing a framework for an identity that crossed ethnic boundaries. It is possible to distinguish three main supercultural musical "umbrellas" under which socialist Yugoslav imagery and its symbolic world were fostered: (1) revolutionary songs, (2) the work of cultural and artistic ensembles, and (3) popular music (the recording industry).[7] Each of these supercultural umbrellas is briefly discussed here in order to describe the way the Yugoslav superculture handled the national question in the domain of music culture. The current use of traditional and religious musics for political purposes, as well as the resurgence of nationalistic songs throughout the former Yugoslavia needs to be interpreted in relation to these past cultural policies.

Revolutionary Songs

One of the most supported and approved means of musical expression in socialist Yugoslavia was the singing of "revolutionary" songs.[8] The songs themselves, usually performed by large uniformed choirs, differed greatly in style. Simple, catchy tunes, popular folk songs, songs composed in pompous "revolutionary" style or more subtle artistic forms in the classical musical idiom were produced to suit the varied tastes and musical backgrounds of Yugoslavs.[9] "Revolutionary songs" were intended to become music for everybody, a way of strengthening unity and brotherhood among nations and of celebrating the Yugoslav government and its socialist ideology. These songs were directed toward maintaining social cohesion and developing patriotic feelings and a socialist Yugoslav identity. This genre contained little or no subcultural reference, as it was a product of the socialist revolution and the new ideoscape — to use Appadurai's (1990) apt term. Subcultural sounds — that is, the musics of different ethnic and regional groups — had to be handled with special care. These musics were remodeled and labeled with expressions like "cultural heritage" or "traditional folk treasure," the terminology itself suggesting their value as museum pieces rather than living musical expressions of a particular national (ethnic) group.

Cultural and Artistic Ensembles

The fostering of "traditional music" was assigned to "cultural and artistic ensembles," melting pots in which all Yugoslav nations could, and should, gather and blend. Cultural and artistic troupes were amateur institutions founded and supported by the government. The importance of these ensembles in providing a sense of community and common identity among its members was enormous. By practicing each others' folk dances and songs, the youth were learning to respect and love the "differences" that should connect, and not divide, people.[10] Membership was always on a territorial basis, not on a national one, and ethnic diversity had to be ensured. The performances of these groups were a potpourri in which each of the Yugoslav nations had to be represented by a perfected and polished "folk" piece, estranged from the actual performance practice of a particular ethnic group.[11] The emphasis was shifted from confirmation of a single national identity toward egalitarianism and unity. The well-rehearsed public performances represented a unification of cultural diversity, not only through musical content but also through the visual appeal of participants dressed in different national clothing, hand in hand with each other, acting as one.

The traditional rural music of the former Yugoslavia has a highly local character. Often members of one national (ethnic) group have more in common musically with members of other national groups from the same geographic region than with members of their own group who live farther away. The traditional rural music thus confirms a local rather than a national (ethnic) identity. For this reason it has never been considered dangerous to the supercultural ideology and so was not placed under its strict control. However, if such rural music appeared in folk festivals or the mass media, it was wrapped in the same unifying packaging as arranged folklore, and organizers made sure that all ethnic groups were equally represented by adequate musical forms.[12]

Popular Music

The third overarching mode of musical expression in former Yugoslavia was popular music. Although many genres of popular music can be viewed as subcultural sounds and discussed separately (see Rasmussen in this volume), here priority is given to their common feature: the capability of grouping people in categories other than national ones. Thus, the term popular music is used here as an inclusive, general term for all genres. Due to its (nationally) "neutral" character, popular music was seen and used by the superculture as a benevolent force. Even though the institution of censorship did not officially exist in the former Yugoslavia, the state occasionally imposed controls on rock musicians when their songs were perceived as threatening to the socialist order. To the best of my knowledge, there were no obvious attempts to address a particular national audience through mass-mediated music that would have encouraged the state to "intervene" against nationalism.

Religious Music

All three of the above-mentioned overarching modes of musical expression are in the domain of secular music. Religious music was restricted to closed spaces, religious institutions, or households. These subcultural sounds of all three main religious groups in Yugoslavia — Christians (Catholic and Orthodox), and Muslims — were never publicly performed or broadcast. Even though religious communities were given a legal position by a federal law in 1953, "this law established restrictions on the use of religion or religious organizations 'for political goals' . . . it also specified the scope of permissible religious activity and thereby formally sanctioned specific forms of religious activity" (Burg 1983: 25). Thus, none of the religious holidays were national holidays, and all large religious gatherings had to report to and be approved by local authorities. In this way the superculture controlled religion and religious music.

Collapse of the Superculture

The disintegration of Yugoslavia in the economic sphere (caused by changes in International Monetary Fund policies, restructuring of the European market, failure of economic plans, big misinvestments, hyperinflation, and the collapse of the economic system as a whole) and in the political sphere (increasing mistrust of the words and deeds of the Communist party leaders, the final breakdown of the Communist party and one-party system in general) was accompanied by dissolution of the symbolic world and a great identity crisis for all those Yugoslavs with socialist Yugoslav identity. Rebelling and denying all the values of the Communist party became the main way to gain the sympathy of the masses. Many political leaders refreshed their red Communist outfit with different national colors.[13] "The nation" became "predominantly a political category and a marvelous medium of political manipulation" (Sekelj 1993: 6). The old genies, kept in the bottle by the Yugoslavian superculture, were there to be pulled out by national leaders. There was no place for social cohesion except on a national (ethnic) basis,[14] which resulted in the urge to "form" national imagery. Unlike Serb and Croat nationalist parties — who in 1990 turned to their independent histories for songs, flags, and other national symbols — the Muslim national party turned mainly toward Islam.

The Bosnian Muslim Subculture

Bosnian Muslim subculture attained the status of superculture in Bosnia after the Muslim national party, SDA (Party of Democratic Action), won the elections in the fall of 1990. These events must be understood in the context of the specific historical processes that enabled them.

Bosnia and Hercegovina was under the rule of the Ottoman Empire from 1463 to 1878. During that period a large proportion of the native South Slavic population was Islamized. As of the start of the Bosnian war in 1992, more than 40 percent of the Bosnian population was Muslim. Although there are Muslims in Yugoslavia that are of non-Slavic origin,[15] the majority of Bosnian Muslims are descended from converted Christians (mostly Croats and Serbs) who adopted Islam during the long Turkish rule.[16] Their native language is Serbo-Croatian.

Over the centuries Bosnian Muslims developed specific modes of cultural expression that provided a distinct cultural identity, defined largely by adherence to Islam.[17] A number of educational, cultural, economic, and political organizations of Bosnian Muslims under the Austro-Hungarian rule "hastened the transformation of the meaning of self-identification as 'Muslim' from the narrowly religious to the national" (Burg 1983: 12). This process of transformation reached its peak in socialist Yugoslavia, where Muslims were first recognized as a distinct "ethnic group" and later given the status of a "national" group, equal to Serbs and Croats.[18] Even though Bosnian Muslims speak the same language and share common history, territory, and cultural roots with Croats and Serbs, their "forms of social behavior, moral attitudes, and specific types of artistic expression contributed to a distinctive national identity which contrasted with that of other Slavic nations of Yugoslavia" (Petrovic 1989: 128).

How did Muslims express themselves musically? It should be clear from the first section of this essay that Muslims were grouped under the aforementioned three supercultural umbrellas on an equal basis with all other nations. As far as particularly Muslim music is concerned, we must first of all acknowledge the diversity of musical expression among rural and urban Muslims. There is a big gap between rural and urban cultures throughout the former Yugoslavia, with different styles of life, different amounts of exposure and openness to outside influence, and — relevant for this case — different extents of penetration of Islam into the daily life of Bosnian Muslims. The secular rural musical repertoire is determined far more by locality than by nationality or religious affiliation. It supports a rather narrow, local, rural identity, usually connected to a village, valley, or mountain. Thus, rural Bosnian Muslims share much of their (secular) music with other Slavic nations from the same region. It should be noted that this kind of geographic rather than national (ethnic) musical segmentation was not created recently by the Yugoslav superculture, but rather by long-standing environmental, historical, and social circumstances.

The extent to which Islam permeates the life and cultural expression of Bosnian Muslims is much greater in the urban areas, which were once directly exposed to Turkish influence.[19] There are traditional urban musical forms that were exclusively Muslim. The most prominent one is certainly the *sevdalinka,* a traditional Muslim urban song whose name originates from the Turkish word *sevda,* meaning love, desire. These highly ornamented, melismatic love songs, once mostly accompanied by the *saz* (a Turkish lute), clearly expressed imagery and values that were not shared by other nations. However, thanks to their popularization, particularly through mass media after World War II, sevdalinkas reached not only a broad audience in rural areas but also fans and performers among other national groups. The mass-mediated sevdalinkas were arranged for stage performance and accompanied by sizeable folk orchestras attached to government-owned radio and TV stations. The songs were shortened, delivering only selected portions of the text; they had a faster pace, were rhythmically more rigidly structured in order to enable coordination between the singer and the orchestra, and adhered to the tempered tuning system. All of this contributed to "westernization" of the genre and fading of its closed subcultural character. The sevdalinka genre became more closely associated with a regional Bosnian than with a national Muslim identity.

Even though widespread and commonly known, sevdalinkas were not suitable for encouraging resurgence of national feelings. They had their place and history within the socialist system and as such they did not symbolize change. Also, the personal, subtle, elegaic nature of this genre made it unsuitable for political use.

The only musical forms that could be claimed as exclusively Muslim and that instantly symbolized political change were religious, even though the majority of the two million Bosnian Muslims "did not think of themselves as religious believers and only followed some of the practices of Islam as a matter of culture and tradition" (Malcolm 1994: 221).

From Muslim Households to Soccer Stadiums

A particular Muslim religious musical form, the *ilahiya,*[20] has played an important role in recent political changes in Bosnia. Converted from a private religious form into a mediated mass music, the ilahiya was used as a powerful tool in forging Muslim national identity and uniting Bosnian Muslims under the leadership of SDA. In this section I provide a broad historical perspective on the ilahiya form itself, then narrow the focus to the present function of ilahiya as a symbol of national identity and to its varied political usage in Bosnia and Hercegovina in the 1990s. My aim is to explain why ilahiyas evoke strong national feelings, why this form was chosen as a symbol of national identity, and what it is that people respond to or identify with in ilahiyas.

The ilahiya is a Muslim religious hymn. As a part of worship, ilahiya appeared in Bosnia together with Islamization. The name originates from the Arabic word *ilah,* meaning God, deity, hence the adjective *ilahi* stands for godly or divine. Ilahiyas were taught in mosques, which resulted in the spread of the genre all over Bosnia, a fact that is significant to its present-day function.

To say that the ilahiya is a song is to imply an outsider's perspective. From the insider's point of view, one does not "sing" (*pjeva*) an ilahiya but rather "learns it" (*uči*). Indeed, ilahiyas are narrative forms with the emphasis on a strong religious, ethical, and educational message for the believer. Basic ethical norms are learned through "singing" ilahiyas.

Ilahiyas are not strictly connected to the mosque, although they can be performed during religious ceremonies as well as during Sufi rituals. The genre is performed by both sexes and by children as well as adults. Bosnian Muslim women often sing ilahiyas to their children instead of lullabies, transmitting the basic moral and aesthetic values of Islam. To ensure the transmission of their religious message, the original texts have been translated from Turkish or Arabic into Serbo-Croatian, because Bosnian Muslims generally can neither speak nor understand Arabic or Turkish. Not only were the texts translated, but new religious poetry in Serbo-Croatian was written to existing melodies, keeping this genre alive.

Due to their religious character, ilahiyas lost their popularity after World War II. In Socialist Yugoslavia, the youth were not closely tied to religious institutions in general. This was especially the case in urban areas. It was not because young people were forbidden to practice their religion, but because being religious was neither socially approved nor encouraged.

How did the ilahiya gain its present-day popularity? The real revival of ilahiyas happened very recently in a certain social and political context in Bosnia and Herzegovina, together with the first postwar elections based on national parties and a real explosion of national(istic) feelings throughout the former Yugoslavia.

In 1988, only two years before the elections, a religious choir from the Gazi Husrev-Bey Medress, a Muslim high school in Sarajevo, recorded a tape called *Ilahiyas and Qasidas*[21] (*Ilahije i kaside*).[22] The tape had no commercial success or public importance in 1988. Obviously, it did not appear at the right time, which demonstrates that the present-day popularity of ilahiyas is not a function of their musical content alone. In this first appearance, the tape could be understood as a purely subcultural product, whose use was limited to a narrow circle of religious people. The tape reappeared in 1990 in audio and video versions under the title *450 Years of the Gazi Husrev-Bey Medress in Sarajevo — Ilahiyas and Qasidas*.[23] This time it scored a great commercial success. What can account for this change? Just as a description of a national flag does not say much about its symbolic value and ability to evoke strong emotional response, the answer to this question does not lie in the music itself. We have to understand it in the context of the disintegration of Yugoslavia in the political and economic spheres and the re-creation of the symbolic world on the basis of single national imageries.

Together with the second appearance of the tape, the choir started giving concerts, first in Sarajevo,[24] the capital, then all over the republic. Concerts were held at soccer stadiums before crowds of eight to ten thousand Muslims from all over Bosnia. It is not by accident that soccer stadiums were chosen as concert venues. First, there is a long tradition of mass gatherings in stadiums, since soccer is the most popular sport in Yugoslavia. Second, a lot of politics and nationalism goes on in soccer stadiums, evident in recent, prewar Yugoslav political ferment. Third, a soccer stadium is the place for the "common folk" and it lends a sense of unity and egalitarianism among the spectators.

Mosques from all over the republic organized transportation for believers to and from the soccer stadiums.[25] This was a sign that the religious institutions, "God's representatives," supported and approved the event as a whole. "Going to a concert of ilahiyas and qasidas" became increasingly ritualized. As an eyewitness to concerts in Sarajevo, I can describe parts of the ritual. The audience first gathered in front of the main mosque and, after common prayers, walked to the stadium through the main streets. A whole river of people flowed toward the soccer stadium. The procession displayed its national imagery in several ways: green flags with the crescent and white star were carried; older women wore *dimije* (harem pants); younger ones were dressed more fashionably, according to the "new" Muslim look, influenced by the styles of Arab countries—long skirts, long-sleeved blouses, and kerchiefs to cover the hair; older men put on "French caps" (berets), usually worn by Bosnian Muslims outside the mosque, or white prayer caps. So the procession denoted not only "going to the concert" but also a certain kind of silent demonstration of "Islamness."[26]

The concerts were preceded by a collective prayer at the stadium. The prayer labeled the event as exclusively Muslim—not only by Muslims but also for Muslims. Communal prayer at the stadium can also be understood as religious approval of the event. In that case "concerts" were not merely concerts but also political meetings and religious services. The performers, the Gazi Husrev-Bey Medress Choir, sat on the stage as they would in the mosque, men cross-legged, women kneeling, dressed in Muslim national clothes. Girls were covered, and their clothing especially recalled ideals of purity and morality, thought to be lost in these modern times in the "faithless" socialist country. The ilahiyas were arranged for the stage. The performance was polished, the form more complex and more musically challenging than ilahiyas Bosnian Muslims used to sing in the intimacy of their households or mosques. The performers were well coordinated and their interpretation evoked the admiration of their listeners.

The ilahiyas performed by the choir were mainly in Arabic or Turkish. This means that the aforementioned transmission of a purely religious message was not important any more. Why? What speaks instead of the language? "When we hear an old and familiar song that is familiar because it is part of our culture," says Arnold Perris in his book *Music as Propaganda* (1985: 6) "even a fragment will arouse the established meaning. Words are not necessary, not even the title." So what is at work in the case of ilahiyas is the totality of the event, including the language, which is not understandable to the large majority of the listeners. Singing ilahiyas in Turkish or Arabic symbolically brings Bosnian Muslims closer to the core of Islam.[27] Even more, singing in another language emphasizes the distinction between Bosnian Muslims and the other Slavic nations.

To summarize: the ilahiya is a religious form, but it is not strictly connected to mosques. It can be performed in secular contexts, which makes it more suitable for political use than any other religious form. Ilahiyas have been present in Bosnia continuously since the time of Turkish rule. They can be found both in urban and rural areas, in the institutions of conventional Islam as well as in the Sufi orders. Muslims are generally familiar with the form, and this continuity is important regardless of the fact that the traditional Bosnian ilahiyas did not find a place in the choir repertoire. At the same time not only is the repertoire new, but the event as a whole and the concept of performing ilahiyas on the stage is also new. In political terms this clearly suggests a radical change to come. The other Yugoslav nations do not share ilahiyas with the Muslims. The form "sounds" Islamic, that is, Turkish or Arabic. The concerts support the imagery of the Muslim nation both acoustically and visually. All of this acts together in making the ilahiya a potent symbol of Muslim national identity and allows for moving ilahiyas from Muslim households to soccer stadiums. It is the event as a whole that provides the sense of unity and "unisonance," to use Anderson's term, among all the participants. The "echoed physical realization of the imagined community" (Anderson 1991: 145) was described by a reviewer of the concert in the local Islamic press this way: "Over twenty thousand people participated in something they will never forget. I do not say watched but participated . . . because everyone was a participant, integral part of the performance, the experience, everyone breathed with one soul and one song" (*Preporod,* March 1990).

In general, the performance, including not only the music but the visual appearance as well, evoked strong national feelings. Even more, it recalled the "good old days" of faith, when Islamic order was much more respected and powerful, when girls were modest and virtuous, and men religious. It evoked nostalgic feelings for an idealized perfect past.[28]

The concerts were not an end in themselves. Several concerts were videotaped. Both audio and video tapes of the events achieved a special symbolic value. During Bayram, an important religious holiday, tapes of ilahiyas and qasidas circulated among Muslim families as the most popular gift, replacing traditional presents like meat or coffee. The tapes, which had been purely a subcultural product in 1988, were played through the loudspeakers on the streets, in front of mosques, and in marketplaces, where they were sold together with Islamic religious items like rosaries, prayer caps, kerchiefs, and Qur'ans. The sound coming from these loudspeakers was defining and claiming the territory as "ours," much like the local graffiti, which contained the abbreviated name of one of the three national parties and which in the early 1990s were "decorating" almost every public building, monument, and traffic sign.[29]

The popularity of "Ilahiyas and Qasidas"[30] was followed by the spontaneous formation of similar choirs in larger mosques all over Bosnia.[31] These groups began recreating the whole ritual in smaller Muslim communities. Although individual choirs had only local importance, these choirs as a whole transformed concerts of religious music into a strong and widespread national movement. They also penetrated more remote rural areas, where the urban-based choirs, accompanied by urban imams and representatives of the SDA Party, not only "visited" but rather took over the religious ceremonies from the local people.[32]

From Subculture to Superculture by Serendipity

When talking about the role of ilahiyas in creating a new political reality in Bosnia in the 1990s, a great amount of serendipity has to be acknowledged. At the time the tapes appeared, Bosnian Muslims were not yet in power, the SDA Party had not even been formed, and, although dying, Yugoslav superculture was still alive. The cautious title of the tape, *450 Years of the Gazi Husrev-Bey Medress,* points to the "folk treasure–like" and "museum-like" coverage commonly used in a secular socialist country to hide religious events behind historical and cultural ones. Even more, the concert was organized and the tape published in coproduction with Radio Sarajevo, the right hand of the Yugoslav superculture. The people directly involved in organizing the concert were not all Muslims, and for some of them economic interest was their primary concern. However, the very fact that having such a concert was possible confirms that there was an acceptable social climate and that the Yugoslav superculture had begun to lose control and

power before the elections in the fall of 1990. The Muslim organizers themselves were not sure of the success of their enterprise. The Islamic press
expressed concern that the attendance at such concerts might be low. There
was discussion about whether to have concerts of ilahiyas and qasidas alone
or to invite popular singers of sevdalinkas as well, to ensure an audience.
The first concerts were carefully composed. Sevdalinkas were sung together
with ilahiyas, but exclusively by famous Muslim singers. They were accompanied by *saz* and accordion, instead of the more usual orchestral accompaniment, which gave an old-fashioned, Muslim air to the performance of
sevdalinkas.[33]

Although it might seem that the concerts of ilahiyas and qasidas were
organized very deliberately, the truth is that many of the events were improvised in process, responding to the reaction of the audience. The first
concert, held in Sarajevo on 17 March 1990, was sold out in advance, and
the decision was made to hold the concert on two consecutive nights in
Sarajevo. Such a high level of audience interest was due to the social and
political climate in the republic and to the novelty of the event, as well as
to the promotion of the concert through religious institutions throughout
Bosnia and their organized transportation of believers from smaller towns
and rural areas to the capital. These first two concerts were not held in soccer
stadiums and were not preceded by group prayer outside of the mosque. The
whole event was thus only gradually transformed into a national and political ritual. It was only after the first concerts that the SDA Party was officially
formed and that it recognized how powerful ilahiyas could be. While the
first concert was attended by the mayor and other officials, not necessarily
Muslim, the following concerts were attended by SDA representatives, and
used as part of their election campaign.

The concerts of ilahiyas and qasidas became real political conventions.
The ritualization of the whole event gave it the importance of a holy mis-
sion. The secularization of the ilahiya as a religious musical form began to
symbolize the sacralization of the future government, surrounding it with an
aura of propriety and inevitability. Under the cover of religious devotion,
political ideology becomes accepted unquestioningly.[34]

What was once controlled and suppressed by the Yugoslav superculture
became favored by the Muslim superculture in the process of creating new
national imagery. In the general climate of the fall of socialist ideology and

the rise of nationalism and separatism throughout the former Yugoslavia, national identity took precedence over the whole set of identifications that previously had framed the personal identity of a Bosnian (Muslim or otherwise) — such as rural/urban affiliation, occupation, level of education, class, age, and gender. The concerts of ilahiyas and qasidas created a new symbolic world based on Muslim national imagery. To attend the concert was to become a part of that world. As a powerful symbol, ilahiyas offered Bosnian Muslims a vision of perfect unity, prosperity, and welfare. In the given sociopolitical climate, Muslims reacted emotionally to that vision, accepting it no matter how different individual perceptions of that perfect vision were.[35]

The concerts of ilahiyas and qasidas played an important role in unifying Bosnian Muslims before they won the elections in the fall of 1990. The concerts helped initiate a widespread national movement embodied in the activity of numerous choirs. Once the SDA was in power, these choirs, now existing not only in Bosnia itself but also in refugee camps and immigrant communities outside of Bosnian borders, brought ilahiyas back from the soccer stadiums to the mosques and local communities.[36] This process was supported by a widespread religious revival, which is evident not only among the Muslims but among all three major denominations in Bosnia. In the same way the Bosnian war forced many Bosnians to identify themselves along national lines, it turned a large number of people toward their respective religions.[37]

After war broke out in March and April of 1992, there was no immediate need for maintaining in-group cohesion among Bosnian Muslims, since they were forced to experience their national identity as their primary and often the only one. The cultural politics of the Bosnian government shifted toward intergroup relations and the maintenance of a symbolic world with which non-Muslims loyal to the Bosnian government as well as non-religious Muslims could also identify. The Bosnian national flag (yellow lilies on a blue background) is void of any Islamic imagery. Based on a medieval Bosnian royal emblem that predates Turkish rule in the region, it points to autonomous Bosnian identity. Sevdalinkas and genres of popular music that emphasize the secular, multiethnic aspects of Bosnian society took the place of ilahiyas in the political arena. This cultural policy reflects the diverse needs of Bosnians and is congruent with the government's advocacy of a multiethnic, federal state.

While presenting Bosnia as a secular, pluralistic, and democratic state to the West, the Bosnian government also emphasizes its adherence to Islam and appeals to the Islamic world for help and support. Beyond being a search for alliance this is perhaps indicative of a struggle between different understandings of Bosnian identity, both among the public and within the Bosnian leadership. In this light it is interesting to mention briefly the search for a new national anthem of Bosnia and Hercegovina.[38] The song that was temporarily chosen as the national anthem had previously been made popular by the Gazi Husrev-Bey Medress Choir. Whether or not it was an actual arrangement of an existing ilahiya, the nasal, ornamented style of singing, as well as the close associations between the choir and the genre, made the song recognizable as Islamic. However, this anthem has been replaced by an arrangement of a well-known sevdalinka that has been given new lyrics and is performed by a popular rock singer instead of the Gazi Husrev-Bey Medress Choir. These deliberate "musical" choices need to be understood within the context of Bosnian internal and external politics, and the situation in the country. They demonstrate how tightly music and politics intersect.

As Bosnia continues to undergo the convulsive changes that mark its current history, the musical needs and choices of Bosnian citizens and their government are bound to continue to reflect and shape Bosnian reality as well as its relationships with the rest of the world.

Notes

I thank Mark Slobin, Tim Eriksen, Keith Moore, and Dane Kusić for insightful comments upon earlier drafts of this essay.

1. The Yugoslavian superculture was not only weakened but eventually ceased to exist.

2. To avoid confusion, let me draw your attention to the emic use of the term *nation,* which is different from the conventional understanding of the word and only roughly equivalent to the term *ethnic group.* For example, Bosnian Muslims were considered an *ethnic group* before they were given the status of a *nation* in the former Yugoslavia. Rather than get involved in complex terminological (and political) issues I use *nation,* the cognate of the local term *nacija,* when referring to Muslims, Croats, Serbs, etc.

3. For definitions of the terms *superculture, subculture,* and *interculture,* see part 2 in Slobin (1993: 27–82).

4. This simply means that the rise of national movements and political parties based on

single national ideologies would have been unthinkable in the heyday of Yugoslavian superculture. Providing an understanding for resurgence of nationalism in the particular historical circumstances goes far beyond the scope of this paper and my area of expertise.

5. See Banac (1984).

6. Songs that could evoke resurgence of national feelings were forbidden by law, and the singers were prosecuted. For example, the songs of Serbian soldiers in World War I — like "Tamo daleko," "Krece se ladja francuska," and "Oj, vojvodo Sindjeliću" — were forbidden. The Croatian song "Ustaj bane Jelačiću" as well as the Croatian anthem "Lijepa nasa domovino," which is now the official Croatian anthem, were also forbidden. All of these "forbidden songs" became top hits during the recent national movements.

7. I have omitted classical music from this list partially because it enables identification along international rather than national lines and also because it has a limited impact on the masses. The most widely known works of Yugoslav composers written in classical styles are the ones that can also be classified as revolutionary, patriotic ones.

8. "Patriotic songs" would be a more conventional term in English. My reason for keeping the literal translation of the term *revolucionarne pjesme* is to emphasize that the content of the songs was devoted exclusively to the socialist revolution itself and events of recent history.

9. The artistic value of the texts also differed greatly, but in any case they emphasized a limited set of values — praising President Tito, the socialist revolution, battles and heroes of World War II, or contemporary achievements of the socialist country. The pre–World War II history of the Yugoslav peoples was, deliberately, completely neglected and a new set of values and symbols was offered.

10. These differences were presented as building blocks for unity rather than entities in themselves.

11. It is hard to tell what the connection is between the intentions of the superculture and the immediate effects of certain decisions. It is unclear whether the superculture intended to estrange musical forms from the ethnic group to which they belonged or whether adapting these forms to a staged potpourri performance stripped them of national connotations.

12. The editors of radio or television broadcasts had to be particularly sensitive not to favor one regional, ethnic, or national group.

13. All of the nationalist leaders of the new independent states in the territory of the former Yugoslavia were Communist officials, with the exception of the Bosnian Muslim leader Alija Izetbegović.

14. As Cohen (1992: 3) points out: "Both the newly elected political authorities and the bulk of the opposition forces in all regions of Yugoslavia were committed to programs of regional and ethnic nationalism."

15. Mostly Albanians, Muslim Gypsies, and some Turks.

16. Some historians argue that a portion of Bosnian Muslims also descended from the Bogumils, members of a Christian religious sect that existed in the Balkans from the tenth

century. The origin of Bosnian Muslims is a highly politicized issue. For a summary of these issues as well as more detailed information on the process of the Islamicization of Bosnia, see Malcom (1994: 51–69).

17. As Burg (1983: 38) points out: "Muslims have a consciousness in which the national and the religious are often interwoven and reinforce each other (more explicitly than among other [groups])."

18. In 1961, Muslims were recognized as a distinct "ethnic group." The 1963 constitution for the Republic of Bosnia and Hercegovina gives Muslims status as a separate "nation." The Constitution of the Socialist Federate Republic of Yugoslavia of 1974 gives them official recognition on the federal level.

19. However, it was the urban Muslim intelligentsia that contributed to the establishment of a secular Muslim identity in the Socialist Yugoslavia, while the rural Bosnian Muslims remained closer to Islam during this period.

20. In Serbo-Croatian, the word is spelled with a "j" (*ilahija*); the term used in Turkey is *ilahi*.

21. There are other spellings of this word, such as *quasid* or *kasida*.

22. According to the *Encyclopedia of Islam* (1934: 713): "the Arabic kasida is a very conventional piece of verse, with one rhyme, whatever its length, and in a uniform meter." *Qasida* is a form of classical Arabic poetry. In the modern Muslim world *qasida* is a popular religious form, devoted to Allah or Muhammad. *Qasida,* both as a term and religious form, is unknown to the majority of Bosnian Muslims and its significance is not comparable to ilahiyas.

23. Interestingly enough, the Gazi Husrev-Bey Medress was built in 1537, so this anniversary was already three years late.

24. The first concerts were held in the Olympic sport hall (ZETRA) on 17 and 18 March 1990.

25. The concerts were targeted at not only Bosnian Muslims but also Muslims from Sandzak, the area divided between the Republics of Serbia and Montenegro. For example, the first concert was attended by "several hundred Muslims from Sandžak," according to *Preporod* (March 1990). It would be interesting to know whether Albanian-speaking Muslims found any religious, cultural, or political interest in attending the concerts in Bosnia and Hercegovina.

26. An ecstatic review of the concert in the Islamic press reported: "Happiness was in the very act of arriving, when the streets and squares of Sarajevo, especially on Baščaršija and around the mosques, became a colorful palette of costumes, faces, movement" (*Preporod,* March 1990).

27. Islam was brought to Bosnia during the Turkish rule of the region. Hence the historical ties of Bosnian Muslims with the Turks. After World War II and the secularization of Turkey under Kemal Ataturk, Yugoslav Muslims looked toward Arabic countries as the real Islamic, sacred lands. A number of Bosnian Muslim students, mostly graduates of the

Gazi Husrev-Bey Medress "have received subsidies from the host governments for study at higher religious educational institutions in Egypt, Iraq, Libya, Morocco, Saudi Arabia, Kuwait, and the Sudan" (Burg 1983: 32). These students, some of them now faculty members of the Gazi Husrev-Bey Medress, brought the ilahiyas and qasidas back to Bosnia. The choir repertoire is imported and does not include the ilahiyas traditionally sung in Bosnia. Religious choirs performing ilahiyas and qasidas appear to be widespread throughout the Islamic world.

28. The time when Islam was the dominant religion was also the period of Turkish rule over Bosnia. During the Austro-Hungarian rule and in the Yugoslavian kingdom, Islam was not the dominant religion, even though religion then had a much more prominent role in social life than it did after the socialist revolution. Bosnian Muslims gained more political power during socialism, but that power was not realized through nor connected with Islam.

29. All the resurrected, borrowed, and/or appropriated symbols used in the early 1990s for various political purposes by all the national parties running for the election had an almost shocking quality of "novelty." Their appearance in public spaces had been unthinkable only months before, and it was understood as the most obvious evidence of dramatic changes in the society. As a reviewer of a concert of ilahiyas and qasidas points out, "this kind of performance could not have been even imagined, since the very thought would have resulted in several years of imprisonment, not years, but months, or rather days ago" (*Preporod,* March 1990)." A Bosnian Serb counterpart to the concerts of ilahiyas were concerts and festivals of epic singers accompanied by *gusle* (one-stringed bowed lute) and the increased popularity and number of *gusle* players' societies.

30. The term is used not only for the tape but for the choir as well.

31. One of these choirs, Sabahski Ezani, recorded "The Song of SDA," combining the "newly composed folk music" style of the solo singer Esad Mulaomerović with an ilahiya-like chorus sung by the choir. This tape was blasted through the loudspeakers well into 1991, that is, months after the SDA won the elections in Bosnia and Hercegovina.

32. For an example, see Laušević (1993: 107).

33. The inclusion of sevdalinkas, which are secular Muslim expressive forms, contributed to an understanding of Bosnian Muslim identity as not only a religious but also a secular one, which enabled nonreligious Muslims to identify with the event as a whole.

34. This is certainly not to say that there are no devoted religious Bosnian Muslims for whom ilahiyas are expressions of true religious feelings.

35. Reducing a complex and diverse society to "the Muslims," "the Serbs," and "the Croats" obscures differences between members of the same group and also similarities and connections between members of different groups. The rhetoric of nationalism on all sides depends on presenting three rigidly circumscribed groups, each having clear and inherent national interests. This rhetoric has been largely accepted and perpetuated in the West as well.

36. The *BiH Eksklusiv* (18 March 1994: 11) reports that "Ilahiyas and Qasidas are most commonly performed at humanitarian concerts in clubs and refugee communities."

37. For example: "Mustafa Ceric, the spiritual leader of the Bosnian Muslims, said the Bosnian Serb leader, Radovan Karadžić, had caused more people to reaffirm their belief in Islam than fifty years of missionary work" (*New York Times,* 10 Oct. 1994).

38. The analysis of the new national anthem is a topic in itself and exceeds the scope of this paper.

Nationalism on Stage: Music and Change

in Soviet Ukraine

Exactly eight days before the failed coup of 1991, which brought down the Soviet regime and unraveled the Soviet Empire, a Ukrainian nationalist song festival opened in a highly Russified region of Ukraine. Through the medium of music and the intercultural connections it provides, the Chervona Ruta[1] Music Festival showcased aspects of the Ukrainian historical experience that had been suppressed, marginalized, or discredited by the Soviet regime. In this Russified area of Ukraine, the festival became a site of transmission of an unofficial past, a past that glorified Ukraine and its suffering under Soviet rule. By portraying an alternative historical interpretation not sanctioned by the Soviet state, organizers of the festival hoped to raise Ukrainian national consciousness among a primarily Russian-speaking population and challenge Soviet power by recruiting converts to the nationalist cause.

In 1989 the first Chervona Ruta Music Festival was held in Chernivtsi in western Ukraine.[2] Because the western provinces were annexed to Soviet Ukraine by Stalin's Red Army only during World War II, Soviet culture was imported much later. Therefore, Ukrainians in western Ukraine managed to keep alive national histories and to continue using the Ukrainian language to a greater degree than in eastern Ukraine in spite of the Russification policies implemented by the Soviet regime following annexation. Chervona Ruta was the name of an immensely popular love song written by Volodymyr Ivasiuk, a pop culture icon. The song was a top hit played throughout the former Soviet Union and was widely known by Russians and Ukrainians alike. Ivasiuk was frequently persecuted by Soviet authorities, and in 1973 he was found hung in Chernivtsi. The authorities claimed that he committed suicide, but it was widely believed that he was murdered by the KGB. Holding the festival in Chernivtsi, the town where Ivasiuk was born and died, and naming the festival after his most renowned song created much emotionally charged symbolic capital.

A rendition of the song "Chervona Ruta" opened the festival, with many in the audience singing along. Featuring traditional folk balladeers and Ukrainian rock, this initial festival was a celebration of Ukrainian culture and aimed to promote the Ukrainian national revival that was already underway. Kobza, a Ukrainian-Canadian joint-venture company and one of the festival's main sponsors, insisted that all songs be sung in Ukrainian. The festival was considered a raging success and generated considerable momentum and support for Rukh, the Ukrainian Popular Movement for Restructuring. The festival followed on the heels of Rukh's inaugural congress, which was held 8–10 September 1989 in Kiev. Within a year of the festival, Rukh emerged as a burgeoning umbrella opposition movement that effectively united a variety of national, ecological, gender-, and religion-based anti-Soviet groups under the banner of Ukrainian independence.

Technology has given the first Chervona Ruta Music Festival a multiple and long-lasting life. The 1989 festival was videotaped and recorded. In addition to being sold in Ukraine, the audio and video recordings were widely marketed to the Ukrainian community in the West. From the comfort of their living rooms, through the medium of music, diaspora Ukrainians took part in the struggle for Ukrainian independence and thereby reaffirmed their Ukrainian origins and commitment to an independent Ukrainian state.

This initial success coincided with the increasing vulnerability of the Soviet state, as the policy of glasnost unleashed an unforeseen barrage of heated criticism of the Soviet system. This combination of factors influenced the decision to move the next festival to eastern Ukraine, where a Ukrainian music festival would find a less receptive audience. In 1991, Chervona Ruta was held in Zaporizhzhia, a provincial, industrial, highly Russified, Communist Party stronghold. Throughout the Soviet era this region was heralded as the "cradle of the proletariat." Although the political and cultural realities of this region in Ukraine were comparatively inhospitable to a Ukrainian nationalist song festival, Zaporizhzhia is a rich site of historical myth and legend. Choosing Zaporizhzhia, the historic "home-

land" of the Cossacks, as the second location for the festival held out the
promise of softening local antagonism to a nationalist agenda by evoking
the appeal of historical nostalgia through the medium of music.

Using the intercultural allure of music, the festival provided the possibility of extending membership in the Ukrainian nation to Russians, Jews,
and Russified Ukrainians — all of whom knew by heart the words to the famous song "Chervona Ruta." The term Russified Ukrainian refers to those
living in Ukraine who are Ukrainian by nationality but who speak Russian
as a first language. Most of the Ukrainian population is bilingual. However
many in the large urban centers and in eastern and southern Ukraine have at
best a passive knowledge of Ukrainian.[3] Although the atmosphere at the
second music festival established sharp boundaries between Ukraine and
Moscow in an anti-Soviet tenor, the essentialist "we" that it posited was an
inclusivist one, which hinged largely on the intercultural connection of
music. Ironically, the festival closed the day before the coup attempt on
19 August 1991, which led to the demise of the Soviet state. This Chervona Ruta Festival was the last event orchestrated by Ukrainian nationalist
groups in an oppositional mode to Soviet rule.

The Beat of the Nation

The opening performance of the 1991 Chervona Ruta festival presented a
barrage of symbols, derived from both a reinterpretation of the past and a
reassessment of the present, in a highly charged political context. The performers tried to channel the anti-Soviet feelings of anger and disillusion-
ment into hopes for empowerment by advocating Ukrainian independence
as a save-all strategy to the ills currently plaguing their society. By presenting symbols of what an independent Ukrainian state would stand for, in
contrast to its nemesis the Soviet Union, nationalist supporters hoped to
generate enthusiasm for Ukrainian independence among an alienated, Russified population.

Riding the wave of new-found popular interest in the spiritual world and
emphasizing the symbiotic relationship between religion and nationalism,
Rukh wanted to begin the opening ceremony of the festival with a mass
conducted by a priest from one of the two historically national churches,

either the Ukrainian Greek-rite Catholic Church or the Ukrainian Auto-cephalous Orthodox Church, both of whose clergy were severely persecuted by Soviet authorities. By 1946, both churches had been officially outlawed and driven underground. Paradoxically, Zaporizhzhia has only Russian Orthodox churches. As an enduring sign of the tenacity of Tsar Nicholas I's proclamation of the indissoluble unity of autocracy, orthodoxy, and nationality, local Communist Party officials refused to allow the local Orthodox church to be outcast. With the notable exception that the Greek-rite Catholic Church submits to papal authority, there is great similarity in the rituals, symbols, and architecture of the three churches.[4] The critical distinction is their different political visions. Previously, the decision to practice religion was a political statement, regardless of one's faith. Today the church with which one chooses to affiliate carries strong political overtones.

The dispute proved irresolvable and the plan to launch the music festival with a mass was dropped. The organizers opted instead for clerical participation in the opening ceremonies. Thus, the rock concert began with a religious procession. A stream of priests solemnly entered the soccer stadium walking along the track in long black robes carrying candles and crosses. In this way, twenty chanting priests introduced, so to speak, the first rock band. Subsequent songs were interspersed with priests from both churches saying prayers and giving speeches that emphasized the necessity of a Ukrainian cultural revival as an antidote to Sovietization.

Beginning the music festival on this sacred note challenged the "naturalness" of the historic links between a pan-Slavic identity and Orthodoxy. By undermining the authority of a pan-Slavic organization such as the Russian Orthodox Church, the organizers extended a parallel challenge to the legitimacy of the Soviet Empire in the age of the nation-state. By insisting that the Ukrainian national churches participate, Rukh lent its support to the nationalizing of religious institutions, inverting and at the same time perpetuating the historic link between identity and religious affiliation in this part of the world.

Following the priests, a lineup of rock bands mixed with folk singers was the featured entertainment for the opening night ceremonies of Chervona Ruta. Rock music helped to combat the prevailing stereotype that contemporary Ukrainian culture is marginal, on the brink of extinction, and interminably locked into its peasant origins. Over time, the Soviet acknowledgment of national differences had added up to no more than caricatures of nineteenth-century peasants performing in folkloric dance troups, theaters, and choral groups around the Soviet Union. By confining Ukrainian culture to the realm of folklore, Ukrainian musical groups were left with little appeal beyond evoking nostalgia for innocent days past.

In contrast, the heavy metal music of long-haired, rebel guitarists was obviously meant to debunk this stereotype and to appeal to eastern Ukrainian youth. Rock groups also showed that Ukrainian pop music had kept pace with the West. The ability to mimic the Western pop music tradition lent some credence to nationalists' claim that Ukraine is an Eastern European country and does not belong in an "Asiatic Empire," as many independence supporters refer to the Soviet Union.

Like Western performers, these rock musicians sported the same long hair, passion for black clothing, and rebel attitude, which permeated their appearance and conduct on stage. Yet even while mimicking the Western rock music tradition, these rock groups emphasized their Ukrainianness. Indigenous characteristics were made to overlay a Western musical style that could be embraced by a broad audience, including ethnic Ukrainians, Russified Ukrainians, Russians, diaspora Ukrainians, and other Westerners. Every step of the way, through their critical lyrics and irreverent comments about Soviet life, the musicians were testing the limits of official tolerance before a multitude of uniformed police officers, who stood around the track lining the bleachers.

During the third song of the opening ceremony of the festival, as the feeling of solidarity and euphoria accelerated, most of the audience poured down from the bleachers onto the soccer field to dance. They broke the traditional segregation of performer and audience and joined hands or elbows in a human chain, encircling the singers on stage and each other. Some formed spinning circles of twenty or more people all holding hands. Others formed swirling chains connected by interlocking hands and traveled up and down the length of the soccer field. The musicians were warmly received as children of the nation, proof of their collective talent. The soccer stadium became the central town square as the "imagined community" of Ukrainians, at least for one night, was reified and celebrated in music and dance.

The cosmopolitan appeal of Western-style rock music provided an inclusivist mode in which to present the often fiercely nationalistic and exclusivist lyrics of the performers. For example, one of the most well received rock bands, the Snake Brothers, who integrate an anarchy symbol into the written name of the band, sang a song titled "Peace and Order in Ukraine," which criticized both the Russification and Sovietization of Ukrainian people. The lyrics, which incorporated several Russian words to stress the point, told of a people whose spirit had been broken:

> The oppressed and the hungry have gone to sleep
> Whoever was no one has become nothing
> That's the way it will be tomorrow and today
> If you don't want to sleep, lie down and be quiet
> Peace and order in Ukraine
> The nightingale is chirping
> The Party and God are with us.[5]

Many audience members who had long feared being accused of espousing nationalist ideals, a crime often punishable by years in prison, began shouting nationalist slogans and denunciations of the Soviet regime as the police stood idly about. The familiar Soviet-imposed taboos on social and political criticism in the public sphere appeared to have been suspended. As the musicians sang, all the while encouraging members of the audience to disassociate themselves from the Soviet regime and from the Soviet experience, more and more blue-and-yellow Ukrainian flags popped up. Some members of the audience began waving them from the bleachers, while others danced around on the playing field with the flags blowing in the wind behind them.

In another of their songs, the Snake Brothers confronted one of the most controversial and inflammatory moments in the history of Ukrainian nationalism by performing their song "We're the Boys from Banderstadt," referring to L'viv, the cultural center of Ukrainian-speaking Ukraine. Reference in public to the legendary nationalist leader, Bandera, who masterminded Ukrainian nationalist collaboration with the Nazis against the Soviet Red Army during World War II, was forbidden for decades. Additionally, the Snake Brothers used the German word "Stadt" for city to underline the links and heighten the connections among Bandera, western Ukrainians, and the

Nazis. Once the singers had cracked this taboo wide open with their song, a half dozen members of the audience began to wave the forbidden black-and-red flags of Bandera's outlawed organization.

The song, which began with soft distant flutes pierced by angry cries of "Hey!," had the following refrain:

> We're the boys from Banderstadt
> We go to church
> We respect our fathers
> No one knows how to party like us
> Till the bugles don't play
> Till the drum doesn't beat
> Some say we're bandits, hooligans
> From this swamp
> There won't be human beings[6]

The fiercely critical lyrics and the highly vocal reaction they drew from the audience provided a forum in which to reject the Soviet definition of what it means to be Ukrainian. No longer marginalized subjects of a suppressed history, the band's songs tried to reposition Ukrainians as agents participating in their own historical experience.

In sharp contrast to these contemporary rock performers, the folk music that followed catered to an age-old tradition of singing minstrels, immortalized in the work of the national poet Taras Shevchenko, and harked back to an "authentic" and unique Ukrainian cultural tradition. These folk performers, who ironically carried forward — and in doing so, endorsed — the Soviet image of a Ukrainian "peasant" culture, were dressed in traditional folk costumes. They performed a round of peasant ballads using traditional string instruments, such as the *bandura.* But here too, there was evocation of the West. The four groups of folk performers, all dressed in nineteenth-century Ukrainian peasant costumes, were from the diaspora community. With cries of "Slava Ukraini!" ("Glory to Ukraine!"), they brought greetings and signs of solidarity from the Ukrainian communities in Canada, the U.S., France, and Australia. Their performance suggested that the "real" and "authentic" Ukrainian culture, protected from the ravages of the Soviet experience, was viable and thriving in the West. The appearance of Ukrainian-speaking, diaspora folk performers also showcased the breadth and strength of the Ukrainian nation outside Soviet borders, suggesting the existence of a worldwide network of Ukrainian independence supporters safeguarding the Ukrainian cultural heritage. All except the group from France introduced themselves and addressed the audience in Ukrainian. The French group, a highly accomplished four-piece instrumental band of guitars, *bandura,* and percussion, called themselves Les Banderistes.

The decision to mix folk ballads with rock music is a critical one. It is important for nationalist leaders to keep the peasant motif alive. Among other things, it supports nationalist claims that, since Ukrainians were a peasant people, Stalin's brutal policies of collectivization — which triggered a sustained famine that took the lives of an estimated six million Ukrainians in 1932–33 — amounted to genocide. The famine and the devastation it wrought on Ukrainian peasant culture have become the definitive Ukrainian national myth of the twentieth century. The Famine, like Chernobyl, is submitted as evidence of the victimization of Ukraine at the hands of a Moscow-based government.

Rukh chose the city of Zaporizhzhia in part because it is the historic "homeland" of the Cossacks. Many scholars have noted that nationalists inevitably refer to a glorious past to evoke images of future grandeur via national liberation (see Anderson 1983 and Smith 1986). For Ukrainian nationalists, this glorious past is Cossack. From this warring group, nationalists have created a myth of a fiercely independent people who successfully resisted subjugation and lived autonomously. Except for the three years following the Revolution, after which a fragile Ukrainian state succumbed to Bolshevik pressure during the Civil War, there is no real period of independent statehood to point to in the modern era. Nationalist leaders nonetheless try to illustrate a (frustrated) spirit of independence and self-sufficiency. The resurrection of a particular historical consciousness fueled by a myth of Cossack heroism was also a goal of the festival and a key reason that Zaporizhzhia was chosen as its location. In commemoration of Cossack warriors, many young men in the audience had their heads shaven the way Cossacks supposedly did, leaving only a long tuft of hair on the top of the backs of their heads.

The myth of Cossack bravery burst onto the scene during the festival in the form of crowd-pleaser improvisation. In spite of the fact that Zaporizhzhia produces vast amounts of electricity, twice during the first song and periodically thereafter the entire sound system collapsed due to power failure. During these moments of technical difficulty, Cossack horsemen, ejected into the arena at a full gallop, performed gravity-defying, life-threatening stunts to the delight of the crowd as they encircled the hordes of Polish technicians desperately trying to jump-start the sound system. (One of the financial backers of the festival brought in technicians from Poland as a hedge against anticipated party sabotage.) One by one the horses galloped around the track at a full speed as the Cossack horsemen dismounted, re-mounted backwards, dismounted in somersault, and remounted again on their hands. As the horsemen raced around the stadium track for the third time, the crowd began to shout "Ukraine without Moscow!" Little did they know that this would soon become reality.

The Illusiveness of Belonging

As jubilant as those dancing on the soccer field were, it quickly became apparent that not all in attendance were able to partake of the euphoria. The notion that the vitality and vibrance of Ukrainian music was directly corre-lated to the vitality of the Ukrainian nation and an independent Ukrainian state failed to carry some members of the audience into the dancing, cele-brating crowds. For those who remained in the bleachers and did not dance in unison with others on the playing field, equally intense feelings and forms of consciousness were generated. Made aware of their Russianness at a Ukrainian nationalist festival, they understood themselves to be trapped in an amorphous colonial space. Suddenly, these people were unsure as to whether they were the colonizers or the colonized.

I had gone to the festival with a Ukrainian woman from Kiev who worked as a nurse at the Higher Party School, a training ground for Communist Party elites. At the outset of the festival she was buoyant in spirit, curious, and ever so slightly beaming with pride that she was at a Ukrainian nationalist fes-tival. Although her family speaks Ukrainian at home and she was educated in Ukrainian through high school, she claims that she understands Ukrainian but does not speak it. For others sitting nearby in the audience who did not understand Ukrainian, she translated the speeches and announcements and words of welcome written on the electronic scoreboard, which here doubled as a message board. The three letters that are unique to Ukrainian and not found in Russian were represented by numerals, adding a sense of displacement and foreignness to finding things Ukrainian in eastern Ukraine. It became undeniably clear at this festival that although Ukrainian by nationality, Natasha was socialized in Russified Kievan society and this is where her allegiances lay. It didn't take long before she felt uncomfortable.

During the third sound system collapse, when the Cossack horsemen raced around the stadium and the crowd chanted "Ukraine without Moscow!" Natasha instantly began explaining that it was unwise for these nationalist hotheads to be advocating such a cavalier policy. She made an emphatic distinction between her unrelenting criticism of the failures of the Soviet system and Russians. She countered that perhaps Ukraine needed economic independence but she was certain that the historic link between Ukraine and Russia would never be — in fact, could never be — broken by political independence. When asked whether she thought it was feasible to have real economic independence (an end to a centrally planned economy) and still politically remain tied to Moscow, she said, "I hope it is possible, because it would be impossible to completely split from Russia. We've lived so long together. It would be like cutting off one side of my body." Ultimately, she was arguing for independence from the Soviet Union, but not from Russia. Twelve days later Ukraine declared independence.

Also with us was Vitalii and his wife Gala. Vitalii is Ukrainian but was born in Vladivostok in eastern Siberia, where his parents were exiled in the 1930s for no apparent reason. Except for university studies in Latvia, Vitalii has lived his whole life in Russia. Of late, he has become very interested in exploring his Ukrainian roots. He joined a recently formed Ukrainian club in his hometown, developed an interest in Ukrainian folk music, and began studying the Ukrainian language with his wife. His newfound enthusiasm for his ethnic origins is what prompted him and his wife to spend the summer in Ukraine. They were delegates from their hometown club to a Ukrainian-language summer program in Kiev. It was through the auspices of this language program that they had come to the festival.

His wife, an ethnic Russian, never lived in Russia until she married Vitalii. She was born and raised in Riga, Latvia. She was clearly aghast by the anti-Moscow chants that erupted when the sound system broke down. She and Vitalii blamed it on the incompetence of the Polish technicians,

whose inability to master the technical difficulties caused a lull in the entertainment in the first place. In a moment of extreme discomfort, Gala claimed
that she had always suspected, but now she was certain, that Rukh was "an
instrument of the KGB." She argued that the KGB staged this festival and
was behind the other Rukh events as well. The KGB used Rukh, she explained, to stir up nationalist sentiment so as to have an excuse to send in the
army and crush Ukrainian separatism. Vitalii told her that she was very
naive and glared at her in such an uncharacteristically aggressive way that
she knew not to voice other opinions on Ukrainian politics that night. Each
of the three wanted so much to feel the euphoria of celebrating Ukraine,
but they just couldn't. Condemning Russia was too mixed up in the process. This heightened consciousness of being different from the Ukrainians
around them, triggered by the performers' lyrics and use of symbolic imagery that was alien to them, gives insight as to why the abundant pleasure the
music was bringing to others failed to carry these three and others like them
into the performance space. For most of the concert they sat stone-faced,
their empty eyes following the intertwining chains of line dancers circling
the performers.

The multiple and fluid qualities of nationality in the Soviet Union begin
to explain the ambivalence Natasha, Vitalii, and Gala felt at the Chervona Ruta Festival. Why couldn't they and the others who remained in the
bleachers celebrate Ukraine? In part, their ambivalent attitude toward their
own nationality has deep roots in the structure of the Soviet system.

According to the 1989 census, approximately 73 percent of the Ukrainian
population is Ukrainian by nationality, 22 percent is Russian, and 5 percent
are of various nationalities. Yet, an exclusive look at nationality does not in
any way portray the very intricate and difficult task of building national
consciousness among Ukrainians on the eve of the breakup of the Soviet
Union.[7] The privileging of blood ancestry over actual cultural practices in
Soviet bureaucratic national designation served to undermine the experiential meaning of nationality.

Under Stalin, a statewide process of cultural integration — which amounted,
in essence, to Russification — was advocated as a means to realize the goals
of communism sooner. The methods employed were numerous: Russian
language was granted a privileged status, especially in education and state
bureaucracies; religion was suppressed; historiography served the political

machine exclusively; and in-migration of Russians to the republics was encouraged. When the process of Russification met with "local nationalist" resistance, state officials swiftly resorted to the KGB and the Gulag to stifle opposition.

However, by recognizing national groups along the Empire's borders with a republican political structure (in essence, a proto-state), the Bolsheviks allowed an alternative regional identity to develop, supported by regional social institutions, such as schools, the press, academies of sciences, and unions of artists.[8] Such institutions functioned to perpetuate regional cultural practices, including language, and, paradoxically, a non-Soviet source of identity. The efforts of the Soviet leadership to craft a Soviet identity as they simultaneously created nationally based cultural institutions resulted in a bifurcated sense of identity and allegiance among many members of the Soviet populace.

The practice of adopting the nationality of one's ancestors — regardless of experiential cultural, linguistic, or residential considerations — linked the concept of nationality to blood, cast it with an aura of ahistorical eternity, and perpetuated an ability to "imagine" the Ukrainian nation. This was, I believe, an underlying motivating factor that brought Natasha, Vitalii, and Gala to the festival. At the same time, Russification undermined the meaning of their Ukrainian nationality and erased its tangible relevance in everyday practice. I would argue that even those at the festival who rushed to embrace Ukraine and Ukrainian culture did it in part to replace Soviet values and Soviet practices, which have been discredited ("From this swamp / There won't be any human beings") by sharp criticism since the policy of glasnost relaxed the threat of retribution.

The nationalist reinterpretation of the Ukrainian historical experience and its accompanying redefinition of what it means to be Ukrainian provided for some a point of orientation to understand present predicaments and future aspirations in a rapidly changing society. Yet, after decades of Soviet discourse that divided the world into "socialist" and "capitalist," attempts to form an experiential "we" in terms of "us" (Ukrainians, the colonized and the oppressed) and "them" (Russians, the colonizers and chauvinists) rang hollow to many Ukrainians. Decades of assimilation, coerced and noncoerced, and comparatively little cultural and linguistic difference between Russians and Ukrainians mean that some cannot dislodge the weight of their past in favor of a new identity quite so easily. The redefinition of the relationship of Ukraine to Russia—and, by extension, of Ukrainians to Russians—for some becomes yet another destabilizing factor.

Why did advocates of Ukrainian independence turn to music to recast the critical relationship between Russia and Ukraine? The demarcations between musical styles, genres, and performances, while nonetheless reflective of a cultural tradition, are infinitely more porous than other avenues of culture that also inform identity. Other cultural elements that were also part of the opening performance of the festival—such as religious affiliation, historical memories and myths, and language—do not command the immediate acceptance and visceral reactions that music has the power to trigger.

Although presented as a music festival, for analytic purposes Chervona Ruta could best be conceived of as a cultural performance, as it united a multitude of cultural elements in a performative setting.[9] The opposition's use of cultural performance was distinguished from that of Soviet authorities by its voluntary, interactive, and improvisational nature. In contrast, the highly predictable and prescribed nature of Soviet rituals was designed to reinforce the established social order.[10]

Victor Turner argues that cultural performances are a form of performative reflexivity: they do not merely "reflect" or "express" a given social order or cultural configuration, rather they are "active agencies of change." In particular, Turner identifies the dialectical and reflexive qualities embodied in the critiques they deliver of the way society handles history (1988: 22). The public liminality created by the festival provided a forum in which individuals could publicly reject the Soviet definition of what it means to be Ukrainian and articulate an alternate version. The performers accelerated this process by encouraging members of the audience to disassociate themselves from the Soviet regime and from the Soviet experience, prompting for some a change in historical and national consciousness, as they imagined themselves belonging to a different community.

Identity through History

The significant use of historical representation in popular attempts to galvanize Ukrainian nationalist sentiment and challenge Soviet authority on

Ukrainian soil began in 1988 with the celebration of the Millennium, the 1,000-year anniversary of Christianity in Kievan Rus', which shone a glaring light on the repression suffered by religious institutions. The festivities surrounding the Millennium were followed by a round of fiftieth anniversary commemorations of various Nazi atrocities, most notably the Babii Yar massacre, in which over 200,000 Jews and Ukrainians were executed. On 22 January 1990, the anniversary of Ukraine's declaration of independence in 1918, Rukh organized a human chain from L'viv to Kiev, in which over 400,000 people participated, to highlight how the nascent Ukrainian state was struck down by zealous Bolshevik ideologues following the Revolution. Each commemoration revived memories of suffering and destruction on a colossal scale.

The transformation of an ethnic community into a politically conscious nation occurs as nationalist leaders assess the significance of their historical heritage. This was a complex process in Soviet Ukraine, where historiography had been manipulated to serve the Soviet political machine. According to Anthony Smith, without myths there would be no nations, only populations bound in political space (1986: 15). In the process of myth making, a double dynamic is operating on the manipulation of history: first, selective historical amnesia becomes political capital; and second, political and intellectual leaders give voice to a heretofore disqualified interpretation of historical experience. Historiography at this point becomes the critical ideological battleground for national identity. This is particularly true for a population as fractured and as culturally diverse as that of Ukraine.

Recalling images that hark back to experiences seemingly shared by members of the audience can ignite certain forms of historical and national consciousness. In such situations, the images recalled represent a redemption of the hopes of the past, an attempt at "rescuing" what is past for the present. The images meant to inform collective representations of the past at Chervona Ruta were of two types: either they were historical images from revered myths of national genesis, or they were from the more recent, consciously experienced past and therefore were used to contextualize the past as a steady stream of destruction. National grandeur was brought to life by Cossack mythology in the form of acrobatic horsemen and by the young men in the audience who shaved their heads and dressed in imitation of Cossack warriors. The use of peasant motifs to illustrate the more recent past, expressed by performers and audience members dressed in national costume, underlined the peasant base of Ukrainian culture and indirectly supported the claims of Ukrainian genocide due to the Famine of 1932–33, which Stalin's policies of rapid industrialization both triggered and sustained.

At Chervona Ruta the Soviet past was represented as an undesirable other, much like Walter Benjamin's Angel of History, who moves away from, yet faces, an ever-growing pile of senseless human tragedy, otherwise known as history (1968: 257). From among the smashed bits and pieces, nationalist advocates scour the past for events that could redeem the popular hopes of the present and legitimate their present political aspirations. Instances of victimization and betrayal are selected and made to represent the Ukrainian-Russian historical experience, so as to argue more cogently for an independent Ukrainian state.

Realigning this relationship and infusing the categories of "us" and "them" with new meaning will not be easy, judging from local reactions to the festival. The audience at the Chervona Ruta Music Festival on the eve of the breakdown of the Soviet Union was made up primarily of diaspora Ukrainians, supporters of Rukh from the western provinces who arrived specially for the festival, and some Ukrainians from the area. But judging by the fact that only a third of the stadium was full on opening night and successive performances were even more sparsely attended, it is safe to conclude that the festival had minimal appeal for Russified eastern Ukrainians. I am quick to note, however, that unexpected concert delays, some of which lasted up to nine hours, last-minute schedule changes, such as performances starting in the evening, breaking for the night, and finishing up the following morning, and overall poor communication about the time and location of events also diminished local interest in the festival.

Attendance at formal events, however, is but one avenue of exposure to nationalist ideas. Such cultural performances derive their power through their ability to communicate multiple messages in a variety of expressive forms. For the residents of Zaporizhzhia, the festival most likely represented the first time in their lives that they had seen their city draped in the Ukrainian national flag. From flag-toting pedestrians, to bumperstickers, to makeshift fliers, to buttons (*znachki*), the national symbol of Ukraine, the tryzub, and the Ukrainian blue-and-yellow flag were everywhere apparent.

In addition, a half dozen disgruntled residents decided to capitalize on the attention and influx of foreigners generated by the music festival to launch a group hunger strike in protest of the abominable environmental conditions produced by a sea of Zaporizhzhian smokestacks belching gray air. The pitiful sight of disempowered individuals in makeshift tents sleeping and literally starving in the center of Great October Revolution Square under-lined the failures of the Soviet system and heightened consciousness of the environmental devastation it has wrought on Ukraine. In a very real sense then, the festival, its very occurrence a voice of opposition, opened the flood gates of protest so long hammered shut.

The former Soviet Union is a land of ironies and paradoxes. One of the greatest ironies surrounding the Chervona Ruta Music Festival is that it provided a rare public forum in which to express spontaneous support for Ukrainian culture in the modest hope of advancing the struggle for an independent Ukrainian state. As I stated earlier, the festival achieved mixed results, alienating some Ukrainians and embracing others. Yet, the festival promoted Ukrainian music up until the night before the beginning of the August Events, as the putsch is euphemistically called. On the morning of 19 August 1991, as the news of the coup became public, those who were involved in the staging and promotion of the festival went underground, fearing retroactive punishment and a return to the pre-glasnost policies that forbade public expression of anti-Soviet agitation. Within three days, how-ever, the coup had failed and the irreversible process of dismantling the Soviet Union and its social system had begun. Ironically, the end of this modest Ukrainian music festival coincided with the end of the Soviet era.

The Past in the Present

Attempts were made to perpetuate the tradition of Chervona Ruta in post-Soviet Ukraine. In 1993 the festival was held in Donetsk, a town similar to Zaporizhzhia in its ethnic and economic make-up. Donetsk, a highly Rus-sified, immense industrial center, is located in the Donbas region of eastern Ukraine. The 1993 festival was plagued with problems of all kinds from the start. The festival became quite controversial when the organizers decided to bar Russian-speaking groups from performing. Up until a month before the festival was scheduled to begin, it was unknown whether local opposition and financial and organizational difficulties would prevent the festival from occurring at all. In its brief, six-year biennial existence, the festival diminished rapidly in its appeal to local and national audiences, which was reflected in declining attendance and vanishing media coverage. At the festival, as in the other anti-Soviet, pro-Ukrainian commemorations and spectacles realized before Ukrainian independence, unofficial histories and alternative remembrances were represented and reexperienced. Such events gave a physicality to alternative historical representations and provided a site of voiced opposition to Soviet rule. Interestingly, these one-time dramatic enactments of alternative histories, designed to generate new forms of historical and national consciousness, have all but ceased in post-Soviet Ukrainian society.

Now that an independent Ukrainian state has been established and the Soviet Union recedes into memory, these unofficial histories and unsanctioned recollections of the Ukrainian experience of Soviet rule are becoming institutionalized. No longer presented as spectacle, the unsanctioned, unofficial perspective of the Soviet period has now become the standard rhetoric of the new Ukrainian state. The historical representations seen at the Chervona Ruta Festival — such as Cossack mastery, religious devotion, and folklore — are essentially mythic images that ignore chronology and historical accuracy. These elements, however, are being integrated into new national historical narratives and national charters. Formerly unsanctioned historical representations now find a home in the post-Soviet curricula in schools, in new state holidays and commemorations and in monuments, to name some of the more visible sites.

However, just as official histories advanced by the Soviet regime never precluded the construction and transmission of alternate interpretations, correspondingly, Ukrainian state-sponsored historical narratives are vulnerable to the challenges of alternative histories by groups that remain or have become excluded. Indeed, a multitude of subnationalisms fueled by diverse regional, ethnic, and religious allegiances have spurred various new histories that challenge the legitimacy of the unofficial-turned-official historical representations in post-Soviet Ukraine. Demarginalizing one group by creating state-sponsored representations of "our past" inevitably disenfranchises other groups. Constructing historical representations that reflect the Soviet experience and resonate at the individual level is proving to be a difficult task. Oppositional events in the late Soviet period, such as the Chervona Ruta Music Festival, merit our attention because the historical representations showcased in an anti-Soviet mood became the raw material from which new histories are being written and public remembering is being practiced in post-Soviet Ukraine.

Notes

I would like to acknowledge support received from the John D. and Catherine T. Mac-Arthur Foundation, the Harriman Institute, and the Department of Anthropology of Columbia University. I also benefited from the insightful comments and criticisms of Kathryn Dudley, Katherine Newman, Paula Rubel, Michael Taussig, and Adrian Wanner. The translations of song lyrics are my own.

1. "Chervona Ruta" is the title of an immensely popular love song. It literally means "red rue," a strongly scented, henna-like herb that grows only in the Carpathian Mountains in Ukraine.

2. For an overview of contemporary rock music in Ukraine as well as a discussion of the 1989 Chervona Ruta Festival, see Romana Bahry's essay "Rock Culture and Rock Music in Ukraine" in *Rocking the State: Rock Music and Politics in Eastern Europe and Russia* (Bahry 1994).

3. When the 1926 census instituted categories for nationality and language, the extent of "denationalization" among certain nationalities was recognized. The term "Russified Ukrainian" essentially indicates a linguistic designation, but it also implies a cultural orientation that usually follows closely behind language use. In keeping with the Bolshevik policy of *korenizatsiia* (indigenization) implemented following the Revolution, Russian-speaking Ukrainians were obliged to learn their "mother tongue." However, in spite of this tacit acknowledgement of national differences and the rights of national minorities, Russification, especially in education, continued unabated throughout the Soviet period. According to state censuses, in 1970, 14 percent of the Ukrainians claimed Russian as their first language, compared to 17 percent in 1979 and 19 percent in 1989. In 1970, 36 percent claimed to have proficiency in Russian; in 1979, it was 50 percent; in 1989, 56 percent. In addition, by 1989, 22.1 percent of the population in Ukraine was Russian. The level of Russian in-migration to Ukraine is exceeded only in Estonia and Latvia (*Rahva Haal,* 19 September 1989, citing Naselenie SSSR).

4. The Ukrainian Autocephalous Orthodox and the Ukrainian Greek-rite Catholic

churches historically have served as institutional bases for the expression and maintenance of nationalist sentiment and political agitation. Such religiously based nationalist
ferment bumps up against the large Orthodox community. The Ukrainian Orthodox
Church was incorporated into the Moscow patriarchate of the Russian Orthodox Church
in 1686. The Russian Orthodox Church consistently positions itself as a Slavic institution.
Metropolitan Filaret, the leader of the Ukrainian eparchies and second in rank to Patriarch
Pimen, often represented the Russian Orthodox Church abroad. Filaret has since left the
Moscow-based Orthodox church, claiming that a Ukrainian Orthodox Church should be
established, in keeping with the Orthodox tradition of organizing along national lines
(e.g., the Bulgarian, Greek, Romanian Orthodox churches). Exactly how each of these
Orthodox churches will relate to one another and which one, if any, will be able to position
itself as the Ukrainian Orthodox church remains unresolved as of this writing.

5. Following is the Ukrainian text as transcribed from the album *My Khloptsi z Bandershtadtu,* recorded in 1991 and distributed by Audio Ukraina: "Zasnuli hnani i holodni /
Khto buv nikym toi stav nichym / Tse bude zavtra a s'ohodni / Ne khochesh spaty to lezhy
i movchy / A na Ukraini lad i snokii / Shchebeche soloveiko / Z namy Partiia i Boh."

6. The Ukrainian text, as transcribed from the album *My Khloptsi z Bandershtadtu:* "My
khloptsi z Bandershtadtu / Khodiemo do tserkvy / Shanuiemo bat'kiv / Nikhto tak iak my
ne vmie huliaty / Poki curmy ne zahrali / Baraban ne zbyv / Ie khto hovorit' bandyty,
khulyhany / Z toho bolota / Liudei ne bydie."

7. Maurice Bloch (1989) has argued that an important factor in Western nation-building
has been an identification by the elite with a particular territory, as represented by a single
name. Ukrainian lands were initially called "Rus' " during the period of Kievan Rus' from
the ninth to the eleventh centuries. In the seventeenth century, however, the Cossacks
referred to "Ukraina," which means borderland. In the eighteenth century, this gave way
to "Malorossiia" ("Little Russia"). Two centuries later with the formation of the Soviet
Union, the territory once again became known as Ukraine. When the parameters of the
group and the implications of membership consistently shift so widely, its appeal is
diminished.

8. For decades, Stalin's definition of a nation, written before the Revolution in 1912, was
a critical determinant of nationality policy in the Soviet Union. Stalin wrote that a nation is
"an historically formed and stable community of people which has emerged on the basis
of common language, territory, economic life, and psychological make-up, the latter being
manifest in a common shared culture" (cited in Hobsbawm 1990: 5; Stalin 1972 [1936]:
8). In spite of the fact that nations are constantly emerging, evolving entities, this list of
static, ahistorical criteria was rigidly applied to determine whether a cultural group was a
nationality or not, and if so, to establish ethnoterritories.

9. The term cultural performance was first used by Milton Singer (1955), who expanded
the concept of performance to include social drama as well. Singer argues that performative genres (concerts, plays, rites, ceremonies, festivals, etc.) are often orchestrations of

various nonlinguistic modes of communication and as such provide a window on how "cultural themes and values were communicated as well as on the processes of social and cultural change" (1972: 77).

Building on Singer's initial cultural performance concept, Victor Turner (1988) argues that cultural performances create a space of public liminality. Liminality is the "betwixt and between" antistructural stage of the tripartite ritual process and the point at which new forms of consciousness can be created and a change of status can occur. The entire audience, by virtue of its attendance and/or participation in the festival, is thrown into public liminality.

10. Many interesting parallels can be drawn between contemporary nationalist use of mass cultural performance for political purposes and the Bolsheviks' use of mass spectacles following the Revolution of 1917. See von Geldern (1993), Stites (1989: esp. 70–100, "Festivals of the People"), Deak (1975), and Hedgbeth (1975).

The Romanian Revolution of December 1989 and Its

Reflection in Musical Folklore

Folklore is a living archive, rich in productions that stand for the quintessence of events experienced by a community, and Romanian folklore studies have always closely followed the expression of great historical events. The main purpose of this essay is to describe the musical folk creativity in the period immediately following the 1989 Revolution in Romania, the most important historical act in the existence of the Romanian people in the last fifty years.

Within the process of folk creation and circulation, folklore carriers feel the need to transmit to their community the deep affective resonance of what they have lived through at important moments. The humiliation and pain experienced by the entire Romanian nation under Nicolae Ceauşescu's Communist dictatorship led to an explosion of people's anger. The Revolution of December 1989 was a time of heroism and blood sacrifice of the masses, particularly of the younger generation. Therefore it is natural that this historic event is reflected in folk culture as well. Collecting new musical material that appeared spontaneously at that time has given us a good opportunity to study the creative process as a direct echo of the events. Our research method, which followed specific laws of folklore, took into account the function of these creations. Special attention was paid to discussions with the creators of the songs and to elaborating their autobiographical "cards," which contain name, age, birthplace, education, professional status, and notes on the interpreter's integration into rural folk events. The music was collected mainly in the studio of the Institute of Ethnography and Folklore, and included sound recordings and data on the songs' origins, such as whether the music and lyrics were created by the singer or came from other sources. Some songs were also performed by the singers on radio and television broadcasts produced in commemoration of the heroes of the Revolution.

The eight pieces discussed below come to us directly from singers in the following counties: Argeş, Bistriţa-Năsăud, Cluj-Napoca, Giurgiu, Hunedoara, and Suceava — all areas well represented in the Institute's Archives, so very good reference material was at hand. We have tried to convey a rich range of issues and to embrace, insofar as possible, all the aspects suggested by the material. We consider the accounts of the singers and the musical examples presented to be a genuine sample of contemporary folk music, representative of a much wider phenomenon generated by the Revolution. We worked with two categories of informants: those who watched the Revolution as it was transmitted by the mass media and those who personally lived through it. These categories are significant because they correspond to differences in the informants' creativity and direct participation in the act of creation. For those who absorbed the events from the mass media, imagination played the main creative role, whereas for direct participants, affective impulses were spontaneously involved in the creative act as the event developed. Unfortunately, not all the creators gave us comprehensive information (as some of them were only passing through Bucharest, they had very little time for recording), but the material gathered is sufficient to reveal the singers' poetic capacity, their authentic musical interpretation, and the specific style of their ethnofolkloric region.

Voichita Stoian (age 54). Born in Dambovicioara commune, Arges county, she is a shepherdess and a valuable interpreter and creator of folksongs. She is recommended by the community of the village where she lives as a gifted singer and a good source of folk songs, with a rich local repertoire. She was discovered and recorded by folklorists as early as 1954, when she was 19 years old, and was recorded in follow-up sessions in 1956, 1973, 1978, and 1987; thus, by 1990 her repertoire was well-known. Stoian connects her creativity to her isolated profession, which involves living in a natural environment for long periods of time and which creates a spiritual space necessary for the production of her songs. As a shepherdess, living far from the urban context, she interprets a historical phenomenon according to her

own cultural background, but mostly filtering it through her special sensibility. From the top of the mountain, Voichita Stoian tries to understand
and to imagine how the young people in the capital managed to overthrow
Ceauşescu. With a mentality dominated by myths, beliefs, and superstitions,
she tries to explain this unexpected event by means of miraculous, divine
intervention that led to the liberation of a people who had suffered so long. It
is not by chance that this woman, who lives within a religious system of
thought, connects the disappearance of the dictator to the Holy Day of
Christ's birth, seeing it as immanent, divine punishment for all the crimes
committed by the tyrant. Wishing to leave her song as a creative legacy,
Voichita Stoian says: "Like history, ma'am! A song is history too, you
know — true history." A careful, analytic reading of Voichita Stoian's comprehensive information card offers the ethnomusicologist valuable information about how she perceives the historical event, taken over from the mass
media and filtered through her own sensibility and creative imagination.

Well, you see, it simply came to my mind. Because these things were true. Now
we need no longer to learn history from books. That is, I saw it, I heard it again and
again on radio. I saw it on TV, directly shown and retransmitted, you know, with
Ceauşescu's death, I wrote down everything. As it happened . . . and one day, I put
all this together. I was no electronic [brain], but still I put down many words on all the
sheets of paper and then I put them in the notebook. Maybe I was curdling the milk,
maybe I was cooking lunch or whatever . . . I wrote "Timişoara is now crying /
Bucharest and all the country / And the grieving mothers / With hearts torn apart." I
couldn't simply write about . . . each town or each place. . . . What a lot of things
you can hear even now. I heard a mother talking about how her daughter died in the
Revolution. She wouldn't have died. She would have been saved. But those rascals
caught her and beat her with their rifles.

As I wrote, "They were raised up in pain / They became learned people." That is
true. This is how it happened. And afterwards I said . . . "Ceauşescu, you rascal /
With a dog's heart / You had no heart in your chest / For such a lot of youth / Whom
you entirely destroyed" — that's those from Timişoara and Bucharest. Afterwards
the youngsters went to the revolt. Then he got his reward and we got our liberty . . . I
called the song "Romania, Romania!" This brought me to Bucharest on the ninth of
January 1990, to the Institute. I myself came through rain, through the revolution. I
wanted to leave that very moment on December 26, 1989, to sing my *colind* [carol],

you know, I wanted it to be around New Year's Eve. And my husband didn't let me go. "Where are you going? The terrorists will shoot you." "Let them shoot me. I want to die as a hero."

The tune is from a war song, from after the war in '47. That tune my brother used to sing, as he was on the front. He would sing "The country and Transylvania are weeping / And we're weeping for our grief / The mountain top is weeping / For the pain of the lads." This is all I know. As a child, I first heard the song, a widows' song, sung by Jean Busuloc, Satic, Rucăr. Her husband had died in Stalingrad and she had been left with four children.

Voichita Stoian's Song "Romania, Romania"

> Romania, Romania
> Be proud, Romania
> You have broken free from bondage.
>
> You have sacrificed
> The flower of your youth.
>
> Timişoara is now crying,
> Bucharest and all the country
> And the grieving mothers
> With hearts torn apart.
>
> The mountain top is crying
> With grief for the lads
> Who died in duty
> For their beloved Romania.
>
> Ceauşescu, you rascal
> With a dog's heart,
> You had no heart in your chest
> For such a lot of youth
> Whom you entirely destroyed.
>
> They were raised up with pain,
> They became learned people,
> but you gave them no justice.

> They could bear it no longer,
> The burden that oppressed them,
> And they rose up in revolt
> To set their country free.
> They did gain freedom
> At the cost of their spilt blood.
>
> Now you've got your reward
> And we've got the freedom
> To live in joy
> In beautiful Romania.
>
> Our brothers from abroad
> Keep sending us aid.
> We gratefully thank them
> For their good soul.
> God protect them
> From thievish rampage.

The second piece that Voichita Stoian presented to us is a traditional New Year's Eve *colind* (carol), to which she adapted a text referring to the events of December 1989. She preserved only the first two lines from the original text.

The lines just came to my mind. How could they not come on our Lord's Birthday? And about peace too, how it came on that holy day. I modified the *colind* "Saint Vasile" because then there was the Revolution and I wanted to do something for it . . . and for God, as I was finally allowed to utter that word, Saint Vasile, and for the Revolution, for this storm that had come over us, as it came by New Year's Eve, on our Lord's Birthday and . . . the dictator died. And who sent the young people there? Who pushed those young people who died in the Revolution by that New Year's Eve? Well, I had to make that connection, as God's Mother from above had pushed these youngsters forth. And I changed that *colind*. My mummy would sing it to me and we girls would sing it too. We were four sisters. We used to go and sing *colinde* too. Out daddy's name was Iosif and he would celebrate Saint Vasile, and we were bound to sing *colinde* to our daddy on New Year's Eve.

Original text of colind

Saint Vasile, Saint Vasile
On your blue foaming stallion
Shut up, son, stop crying.
The flowers on the earth
I gave them all to you.
Only the sunflower
And the vine of the hill
Stay at Heaven's gate
And judge the flowers
That made the scents.
The flowers confess
That they can find scent no more
As rain and wind have come along
and have laid them to the ground
As rain and sun have come along
And have raised them up
At the mailcoat well
The sun has risen
He is not a risen sun,
He is a big-blossomed tree
With silver blossoms,
And it's him that we gave as a gift.

Modified Colind *by Voichita Stoian*

Saint Vasile, Saint Vasile
On your blue foaming stallion
You have come in winter's dawn
To enlighten our land
With your holy staff
To bring peace upon the earth
To tell us who sent you here:
God's Mother from above,

To come forth to our help

To support our brave people

To the soldiers of our homeland

Who keep watching day and night

For the freedom of this country.

Elena Brustureanu-Cucu (age 38). Born in the Horodniceni commune, Suceva county. Worker at the Zimbrul Knitwear factory in Suceava. Married, three children.

I started singing in my family, when I was a little girl. My father would sing and is still singing. We were four children; we all sing, draw, and write poems. My mother doesn't sing; she writes verse. She likes making verse irrespective of its nature, be it folk or poetry. As soon as I realized that I could write verse myself, I found a good support in my own mother. . . . From my father I took . . . the ballad. My father had learned these ballads from some old people in Cornu Luncii.

Now as it happened with this Revolution that was made . . . it came to my mind to make some verses for all that happened. Yes. After all those events that happened in Timişoara, those terrible things we heard about, which they showed on TV . . . In the evening of December 19, I was in Suceava, at home, with my children . . . some lines came to my mind . . . and it was an impulse of my soul . . . and I started writing. And then I asked myself: "Romania, my mother / How could you bear this all / Didn't you see that he wanted / You to be his obedient servant?" Hearing the first news about Timişoara and all that happened in the land of Banat, I said: "And the Romanians in Banat / Transylvania and Bucharest / All got out, could bear it no more / And made justice for themselves." And then I made the connection with the other lines that I had made in '89 during the Revolution too. That is, now there was another, more important event with the fall of the government . . . .: "Romania, good mother / You are free and your own master / You are no longer under the dictator / Your people are free now." And then I said to myself, this people of ours, the Romanian people, had no right while he was reigning, this is what I thought, that we'd never had the right to speak, and I said: "And the enemies were enemies / They took land and money from us / And the right to speak / And our daily bread."

And afterwards I thought why shouldn't I add some lines connected to nature besides these lines. How nature comes into being. How the field gets green. About man, how handsome and how wise he is . . . since he's born until he dies. And how death comes and doesn't care, whether fields were green and people were handsome . . . and it withers them all and simply sends them to the grave. And then I thought that I should say something about death too. Why did it take our children, who died in the Revolution . . . why didn't he take that woman who tortured and oppressed this people, this house of ours in which we live. And I cursed death.

Afterwards I gathered all these lines together and I ordered them as it seemed proper to me. And I said to myself that well, these words would be good to sing. To make a song. But how should I sing them? In what way? And I thought of making a *doina* [an expressive Romanian folksong genre, often improvisatory and sung by women], as I like the *doina* anyway. I thought it should be a lamenting *doina* or a *doina*-like lament. And out of that poem I only picked several stanzas that I needed at that moment and I put them into this . . . lamenting *doina* that I made. When I made the poem, it was an impulse of my soul. The impulse was spontaneous, of course. And afterwards I wanted to show it to somebody . . . and I showed the poem to an engineer in our factory, Engineer Butnaru, and to the music teacher Palade in Suceava. And they told me, "Ileana, your poem is fine, but in order to get some resonance from it you must sing it. And you must find a way . . . to make it a tune as well." And I made a tune too . . . taking as a model the lament by which they mourn the dead in my village, Horodniceni . . . They mourn the dead in various ways, both in a *doina*-like manner and prevailingly recited, in words. This means, one's grief when one's relative dies and, at some moment, they tell the dead strong words, as if trying to bring him or her back to life . . . Sometimes they even shout. As this is how they call the dead, who never come back, properly . . . Well, that lament from that place, I took it over, and I put in those words I had made for the Revolution, for those who died for freedom and for this democracy we now have. I called it "God, How You Gave Death to Us."

Song Adapted from a Folk Lament by Elena Brustureanu-Cucu

(*recited*)
Before the brilliant cross
Children of different mothers
Are kneeling now all over the country,
Singing the hymn of resurrection.

(*sung*)

Oh Lord, ever since the world existed,

Life has been sweet

Among blooming fields

And blossoming forests

Among good and wise people

With kind open hearts.

But you, death, wither them all

And put an end to their lives

You, death, be damned,

For you have never chosen

The people when you took them

And sent them to death.

Why haven't you, death, taken

Those who deserved it?

Death, the wicked enemies,

You have never taken them.

You left them to enslave us

And torture our lives.

They gave us nothing more

Than two meters under the ground.

But the enemies were our enemies.

They took land, money from us

And also the right to speak,

And also our daily bread

And they reigned unlawfully

Over people, land, and all.

Romania, my mother,

How could you bear this all?

Didn't you see that he wanted

You to be his obedient servant?

But you simply bore it no more

And one day you rose up in revolt

And the Romanians in Banat,

Transylvania, and Bucharest

All came out, could bear it no more,

And made justice for themselves.
And one day in Timişoara
The spark burst out into a flame
And everyone, child or man,
Asked for their right to the sun.
Oh Lord, death, what have you done?
You've put our children in the ground.
Their frozen souls
You've sunk into graves.
Parents are going to graveyards
To weep for their children
That died for the people,
For their freedom.
Weep, you eyes, and shed tears.
Water our land.
As long as we live on earth
We shall remember the martyrs.

Eugenia Ilieş (age 35). Born in Turda, Cluj county. Married, housewife, three children. She lives with her family in Cluj-Mapoca. She states she has taken her talent and repertoire from songs of her family environment, as well as from her village community.

From my grandmother, my mother's mother, Nastasia Iui Bondea, and from Granny Anica and old Bucu, on my father's side. I learned the songs from them and from the villagers, Aiton village where my parents came from. They are both dead now . . . During the Revolution I was at home, with my children. We were watching TV. And we saw corpses . . . and such a great grief came upon me and I started crying and I started singing, mourning the dead: "I would lament, but I can't really / Because of tears and sighs." And then I said: Just as I made "verses" for my mother and father when they died, I will make it for these boys and girls who were young and died. For all the martyrs of the Revolution. And I started composing it. While singing *mortăşte* (in the mourning way), the ideas would come to my mind. Otherwise they wouldn't. I composed no line without singing it first. And I didn't give up until I completed it. It was on December 22, on Friday [inaccurate date], when it started in Cluj. When the battle was fiercest in the Manastur side, all night I didn't go away from the TV set. I kept watching and writing, composing. It all remained like that. As I had done it at that time.

Eugenia Ilieş's Lament for the Revolutionary Dead

I would lament, but I can't really
Because of tears and sighs.
I would lament day and night,
But my heart can bear no more.

Oh land, green grass,
There's so much youth in you.
Oh land, dried ground.
So many of our lads you've eaten.

The bell ringers are ringing bells
And the lads are dying.
And instead of learned priests,
Guns are tolling at their heads.
They have neither shrouds nor coffins;
Neither do they have four bulls [to draw their hearses].
They only have a dark house
Made of black clay and stone.
This is the holy Christmas day
Bullets are flying out of cannons,
A cannon is tolling day and night
And death is raining from the sky.

Be eaten by fire, you tyrants.
How you paid them in good money.
You gave them gold and coins
To slay the people.

Ever since the beginning of time
Never has such a wonder occurred:
Such a great wonder
That brother should kill brother.

Romania is all bleeding,
And every man in the country is weeping.
Romania is all on fire,
And the dead are all over.

Mothers are mourning their sons,
Wives, their husbands,
And girls, their lovers.
How they died — poor ones!

Children are sitting on the stove
And keep asking for their fathers;
Many mothers are wailing
And cannot find their dead.

Bring on rains, oh Lord,
Wash out the bloom on the road,
Wash out the innocent blood
That was spilled for our country.

For our country and our people
To get rid of that bitter life.
To live better, all of us,
Not in tears and sighs.

My brothers, my Romanians,
Let us pray for them,
Let us bring them burning candles
To rest in peace under the ground.

I pray to God
To forgive my people,
The martyrs who died
Sacrificed themselves for us.

Ana Banciu. (age 32). Born in Cerbia village, Zane commune, Hunedoara county. Zincograph worker at the printing house in Deva. Married, with a child, lives in Deva. A passionate collector and gifted interpreter of songs from Tara Zarandului, Almaş Valley, she has in her repertoire ballads, *doinas* of *dor* (longing), and grief, dance, and entertainment songs.

Immediately after the Revolution, I was particularly impressed by a woman who was pregnant and about to give birth. Her husband was in the army and didn't come back. The reasons are known. The woman was from Orastie, and . . . of course, he was shot. This is all I know. I don't know any details . . . It seems that he was among those who were not identified . . . This made me determined to create this song about the Revolution in which, in the end, I meant to point out the fact that the father didn't die for nothing, but he died for the good of this country . . . and he will keep living through his son . . . to whom his mother would give his father's name. I know no more details, but this thing inspired me. It so happened . . . that when I managed to create it . . . the tune already existed. It is a tune, a piece from my native place. It is the *doina* "The Cuckoo Is Singing near the Spring," and therefore, as the tune existed, I considered that this text suited it well. I created the text spontaneously. I don't remember very well when it was, but in any case it must have been in winter. Not immediately after the Revolution, but I kept the subject in my mind and subsequently created the text. Interestingly enough, I created it all. At once. At the moment when I was inspired. It doesn't happen the same to me all the time."

The literary text reminds us of a specific army song. It is a type of song from the old layer (of folk songs), a largely melismatic one.

Ana Banciu's Song

Down upon the vale upon the balk
A wife is weeping longingly
And is cursing the reigning regime
For Ionel is never returning.
As he left and never came back,
Let the fire burn those enemies!
As he left for the battle,
(From which) only one returns from among a thousand.

You Ioan, my own Ionel,
Come tell your little child
To be proud of you
Since you fought for better days.

I am waiting for him to be born

And to name him with your lovely name.

Briduşa Drăgulin (age 30). Born in Chilsteni village, Udesti commune, Suceava county. Technical designer at the Zimbrul Knitwear Factory in Suceava; married, with two children.

I sing merely for the beauty of the songs and in order to purify myself. This is why I love them and I sing them. Not in order to break free from them. I purify myself by means of songs. I appeal to the songs like to an art. I don't use them for certain expressions of my tension. I wish to sing them in order to get out of the state of common everyday life a little bit. And when I start singing, I escape a little bit.

From the informant's remarks, we can appreciate her taste and predilection for songs belonging to the old stratum. Her own stylistic and interpretive evolution is manifested on the one hand by preserving the local style in its most characteristic elements, and on the other by enriching and renewing this style by means of her own artistic vision. To illustrate our topic, we chose her lament "Get Up, Gheorghiţă, Get Up." This piece was not created for a certain person. To the singer, the name Gheorghiţă is a symbol of those who sacrificed themselves in the Revolution.

I shall tell you how I understand lament. Of course, I was helped by those women who accompanied their beloved, whom death had forced into this final turn, this passage into nonbeing. Man discovered lament as the only bridge of communication with the other, as one can never accept that they will be forgotten in our souls. And then, how shall we communicate with them? By means of lament. It seems extraordinary to me. Still as a child, I would repeatedly hear someone say, "Where do you come from, Aunt Floarea?" "Well, I went to talk to Gheorghiţă a little bit." Who is Georghiţă? Her man, husband, child, brother-in-law, or somebody close to the family who was, of course, dead, in the graveyard. And she would come, very serene and natural, and would say she had just been talking to him. How had she talked? Through lament. I think lament supports this state of despair of the mother, wife, sister, as usually women are those who lament, at the moment when this event really occurs. Lament gives her the possibility to communicate with him. We cannot give up those whom we loved. And then, I think, we resorted to this form of communication: lament.

To show her respect for all those who died in the Revolution, for the pain of the mothers who had lost their sons, Briduşa Drăgulin performed this lament in a radio and TV broadcast in April 1990 at the commemoration of the heroes of the Revolution.

Briduşa Drăgulin's Lament

Get up Gheorgiţă, get up
Since spring has come.
You should walk through orchards again
As you are still young
And you didn't like to live.
Make yourself a knight's bow
Since the priests are coming to take you away
To unwalked paths,
Where you've never been before.
Where the priests are taking you now
There's a road with no return.
If I knew it had return
I would sweep this road for you
And I would sprinkle hollyhock on it
To bring you home more quickly.
You, earth, if you're my brother,
Take your clay away
To see how Gheorgiţă is.
You black merciless death,
Why have you chosen me?
You have come in at noon
And left me to sorrow.
You blasted coffin,
You did not ask anyone.
You took Gheorgiţă away.
You, my good dear little son,
How could you so easily
Move to another house
And leave me with mourning heart?

As in any manless house, not even a prop is well fixed.

And wherever a man dies,

No sunshine ever enters again,

There is but pain and sorrow.

Black merciless death,

Why have you come back to me?

Get up, Gheorghiță, get up,

Since spring has come.

(*spoken*) God forgive him!

Lenuta Purja (age 24). Born in Agrieş-Tirlşiua, Bistriţa-Năsăud county; married, one child. Store worker at the silk factory in Bistriţa. From her brief information card we learn that the singer has also created other folk melodies and texts. Out of Lenuta Purja's repertoire, we chose as an example the piece "December 22," created after the events of the Revolution. As regards the creative process, she says, "It was a burial song, but without those trills, and I have updated the text." The musical type of the piece tells us it is a tune from the older stratum, typical for the northern area of Transylvania. It is an amply designed, melismatic tune with a fixed form and four melodic lines.

Lenuta Purja's Song

And I have come to tell you

What our last Christmas was like;

Nobody went to sing carols,

But only wept and prayed.

And suddenly there started

A blood-shedding fight,

And it spread in Timişoara

And then in all the country.

Bega was filled with blood,

The Danube started weeping.

One could hear from Bucharest

The big tale-like battle

You, wicked ground,

How thirsty you were.

You quenched your thirst with blood,

With young and pure blood.

Oh, those poor youth,

How they died, poor ones,

To bring us freedom

And all we needed at home.

We shall never forget you

And neither will the whole country.

You, who exist no more,

Who are sleeping under the ground for good,

Let us honor and love them

And live in peace.

Ion Bădircea (age 31). Born in Toporu commune, Giurgiu county; locksmith at the Dunarea enterprise in Giurgiu, lives in Toporu with his family.

On 21 December . . . I waited for my wife . . . we left the factory, we went home, and together with a cousin of mine from the village, we took a car and went to Bucharest . . . we had some food on us, like everybody . . . We didn't shoot; instead, we gave a hand to bringing food . . . I saw a colleague from Alexandria who fell just next to me, shot in the head. I didn't notice where they shot from. We were busy with something else, to fetch food, as everybody did. We left on the 27th, in the evening when things calmed down a little bit. . . . I was impressed by the fact that life was resurrected. In the Central Library, which had been burnt down, two young people got married. The priest, as is our custom in Romania, came there to marry them . . . and it was symbolic. A girl, another fighter, came there too, and she was their godmother, together with a soldier who had fought in the Revolution too. And this impressed me . . . After the Revolution, in the first days, I didn't really feel in the right mood for singing. But after that . . . together with some colleagues, Irina Severin, a weaver, and others, we thought of composing, of making a text about the Revolution. And so we did. We contributed to it, all of us, as much as we could. As our minds helped us. Later we thought of putting this text to music. To show the world the terrible things that happened here, as we saw them all. I thought the tune should be a lament, a song dedicated to the heroes of the Revolution. And there will be some other songs that will come out too.

Ion Bădircea's Song

On the day of the twenty-second
Thousands of heroes fell:
Children, youngsters, and elders
Who had worked miracles
That no one might have believed.
This is a true story.
They all rose up in arms
To set our country free
From a bloody wild beast
Who was bloodthirsty.
From Sibiu, in Timişoara,
Bucharest and Hunedoara,
Thousands of young people fell
For the country's sweet land.
They did not care,
But sacrificed themselves for the country,
Now, at the end of the year,
To get rid of the tyrant.

Conclusions

In this essay we have not analyzed the specific poetical and musical morphological characteristics of our examples, as this is not our main objective. What seems more important is to point out first the sense of local belonging, which is reflected in the musical types themselves. For example, in our sample the old, local background of the music found in various areas of Romania is represented by the musical types of ballad, song, *colind* (carol), and lament. Second, we notice how the poetical and musical structure and the language are tightly connected to those of traditional folklore: the creators belong artistically to a folklore environment, which corresponds to a regional interpretive style. In this way, our sample reveals the maintenance of authenticity — that is, the preservation of traditional background and the integration of innovation into traditional structures.

Music seems the most constant and conservative aspect of these reflections on the Revolution. Innovation in music stays within the boundaries of folk norms, whereas the texts reflect the more rapid evolution of verbal language. The creative interventions of the interpreters range from slight modification and adaptation of traditional lyrics to creation of entirely new text. Connections to tradition at the structural and musical level range from mere adaptation to the birth of a new tune.

The pieces presented here share a clear thematic unity, all being focused on events of the Revolution. They also evoke the atmosphere specific to particular senses of folk poetry. The themes in the texts are relatively diverse. Most texts are more or less developed forms of the "oral diary" type, resulting from the way the creators thought the songs should reflect real events.

In accordance with the traditional process of folk song creation, spontaneity came to the fore in the creation of many of these songs, propelled by the living, direct impression of events. Many of the artists said the songs came to them "all at once," without needing time for artistic deliberation.

In most cases, the performance style is dramatic, a result of the life-and-death content that had to be expressed. This made possible a rich range of nuance, as well as the ornamentation of the tune with melismas, appoggiaturas, portamentos, and modalities that render the expressive functions of the sounds more sensitive.

The impassioned and often urgent way in which these songs were composed, as well as the special personalities of the creators and performers, shows clearly that they were written to be performed for an audience. In fact, some of them were included in radio and television broadcasts, sung by their creators themselves. The commentaries provided by the creator-interpreters point up the connection between the songs' expressive content and the emotions and frame of mind of the community and the singers themselves.

Since only a relatively short time has passed since the creation of these songs, at the moment we cannot know to what extent they are living their lives within the folk circuit. But we may be sure that they stand as genuine documents of the historical events of the Revolution of 1989.

Note

This essay is an abridged and edited version of an article that appeared in *East European Meetings in Ethnomusicology*, 1994, volume 1, pp. 65–97, published in Bucharest. The editor is grateful to the journal for permission to reprint and edit and to Gail Kligman and Donna Buchanan for identifying and providing the article.

TIMOTHY RICE

The Dialectic of Economics and Aesthetics

in Bulgarian Music

To understand the dialectic between the economics and aesthetics of Bulgarian music from the 1920s to the present requires the thesis that music is not irrelevant to economic, social, and political processes, as some sociologists and political scientists doubtless imagine. Nor is music epiphenomenal to the supposedly real structuring of society determined by the economic base, as some Marxists might believe. Nor is it an autonomous work of art that makes sense only in relation to other works of art without reference to a world, as some scholars of art and literature occasionally maintain. Rather, I argue that Bulgarians of all political and ethnic stripes create and interpret music within symbolic webs of meanings, political struggles for power and influence, and evolving economic structures. The making of music is a making sense of those webs, struggles, and structures and a manipulation of them for the musicians' and their audiences' economic and political advantage. Far from being an irrelevant epiphenomenon, music, particularly during Bulgaria's Communist period, was a site of contestation, meaningful action, and cultural configuration. At stake for musicians and music lovers were economic well-being, ethnic identity, subjugation to a totalitarian state, and emotionally satisfying, aesthetically appealing music.

This essay has three parts. In the first part I provide a schematic review of the way Bulgarian music has changed over the last seventy years. It amounts to an examination of the efficacy of a Marxist model to explain music in a Marxist society. The second part first uses a semiotic approach to explain how music can be said to mean something and what sense Bulgarians were making of their music in the late 1980s, at the end of the communist period. It then employs a hermeneutics of social situatedness to understand how

Bulgarians understood the sharp contrasts in musical practice on the eve of revolution to reference a world of contested and differentially distributed power. The third part presents a preliminary sketch of the way economics and aesthetics continue to be intertwined in the post-Communist period.

Economics and the History of Bulgarian Traditional Music

To understand the forces behind the dramatic changes in Bulgarian musical style of the last seventy years, no theory is more mischievous than a Marxist one. Dave Laing (1978), a well-known British Marxist, has complained that there is not a systematic Marxist theory of art and, worse, that music is mentioned hardly at all in Marxist writings. However, two important principles can serve as the basis for a Marxist analysis of music history: first, the claim that there is a fundamental dialectical relationship between the economic structure of society, the so-called base, on the one hand, and the political, legal, religious, artistic, and philosophical views and institutions of society, the so-called superstructure, on the other hand. The second principle, a corollary of the first, is that "if the base changes or is eliminated, then . . . its superstructure changes or is eliminated; if a new base arises, then . . . a superstructure arises corresponding to it" (Stalin 1972: 80–81). If music is taken as a part of the superstructure, then we have in these two principles a theory of the interrelationship between music and society and a theory of why and how musical change occurs.

If we examine Bulgaria's recent past from the point of view of rural or village economic structures, I would posit the existence of three different bases, each with its own superstructure and in particular with its own manner and means and aesthetics of making music. In chronological order, these are (1) the pre–World War II, family farming economy; (2) the centralized state socialist economy of the post-war period; and (3) from the 1970s to 1989, a mixed economic system in which workers engaged both in state labor and in a significant amount of private petty commodity production. These changes in the economic base have effected major changes in the Bulgarian folk music tradition and in how music interacts with other elements of the superstructure, in particular politics and ideology.

How should such an analysis proceed, however? Which aspects of music are amenable to a Marxist analysis? Given Dave Laing's pessimism, I was surprised to find a Marxist analysis of music by one of the leading intellectuals of the Russian revolution, Nikolaj Bukharin, a man executed in the party purges of the 1930s and rehabilitated in the 1980s in the spirit of glasnost. In his book *Historical Materialism: A System of Sociology,* published in 1925, he analyzes the relationship between music and economic structure by dividing the art of music into six "component parts": (1) genre or function; (2) technique, that is, instruments; (3) the human or social organization of musicians; (4) formal elements such as rhythm and harmony; (5) style or expression; and (6) content or subject. Bukharin argues that all these elements are "ultimately determined in various ways by the economic structure and the stage of social technology." Thus Marxist philosophy of art not only provides us with an explanatory theory but an analytical framework as well, a framework consistent enough with contemporary ethnomusicological theory to be attractive in the 1990s. In the following analysis, I apply Bukharin's components of music to show how Bulgarian music is related to the economic base, and how it has changed as the economic base has changed. The analysis is summarized in Table 1.

The musical superstructure in Bulgaria in the period before 1948, when family farming constituted the primary rural mode of production and barter between families was an important mode of economic exchange, is basically lost to us today. What we know of it must be laboriously reconstructed from the scant ethnographic record and from the accounts and behaviors of living musicians who grew up in this time (see Rice 1994 for one such account). The important genres of music during this period were songs, dances, and instrumental tunes tied to a seasonal cycle of work and ritual designed to ensure the fertility and productivity of the family-owned lands and animals. The musical instruments were homemade products of animals, trees, and plants in the villagers' immediate environment, products of the ecology and technological level of that society. As for their social organization, musicians, dancers, and singers were unspecialized, unmarked social categories. One of the ironies of the history of Bulgarian folk music is that, in this stage of economic development, social organization of labor resembled that envisaged for the utopian future communist society. To quote Marx and Engels, "nobody has one exclusive sphere of activity but each can become

Table 1. Historical Relationship of Village Music and
Economic Bases in Bulgaria Economic Bases

Components of Music	Family Farms (pre–World War II)	State Socialism (post–World War II)	Second Economy (1970s–1989)
Genres	Calendar and family rituals and events	Concerts, festivals, and competitions	Weddings
Technique	Homemade instruments, fabricated using local plants and animals	Addition of manufactured European instruments	Electronic instruments and huge sound systems
Social Organization	Soloists and informal, changing groups	Formal, fixed, large, directed groups	Small groups, "star" soloists
Elements	Pentachordal modes, asymmetric meters, monophonic and drone textures	Addition of European harmony	Jazz harmonies and rhythms, foreign tunes
Style	Freely negotiated in performance	Formally rigid	Improvised, virtuosic
Content	Shared emotions of life experience	Order, cleanliness, beauty	Freedom, hostility to order

accomplished in any branch he wishes; society . . . makes it possible for me to do one thing today and another tomorrow, to hunt in the morning, fish in the afternoon, rear cattle in the evening, criticize after dinner . . . without ever becoming hunter, fisherman, shepherd or critic" (Marx and Engels 1972: 43). This lack of specialization meant that musicians, singers, and dancers assembled casually in constantly re-forming family groups and village neighborhoods, and that people moved easily between roles as singers, dancers, musicians, and audience. As for formal elements such as rhythm and harmony, I take these as given and traditional at this point and will not try to show their relation to the economic base; however, I show later how they change as the base changes. In the Bulgarian case, the formal elements include a variety of pentachordal melodic modes, asymmetric meters, and monophonic or drone-based polyphonic textures.

Bukharin's concept of style seems to involve form as it expresses feelings, thoughts, moods, and beliefs. Looking for the moment only at instrumental music, its form during this period seems to have been relatively free and unfettered by strict notions of form. Although village instrumental music during this period was surely constrained formally, those constraints were beyond discourse; one musician told me that his playing was "unconscious" (*nesûznatelno*) during this period. As for Bukharin's notion of form in the service of expression, the playing seems to have expressed the joys of particular relationships between dancers and solo musicians at a given moment of the dance or fair or ritual. The details of musical form were negotiated on a moment-to-moment basis, much like a conversation between family members, friends, and neighbors. No economic incentives, other than the barter of goodwill, determined the form of particular performances. As for Bukharin's sixth component of music, content or subject, he acknowledges that it is difficult to separate content from form. Here a certain amount of interpretive leeway must be allowed, but I would suggest that this music was about life, life as lived and experienced by these villagers. It addressed their fears and hopes through its song texts; it expressed their joys and satisfactions through the dance it accompanied; it cemented social relationships between families and friends; and it helped them celebrate and ultimately endure the seasonal round of work and ritual. It was fully integrated into the mode of production as an indispensable adjunct to it.

Both the economic base and music as superstructure changed dramatically with the imposition of Soviet-style state socialism. In a period of twelve years from 1948 to 1960 family farming plots were lost to even the most isolated villagers and replaced by huge collective farms (Lampe 1986). Peasants lost control of the means of production and became proletarian wage-earners for state-run collective farms, or urbanized factory workers in a rapidly industrializing economy. A centralized bureaucracy reached into and tried to control nearly every aspect of villagers' lives. An ideology hostile to Christianity and hell-bent on progress of the human spirit specifically forbade the performance of all the seasonal pagan and Christian rituals that underpinned the old village music practice. With a series of more or less simultaneous economic, ideological, and political acts, the old base and superstructure were eradicated. Turning vulgar materialism on its head at the moment of revolution, Marxist ideology determined what the future economic base would be.

The genres based on seasonal rituals disappeared almost completely in traditional practice, first because the peasants no longer had any economic interest in ensuring the fertility of land and animals they no longer owned, and second, because the progressive ideology forbade their practice as backward superstition. In its place emerged a centralized, state-managed, professional folklore establishment, run by an intelligentsia of classically trained composers and conductors. They turned the best of the village musicians, singers, and dancers into wage-earning, urbanized, proletarian workers for so-called "state folklore ensembles." Those who remained in the villages were urged to participate in centrally managed "artistic amateurism" (*hudozhestvena samodeinost,* literally "artistic self-activity"). The new genres for both professional and nonprofessional performers were concerts, festivals, competitions, and recordings that contained acted-out reminiscences and highly edited distillations of the pre-war genres.

As for music technique, the pre-war instruments were retained by these ensembles as symbols of the national past but were "improved" where new industrial technologies could be applied, such as plastic-and-metal tuning pegs on long-necked lutes. Manufactured instruments, such as cellos and basses, were added into the ensembles.

The social organization of musicians mirrored the new state organization and the specialization of labor inherent in the new economic structure. Village musicians, who one proverb said "could not feed a household" in the pre-war economic structure, found full-time jobs and became specialist performers largely alienated from the audience of which they used to be a part. Large, fixed ensembles under the direction of a conductor and artistic director replaced loosely organized and constantly shifting assemblies of family members and neighbors.

Many of the formal elements of Bulgarian folk music, particularly the meters, modes, and tune structures remained largely intact. The basic change was the addition of classical harmonies and the regularization of pitch and intonation in terms of the equal-tempered intonation system of European classical music. The most immediate cause of these changes was largely ideological. While the forms were preserved as symbols of Bulgaria's national identity and heritage, pre-war folk music practice became, for the Communists, a symbol of a dim, unenlightened past on the verge of transforming itself into hated capitalism. A peasant had to be made a "new man" capable of full participation in the communist vision of the future. Literacy and refined appreciation of great art were among the state's educational goals for its citizens. In that context, many composers told me they saw the classicization of the folk tradition as a step on the path to the peasant's greater appreciation of the great works of European music. Thus the elements of music changed as part of an ideological plan for the betterment of man. It is this music we listen to as we hear *Le mystère des voix bulgares*.

The style — which I defined, after Bukharin, as form in the service of expression — changed as well. What had been free and individual became rigidly formal, manufactured by a disciplined work force of trained musicians performing in the tightest possible coordination under the direction of a shop steward acting as conductor. The performances express some nostalgia for the past, and they demonstrate the ability of the individual to subject himself to centralized direction in the service of higher goals, which included a move away from a past beset by poverty and Ottoman domination to a future of economic equality and European cultural identity (Buchanan 1991).

These higher goals, it seems to me, are the content or subject of these performances. Insofar as instrumental music can be said to be about anything, these performances are about order, discipline, cleanliness, and beauty. They express the goals of a state for its citizens in the future, rather than the joys of individual musicians and lines of dancers in the present, and stand in stark contrast to the drab and difficult life many Bulgarians lived during the Communist period.

Finally, the third period was a time of mixed economy, a mix of the centrally planned state socialist sector and a second economy of petty commodity production, the result of economic reforms begun in the early 1970s (Lampe 1986: 210–12). Bulgaria, like other Eastern European socialist states, was not able to proletarianize fully its population. Spaces were left where individuals, in addition to their state labor, sold personal services, handmade items, and the products of part-time work on so-called personal garden plots, rented from collective farms. Among the occupational groups with the most to gain from this arrangement were musicians, who throughout the socialist period had been allowed to sell their services to other private individuals. As the state relaxed controls on this petty form of private enterprise during the second half of the Communist period, more and more money flowed into this second economy, enriching the people who engaged in it in comparison to those who worked only in the socialist economy (Szelenyi 1988). Since the state economy did not supply adequate goods to purchase with this newfound wealth, people turned more and more to the second economy as the place to spend their money, and musicians, squarely positioned there, were among the main beneficiaries.

What kind of music system did this flourishing second economy support? The main genre was wedding music, played at enormously expensive two- or three-day events that required the hiring of musicians, the best of whom were paid enormous sums of money in an ostentatious display of wealth by the richest families. (Of course, wedding music existed in all three periods, but its ideological force and even hegemony in relation to state-sponsored musical styles emerged only in the last years of the Communist period as a function of its economic power.) Of all the traditional genres, the wedding provides the most obvious condition for monetary exchange, as well as being one of the few traditional rituals still performed during the Communist period. As for technique in the form of musical instruments, wedding music features the finest instruments money can buy and international technology can provide: clarinets, saxophones, accordions, electric guitars and basses, synthesizers, drum kits, and above all sound systems. The best musicians have the best sound systems. As one musician told me, "If you don't have a good, loud sound system, it doesn't matter what or how you play." In a socialist state whose isolated main economy made it difficult to purchase first-rate equipment from the West, success at acquiring a good sound system also carried with it mildly subversive economic and political implications as well. The model social organization for musicians of the second economy includes the small, economically viable wedding band of five or six musicians as well as the creation of "stars." These stars attract the largest amounts of money to themselves and confer the most prestige on the families who hire them.

In the 1980s, the greatest star to emerge among these wedding musicians was the clarinet player Ivo Papazov, who in the period before 1984, when Muslim Turks and Gypsies could use their given names, was known simply as Ibryam. Ivo is an astonishing musician who took the Bulgarian music tradition to previously unknown heights of virtuosity. A Marxist analysis, however, would suggest that he could not have emerged as a "star" without the freedom, money, and attention that the second economy provided him. Striking new formal elements crept into this music, including the chromaticisms, arpeggiations, and rhythmic devices of jazz and popular music, as well as the borrowing of foreign folk and popular tunes. This appropriation of formal elements from America and neighboring countries was the musical equivalent of being able to buy Western products produced by capitalist economies either on the black market or in government-run hard-currency stores. Both the Western products and the foreign musical elements carried enormous prestige in a stagnant economy and political system that generated forty-five years of unchanging, conservative music. These foreign formal elements were the new, exciting coin of the second economy's music.

As for style and expression, wedding music represented a continuation of the freedom of the pre-war period, mixed with some of the formal rigors introduced in the socialist period. Improvisation was highly valued, and virtuosity in the form of dazzling tempos, dense ornamentation, complex key changes, and complete command of the range of the instrument became the criterion by which musicians were judged. The playing style often seemed a parody of Bulgarian folk music as it had come to be played in the Communist period. Most of the best players of this wedding music were Gypsies, who, in the repressive climate of the period vis-à-vis Muslim minorities, were required to play Bulgarian tunes even at Gypsy and Turkish weddings. So they played Bulgarian tunes, but with a kind of aggressive ferocity that expressed wordlessly in music their hostility to a planned economy and nationalist politics that offered them very little. In a series of competitive festivals created partially to control this form of free music-making, some of the best groups did not make it into the national finals because their playing was "too aggressive," not "calm" or "sweet" as traditional folk aesthetics supposedly demanded.

What was the music then about? What was its content or subject? I would suggest it was about freedom. One musician even told me, "Music is, in essence, freedom" — in this case an inarticulate, nonverbal, musically stylized cry for the freedom to live in some kind of acceptable accommodation to a sluggish bureaucracy that stifled both economic initiative and the ethnic identity of Muslim minorities.

The Bulgarian folk music tradition at the end of the Communist period was enormously lively, partly because of its rich pre-war heritage, partly because state support helped it to retain some of that richness while advancing its technical possibilities and the virtuosity of musicians, and partly because new economic conditions created by the second economy spurred creativity, invention, and competition among musicians. Thinking about Bulgarian musical life using this Marxist hypothesis and analytic framework helps to explain some of the relationships between the different types of music-making that existed in Bulgaria during the last years of the Communist period and to account, at least in part, for the changes in the components of music during three periods in Bulgaria's recent music history. If we remain uncomfortable with the unsubtle, even vulgar, Marxist notion of the economic base determining the musical superstructure, including important aspects of musical aesthetics, one solution to our discomfort might be to unite music in an economic analysis by reinterpreting music metaphorically. For many musicians, music is economic practice.

The Meaning of Bulgarian Music in the 1980s

A Marxist-style analysis can provide a useful way to understand large-scale structural features of a music system — in particular, music as economic practice and musical aesthetics as partly determined by economic considerations. But such analyses have at least two important limitations. First, their implicit or explicit determinism fails to account for individual and group variation and choice. For example, in the late Communist period, Bulgarian singers, musicians, and dancers had at least three choices: (1) they could stay "down on the farm" and refuse to become professionals; (2) they could accept a job in the state-run folklore apparatus; or (3) they could reject that apparatus and freelance in the lucrative wedding-music market. Some of their choices were certainly based on economic calculation, but they were not determined by them. We need additional approaches to explain the social, cultural, and aesthetic factors affecting these choices. Second, economic analyses ignore — or, in a more sympathetic view, bracket and post-pone — aesthetic issues crucial to the musical experience. Ethnomusicolo-gists clearly need ways to understand the symbolic force and emotional power of music, the appreciation of which seems profoundly nonutilitarian and rather uneconomical, considering the amount of money live and re-corded performances of music can cost. As a correction to the metaphor that music is economic practice, we need to develop other metaphors — for ex-ample, the anthropological one that music is social behavior and the semi-otic one that music is a symbolic system. To provide this fuller understand-ing of the nature of music, the following section looks at music as symbolic behavior in Bulgaria during the late 1980s.

During the last years of the Communist period, 1984 to 1989, wedding music grew in importance not just because of its economic power but be-cause it expressed and articulated opposition to the Communist government and agitation for change. As dissatisfaction with the Communist govern-ment's economic, social, and cultural policies rose, the orchestral and choral arrangements of the "national ensembles of folk song and dance" and of the orchestra and chorus at Radio Sofia became negatively implicated in the ecological and moral decay of the country during the last years of Commu-nism. At the same time, state-supported professional folk musicians articu-lated in interviews with me their confidence that the growing complexity of their musicianship and their arrangements exhibited continuing evidence of "progress," Communist propaganda's most important goal for society.

All of these claims about the link between Bulgarian music and social and political forces in the 1980s imply the fundamental capacity of music to function symbolically. But the question remains, how does it do so, and how can this capacity be explained? How is it possible for music — ostensibly one of the least semantic and referential of the arts — to have a "sense," to have "implications," and to "express and articulate"?

One way to demonstrate music's referential possibilities is through yet another metaphoric reformulation of music, this one borrowed from semiot-ics: music is a symbolic system. As such it shares the properties of other symbolic systems such as language, including paradigmatic and syntag-matic structuring and the possibility of semantic, referential meanings that derive from those structures. Semiotics and other structuralist approaches to semantics have taught us that meaning resides not in individual items of language or symbolic systems but in relationships among these items. So the twin notions that words contain meaning and reference things in the world while musical tones are devoid of meaning and have no reference are both illusions. Both the meaning of words and of musical sounds emerges in their systematic paradigmatic and syntagmatic relations within systems of discourse (*langage*). The favored method for analyzing meaning involves binary oppositions between elements in the system, and music is as amenable to such analyses as is language. And music, like other symbolic systems, has two types of meaning: an internal, structural "sense" and an external, interpreted "reference" (Ricoeur 1981).

The "Sense" of Music

In the 1980s *svatbarska muzika* (wedding music) and *narodna muzika* (folk/people's music) emerged as a conjoined symbolic system that contrasted across virtually every element of musical style and practice (see Table 2). The possibility that music during this period could "express and articulate" aspects of the national political debate lay in these oppositional relationships.

Narodna musika repertoire was constructed as an "authentic" expression of Bulgarian national identity that used instruments defined as "traditional" (*bitov*) and whose presentation and transmission was controlled by state-run media and educational institutions. *Svatbarska muzika* repertoire was a grab bag of Bulgarian, Gypsy, Greek, Turkish, Serbian, and popular music performed on Western, manufactured instruments; stimulated, rather than controlled, by the exigencies of the market; and transmitted at family events and by amateur cassette recordings. *Narodna musika* featured "clean" (*chist*), acoustic tone quality; a "sweet" (*sladko*), legato playing style with mordents; stepwise, diatonic melodies within the range of a sixth; and moderate, danceable tempos. *Svatbarska muzika,* on the other hand, featured a raspy, poorly amplified sound; a "with-gusto" (*s hûs*), staccato playing style with inverted mordents; chromatic melodies of an octave or more with leaps, arpeggios, and syncopation; and incredibly fast tempos that defied either comfortable listening or dancing. Finally, *narodna musika* emphasized pre-

Table 2. Structural Contrast between *Narodna* and *Svatbarska Muzika*

Feature	*Narodna muzika*	*Svatbarska muzika*
Transmission	State-run media	Family events and amateur cassettes
Instruments	"Traditional" (*bitov*) favored	Western instruments favored
Ensembles	Western and traditional instruments kept separate	Instruments mixed
Tone Quality	"Clean" (*chist*), acoustic	Raspy sound, amplified
Repertoire	Bulgarian, identified as "authentic," from the "wellspring" (*izvor*)	Mixed, including Gypsy music, music of neighboring countries, and popular music
Playing style	Legato, with mordents	Staccato, with inverted mordents
Melodic style	Stepwise diatonic within a range of a sixth	Range of octave or more, chromatic with arpeggiation and syncopation
Tempo	Moderate, danceable	As fast as possible
Form	Emphasis on precomposed forms with regular phrasing	Emphasis on improvisation and irregular phrasing
Modulation	Stable tonal center (drone-based aesthetic)	Rapid modulation to unusual keys

composed forms consisting of regularly repeating melodic phrases performed by well-synchronized groups and even orchestras, while *svatbarska
muzika* put a premium on irregular phrasing and solo improvisation.

At one level these differences in style could be interpreted as simply
different ways of making music, and the main implications of the contrasts
could be assigned to the domain of aesthetics — that is, the question of what
sounds good and beautiful in music. *Narodna* and *svatbarska muzika* could
be understood simply as alternative ways of making music that each made
"sense" in its own structural terms and in terms of the way it differed

systematically from the opposite style. Some musicians argued, for example, that studio recordings and the planning associated with them simply sounded better than the music at family events, while others preferred the musical spontaneity of live events and the impromptu cassette recordings of them. Bulgarian composers and musicologists argued for the artistic value of "pure" Bulgarian folk tunes and condemned as "kitsch" more modern concoctions by wedding musicians that mixed a variety of styles. Wedding musicians, on the other hand, argued that those same Bulgarian tunes were too "simple" and preferred their own more "complex" creations. Some Bulgarians (and foreigners) liked the exoticism of ensembles of traditional instruments and the unity of segregated ensembles, while others preferred the tempered tunings of Western ensembles or the sonic variety in mixed ensembles. The remaining contrasts in playing style could also be rationalized aesthetically in terms of a preference for "clean," "pure," "simple," "traditional," "artistic" presentations vs. a preference for a more exciting, technically challenging, complex music demanding more improvisational, creative flair on the part of musicians. So one possible interpretive move in this period was largely a structural one, a making sense of music in terms of its internal properties and a framing of contrasts in those properties in formal, aesthetic terms. In this move, music makes sense largely in terms of its structuring without reference to a world and a way of being in that world. In the late 1980s it was a move used by Bulgarian musicians, composers, folklorists, and critics and by foreign fans and observers, and one could observe them making this move in many of the metaphors they used to describe the two styles, metaphors such as "clean," "sweet," "simple," and "complex."

This explanation of musical aesthetics in terms of musical structure makes it difficult if not impossible to impute semantic, referential meaning to music. However, the ability of music to make structural and aesthetic sense without ascribing additional semantic meaning to it hides or obfuscates its ability to reference a world. In fact, the striking contrast between *narodna muzika* and *svatbarska muzika* seemed to be generating deeply contested referential meanings at the end of the Communist period in Bulgaria. And the key to generating and understanding those meanings lay in both the same sharp structural differences discussed above and the slightly different set of metaphors used to discuss them.

The Reference of Music

The music of this period raised the aesthetic question not just of what good music sounds like — and therefore what makes sense as an absolute, autonomous expression — but the ethical question of what good music should sound like in the specific social and historical circumstances of the late 1980s in Bulgaria. During that period, what good music should sound like was inextricably linked to how the state should treat its citizens. Contrasts in musical sounds created referential meanings, and in the process musicians and their audiences joined aesthetics to ethics.

If structuralist interpretations sometimes seem to make meaning emerge logically from the play of contrasts in the mind of a brilliant analyst, what I would call a hermeneutics of social situatedness suggests that meanings are assigned to those contrasts by individuals or classes of individuals operating within particular social and historical conjunctures. Musicians make differences in musical style partly to make aesthetically satisfying music, but what makes music aesthetically satisfying has partly to do with what the music means, that is, with the world it references. Musicians and audiences choose sides and select one kind of music over another for the same reasons. The question of what kinds of music are the most aesthetically satisfying and deeply meaningful is linked to the possibility that music can act as both a critique of the existing world and as an imaginary construction of a new and perhaps better world.

Each of the stylistic contrasts mentioned above and summarized in Table 2 can be interpreted in terms of the meaning or reference to a world that emerges from the contrast. In the particular social and historical circumstances of the late 1980s, the contrast between state-run media and family events recorded on amateur cassettes generated meanings centered around the contrast between the control, stability, and discipline desired by the state and imprinted on a recording on the one hand, and the freedom and unpredictability inherent in musical events sensitive to audience needs and desires on the other. The contrast between a "pure" Bulgarian repertoire and an ethnically mixed one generated meanings centered around the nature of Bulgarian national identity. The contrast between traditional instruments and Western instruments generated meanings centered around whether folk music performance should present an idealized version of the nation's past or a dynamic version of its present. Keeping ensembles of Western and traditional instruments separate versus mixing them raised issues of the nature and control of tradition versus musicians' needs to satisfy a contemporary audience and thereby earn a living. The contrast between "natural" acoustic sounds and distorted amplified sounds generated meanings centered around acquiescence to the government or loud protests against it. The contrast between legato style with mordents versus a staccato style with inverted mordents generated meanings centered around satisfaction and acceptance versus dissatisfaction and challenge. Finally, stylistic contrasts between (1) narrow-range, stepwise, diatonic melodies and wide-ranging, arpeggiated, chromatic melodies; (2) moderate and fast tempos; (3) regular and irregular phrasing; and (4) precomposed forms and improvisation all generated meanings centered around acquiescence to or freedom from tradition and state control.

One of the best indications that Bulgarian music of the 1980s was not an autonomous, Olympian domain for quiet contemplation of the orderly and beautiful "combination of sounds and tone" was the vigorous response of state institutions to the growing economic power and aesthetic influence of wedding music. The Communists had long understood the power of the arts to configure a new way of being in the world. They had explicitly used folk music as a way to attract people to their verbal propaganda in a way analo-? gous to the capitalist use of music to attract consumers to the advertising of products and services. More profoundly, they had arranged that folk music in ways that constructed iconically a sense of national identity and the future under communism (Buchanan 1991; Rice 1994). As the first part of this essay has shown, post-war folk music contrasted with pre-war folk music in ways that set up the possibility for music to express meanings that the Communists intended as they set out to "build communism." From the state's point of view then, wedding music was seducing the Bulgarian musical public away from both the Party's propaganda and from one of the many carefully constructed images of how the world should work under the leadership of the Party. Bulgarians, whether Communists or not, understood themselves in terms of the symbols that the state provided and controlled — and arranged folk music was one such symbol. If another set of powerful and influential symbols was being produced within the second economy and if those symbols gave people an emotionally charged, noncommunist way of being in the world, then the state would have to respond and try to bring those symbols under its control. If, on the other hand, music were merely a domain of aesthetic play, the state would have no reason to act or assert its control.

Predictably, the state tried to assert its control. Communist authorities understood the possibilities of music to reference an existing or imagined world, and they did not like the world that *svatbarska music* referenced. Produced by Gypsies and using elements of Turkish style that contrasted strikingly with arranged versions of Bulgarian music, wedding music referenced a world of decline, agitation for change, and ethnic oppression rather than the optimistic world of "progress" proposed by the Communists. For some time, the state tried to make illegal the playing of Gypsy and Turkish repertoire. When this proved ineffective, they tried to license and tax wedding musicians through a series of auditions. Whereas the differences in musical style tended to exaggerate the contrast between *svatbarska* and *narodna muzika,* and thus its potential for expressing an anti-state meaning, the state acted to reduce that contrast by co-opting *svatbarska muzika* within its institutional structures in at least four ways. First, it recorded wedding music for the state recording company (Balkanton) in watered-down, arranged versions consonant with the state's aesthetics of "sweet" music. Second, it created festivals that guided wedding musicians away from playing forbidden repertoire toward the playing of supposedly "authentic" Bulgarian pieces. Third, on these records and at these festivals, wedding music was nearly always referred to as *narodna muzika;* by eliminating the label, they hoped to liquidate the possibility of opposition inherent in such symbols. And fourth, musical folklorists began to write articles demonstrating the continuity of *svatbarska muzika* with the continuous history of older forms dating back to the Ottoman period, in the process turning wedding music into folklore and diminishing the possibility that it had anything new to say.

Individual musicians within state institutions also helped reduce the distance and the difference between *svatbarska* and *narodna muzika* in at least three ways, although, to be fair, their motives seemed to be economic and aesthetic rather than political. First, some composers began to write arrangements that employed elements of wedding music, such as Gypsy and Turkish melodic structures. Second, players of traditional instruments attempted

Table 3. Aesthetic Metaphors Used to Describe *Narodna* and
Svatbarska Muzika

Users of Metaphors	*Narodna Muzika*	*Svatbarska Muzika*
Proponents	Clean (*chisto*)	Complex (*slozhno*)
	Sweet (*sladko*)	With gusto (*s hûs*)
	Authentic (*avtentichno*)	Free (*svobodno*)
Opponents	Simple (*prosto*)	Aggressive (*agresivno*)
	Lifeless (*vialo*)	Empty (*prazno*)

to keep up with the innovations of wedding musicians, stretching the possibilities of their instruments; one player of the Bulgarian bagpipe (*gaida*) told me he hoped to turn his instrument, with its limited melodic range and nearly diatonic scale, into a "skin saxophone." Third, many professional ensemble musicians formed their own wedding bands to make money in the second economy. These three "if you can't beat 'em, join 'em" responses show that even proponents of *narodna muzika* were prepared to make sense of wedding music and treat it as a politically neutral aesthetic choice with definite economic benefits.

In fact, the controversy over *svatbarska muzika* was couched largely in aesthetic terms, which had the effect of further burying its potential reference while simultaneously suppressing the reference of *narodna muzika*. The argument was carried forward in metaphors, with proponents and opponents of each genre employing a rather different set (see Table 3). Proponents of *narodna muzika* praised it as "clean" or "pure" (*chist*), "sweet" (*sladko*), "authentic" (*avtentichno*), and capable of "filling your soul." From their point of view and by implication, wedding music was dirty and inauthentically distanced from the "wellspring" (*izvor*) of tradition. They described wedding music metaphorically as "empty" (*prazno*) rather than "filling," and "aggressive" (*agresivno*) rather than "sweet." Proponents of wedding music, on the other hand, believed their music to be "complex" (*slozhno*), "free" (*svobodno*), and played "with gusto" (*s hûs*), and dismissed *narodna muzika* as "simple" (*prosto*) and "lifeless" (*vialo*). Each side in the argument interpreted the two types of music from its own perspective, using contrasting and nonoverlapping metaphors. Although many of the metaphors seem relatively neutral and appear to reference a world of pure aesthetic preference, others betray the sense in which these musical styles were being "read" for their reference to the real world of political action.

In particular, the metaphors "authentic" and "pure," which the state used to praise *narodna muzika,* and "aggressive," which it used to condemn *svatbarska muzika,* reveal a referential, ethical aesthetic. To the state, *narodna muzika* was an authentic representation of national identity. *Narodna muzika* also referenced the world of Bulgaria's self-construction under Communist leadership. As Bulgaria was trying to define itself as purely Bulgarian in the 1980s by wiping out the traces of its Ottoman past through forced name changes, the prohibition of Muslim cultural displays, and the encouragement of mass emigration to Turkey by its Turkish minority, *narodna muzika* seemed ever more obviously a presentation in musical form of that political agenda.

If *narodna muzika* was at least partly about national identity, then it is easy to understand why the state and its minions regarded wedding music's challenge to the aesthetic hegemony of *narodna muzika* as potentially dangerous and "aggressive." The authorities obviously understood that wedding music — while providing a seemingly innocuous, aesthetically pleasing musical experience — contained an engrossing representation of national identity distinctly at odds with their official position. It obviously had to be eliminated or at least controlled, and they took action to do so. On the other hand, when the proponents of wedding music referred to music in their own tradition as "free" and played "with gusto," it doesn't take much of a stretch to interpret the music these metaphors construct as a response to a world controlled by the Communists, where freedom was largely absent and music and other work in the socialist economy was performed not freely but with discipline, not "with gusto" but "lifelessly."

If music is a symbolic system that both makes structural sense and references a world, the interpretation of that sense and reference depends partly on invoking individuals or classes of individuals who have some interest in making sense and generating meanings in particular social and historical circumstances. If structural studies of musical style seem to suggest that music has little or no relation to other realities, then an analysis of musical practice as discourse between individuals or classes of individuals returns to music the possibility that meanings are intended and interpreted in it, that it "applies itself to reality [and] expresses a world" (Ricoeur 1981: 140), and ultimately that propositions that truthfully reference a world are contained within it.

Testing Theories in Post-Communist Bulgaria

I revisited Bulgaria for a month in the summer of 1994 for the first time since the early autumn of 1989, a few months before the fall of communism there. While my impressions are relatively superficial, one of the easiest things to confirm is that individuals continue to treat music as an economic practice. Many of the players of *narodna muzika* in the state-sponsored musical apparatus have ceased to play it. Some have been forced out of jobs by decreased state funding. Others, who have the opportunity for continued state support, have rejected it, believing that the salaries are too low compared to the opportunities in the developing private sector. A number have left Bulgaria for Western Europe and the United States, hoping to capitalize on Bulgarian music's popularity there; others are devoting themselves to starting up small businesses of various kinds. Those musicians who have stayed and continue to play were re-forming themselves into small bands — wedding bands, in a sense — and recording and selling cassettes produced by the many small, private recording companies that have sprung up since 1989.

Studying music as social life and symbolic system would have taken more time than I had, but I did observe the extraordinary staying power of tradition, which speaks if not to the autonomy of music, then to its power to make claim on us — to force us to engage with its rules — even as social, economic, and political conditions change. Radio programming, whether on government stations or some of the new, private radio stations, was dominated by old recordings or new recordings in styles superficially similar to those that existed before 1989. Musicians were not, in other words, heading out in bold new directions, but were carefully bringing along with them the musical styles of the past. The stylistic contrast between *narodna* and *svatbarska muzika* still exists, but I have a feeling that the meanings generated by the contrast are no longer salient. Musicians were undoubtedly using music to construct notions of ethnic and national identity, but precisely how that is working itself out in the details of musical style will have to be studied in more careful future analyses.

While it seemed to me that musical traditions of the past rolled on unimpeded, if with somewhat changed meanings, I did observe at least three new developments in addition to the flowering of recordings of small groups on private cassette labels. First, Gypsy musicians have appropriated African-American rap in the Romany language and have interwoven it rather artfully into songs with more traditional Gypsy stylistic elements. It makes sense musically, and I interpret it provisionally as referencing both a new freedom to consume products from the United States, which enjoys enormous prestige in post-Communist Bulgaria, and the Gypsies' appropriation of African-American "blackness," low social status and high prestige in music and sports, to construct aspects of their own ethnic identity. Second, most radio programs now include a mix of styles rather than segregating them into separate programs on "authentic folklore," "arranged folklore," "wedding music," and so on, as had tended to be the case during the Communist period. This could be interpreted as a sonic representation of the dissolution of the tension between the socialist and second economies and between oppressive state policies on minorities and the reality of their diverse practices and thus as a further example of the metaphors that musical life is social life and music is a symbolic system. Third, a new, private radio station devoted to twenty hours per day of folk music programming, *Radio Signal Plyus* ("with one plus more than the rest"), is broadcasting a large amount of Macedonian music, along with a fair dose of Bulgarian *narodna, svatbarska,* and *starogradska* ("old city") *muzika* intermingled with Gypsy, Greek, Serbian, and even Latin American music. The station's emphasis on Macedonian music stands in striking contrast to the emphasis on Thracian music from southeastern Bulgaria during the Communist period. While Macedonian songs have functioned since the pre-war period rather neutrally and aesthetically as popular songs throughout Bulgaria, it is difficult not to interpret this station's programming emphasis on Macedonian music as a statement of some Bulgarians' interest in the fate of Macedonia in the context of Serbian aggression against its ethnic neighbors in the former Yugoslavia.

Conclusion

This essay, in addition to its focus on Bulgarian music, addresses three general questions about music. First, can music be interpreted properly as possessing or lacking semantic reference? Second, is music an autonomous aesthetic domain or is it linked to social life? Third, is music determined by or does it affect social and economic forces? Rather than argue for or against one or another side of the dichotomies suggested in these questions, my strategy has been to explore the truth of both sides by keeping them in some dialectical tension.

Music is a practice that can be interpreted both with and without reference to a world. In Bulgaria in the 1980s, music clearly referenced the world in which it was being made, but when the government took action to suppress wedding music because it read that music as anti-state political expression, musicians in that tradition could take strategic refuge behind claims that music is simply music. Rather than containing political meanings, music's aesthetic and structural sense is so powerful that it can overwhelm interpretations of reference. Thus scholars' competing claims that music either possesses reference or does not overlook the usefulness to individual actors within a tradition of keeping both views alive and in tension. Certainly music's ability simultaneously to contain and to suppress reference was not lost on Bulgarian musicians in the 1980s, and it should not be lost on ethnomusicologists either.

Similarly, scholars argue about the autonomy of music as an aesthetic form versus its construction within and indebtedness to social life. As I observed musicians trying to decide how to make music in the late 1980s, it seemed as though the musical tradition made certain claims on them and in that sense possessed a certain autonomy. Whether they chose to play *narodna muzika* or *svatbarska muzika,* they had to subject themselves to the structural rules of those particular games. In some sense, the music played them as much as they played the music. In that sense, the music as sedimented in tradition could be understood as an autonomous given. But which games musicians chose to play, which radio stations the Bulgarian public listened to, and the meanings they gave to those choices suggest that a dialectical tension must be maintained in our analyses of the interplay between the individual construction of musical and social life and the constraints on that construction presented to those individuals by a tradition of music-making. Rather than autonomous forms or constructed practices, our analyses should explain the way a dialectical mediation of traditional forms and resources on one hand and social, political, and economic forces on the other produce the musical strategies, practices, and forms we observe during our field research.

Finally, ethnomusicologists often argue about whether music is determined by or affects economic and social forces. Again, I would contend that the truth of both these propositions must be kept in mind. As the brief history in the first part of this essay showed, musical practice is clearly constrained by economic and social forces. On the other hand, individuals shape their own economic and social destinies by making strategic choices about whether to play music, what kind of music to play, and how to play it. When, as in the case of wedding music, those decisions develop enough economic and symbolic power, they can participate in a fundamental re-alignment of economic priorities and in the toppling of an entire system of economic practice. As was the case with the above two contradictions, the actions and strategies of individuals and classes of individuals provide the key to mediating and reconciling these seemingly contradictory propositions. In all three periods of recent Bulgarian economic and political history, plus a fourth post-Communist period, Bulgarian musicians made decisions about whether to become professional musicians or not and what styles to play based on pragmatic assessments of their economic, social, and symbolic rewards. At the same time, their actions participated in the maintenance, advancement, and decline of those systems precisely because, when viewed from the individual's perspective, Bulgarian music was and is, among many other things, an economic practice.

An analysis of Bulgarian musical practice as it has changed during the last seventy years provides an ideal opportunity to reflect more generally on the nature of music. When viewed from the point of view of individual practitioners, music can be understood as economic practice, as social behavior, and as a symbolic system with the powerful ability to make aesthetic sense while hiding meaning; to reference existing worlds; and to imagine new, utopian worlds. Bulgarian musicians and their audiences at the end of the Communist period exploited music strategically to these ends in parallel with other economic practices, social behaviors, and symbolic systems.

Bulgaria in the post-Communist period remains an interesting place to observe music doing its symbolic, social, and economic work. As Bulgarians struggle with economic, social, and political transformation and the creation of new notions of national and ethnic identity, they will recreate old musical styles and practices and create new ones that help both to construct those transformations and to imbue them with meaning and emotion.

DONNA A. BUCHANAN

Wedding Musicians, Political Transition, and

National Consciousness in Bulgaria

This essay examines the interface of political ideology, social identity, and musical expression in Bulgaria during the nation's "political transition," an open-ended time frame ranging broadly from the onset of glasnost in the mid-1980s through the sociocultural fragmentation of the post-socialist era. Throughout this period, the relationship between music, politics, and identity has been sharply apparent in the contradictory and fluctuating government policies and popular attitudes directed toward the eclectic, ethnically syncretic musical styles created by Bulgarian *svatbarski orkestri* (wedding orchestras). Largely because of their association with minority cultures, performers of *svatbarska muzika* (wedding music) became targets of harassment and discrimination by cultural, political, and juridical authorities during the 1980s. At the same time, wedding music was by far the most popular musical genre in the country, despite the fact that it developed and flourished without state patronage.

The controversial position occupied by *svatbarska muzika* and its performers highlights several issues which, although specific to Bulgaria, may be pertinent also to other Balkan political transitions.[1] These factors include: (1) the effect of glasnost on all levels of amateur and professional Bulgarian musical culture; (2) efforts to reformulate Bulgaria's national image — and after 1989, its political ideology and economy — as engaged with Western European society rather than the historical legacy of pre-1878 Ottoman domination; (3) the debate surrounding Bulgaria's "national question," an official euphemism masking the struggle of ethnic minorities for civil and human rights; (4) the urge to eradicate all markers of socialist life; and (5) underlying all of this, how concepts such as tradition, authenticity, heritage, and cultural purity are shaped by political forces and perceived and negotiated by citizens in relation to senses of identity on a scale ranging from local to global.

Clearly, Soviet cultural policy, perceptions of Ottoman suppression, aspirations to Western European lifestyles, socialism, nationalism, politicized ethnicity, and cultural purity have been shaping forces of social identity at various points in Bulgarian history before 1989. Yet at the moment of political transition, these factors, which both generated and informed the events of 1989–90, coalesced in the performance practice of *svatbarska muzika*. My research indicates that wedding music culture, considered within the context of the political transition, exemplifies specific aspects of Bulgarian sociopolitical and sociohistorical discourse. Its development, performance, and valuation represent a contemporary metamorphosis of cultural tropes pertaining to the historicized patterning of ethnic interaction within Bulgaria. By merging elements of ethnic and popular musics characteristic of neighboring peoples, the wedding music style emphasizes historical and cultural ties between these peoples and Bulgaria's own multinational population, thus challenging the socialist administration's assertions of mono-ethnic nationalism. This demonstrates that whether we examine the politics of musical culture, musical style as simply a marker of political change, music as an indexical symbol pointing to deeper conceptual shifts in sociocultural processes wrought by political factors, or music as an agent or facilitator of political transformation, changes in musical and political culture must be viewed as occurring in complementarity with each other and in association with other sociocultural processes in historical context.

I focus my investigation of *svatbarska muzika* on Ivo Papazov, Bulgaria's foremost performer of the genre, and his wedding orchestra, Trakiya. Following Foucault (1980: 98), I find it helpful to consider the actions of individuals in shaping or negotiating political policy, for "individuals are the vehicles of power, not its points of application." Of significance here are the dialectical social, political, and economic relationships between musicians like Papazov, and power-endowed representatives of Western musical culture or the transnational music industry, such as rock stars and recording company executives. Such associations evolved as an outgrowth of the political transition and perhaps served to expedite some of its developments. Throughout the transition period, Bulgarian musicians, cultural administrators, and Western agents of music production have utilized concepts of tradition as bargaining chips in the reformulation of Bulgarian identity within the world economy (Buchanan 1991: 498). Such new commercial alliances transcend the earlier dialectic of power relations negotiated between musicians and the socialist state, and redirect musical expressions of local identity into international channels. The repercussions of this rechanneling can be seen in the current development of a market-based musical economy that is resulting in the fragmentation and regionalization of the wedding music scene.

Wedding Orchestras and Their Music

Svatbarski orkestri belong to the category of *moderni orkestri* (modern orchestras), or urban instrumental groups that utilize *moderni* (i.e., Western European symphonic) instruments for the performance of *narodna muzika* (folk/national/people's music). Classified as *gradski folklor* (urban folklore) rather than *selski folklor* (village folklore), the panorama of *moderni orkestri* also includes *dukhovi orkestri* (wind bands), restaurant and folk tavern bands, and even symphony orchestras that perform arranged renditions of traditional melodies. Contemporary wedding orchestras developed from the small, ethnically mixed, nineteenth-century urban bands known as *chalgadzhii, bandi,* or *svirdzhii,* which were hired by villagers to perform a wide range of ethnic and regional musical styles at *svatbi* (weddings), christenings, name days, local *panairi* (fairs), and Sunday *horos* (traditional line and ring dances performed by communities on festive occasions) — a function that they continue to fulfill (Vŭlchinova 1989; D. Kaufman 1990). While no standard format of wedding orchestra exists, most number between four and ten musicians. The instrumentation, too, is variable, but often includes accordion, clarinet, electric bass guitar, and a trap drum set. To these instruments, electric guitar, synthesizer, trumpet, violin, saxophone, *kaval* (rim-blown wooden flute), *gaida* (bagpipe), and *gŭdulka* (three-stringed, bowed lute with short neck) may be added. The lead instrument is usually the clarinet, although violin, sax, or accordion may also predominate. Most bands also include a vocalist (usually female) who performs songs utilizing a distinctive, wide style of vibrato specific to Strandzha, located in the southeastern corner of Thrace. Several hundred wedding orchestras exist throughout the country.[2]

Contemporary wedding orchestras became popular following the establishment of Ivo Papazov's band, Trakiya, in 1974 in the Thracian town of Stara Zagora. Papazov credits himself as the originator of the wedding music style, which combines highly eclectic and improvisatory renditions of Bulgarian *narodna muzika* with stylistic elements of Greek, Macedonian, Serbian, Romanian, Turkish, and Rom (Gypsy) traditional music, and American rock and jazz (Papazov 1992a). The musical aesthetic calls for *chalga,* or high levels of technical virtuosity coupled with rapid-fire improvisation on traditional musical motifs and scalar passages, as well as extremely fast tempos, profuse ornamentation, very loud amplified sound, the incorporation of multiple themes, frequent key changes, and the use of complex, sometimes chromatic harmonies. Rather than concert fare, wedding music is participatory music. Its structure is loose, spontaneous, and dynamic; the substance and length of pieces depends in part upon the band's interaction with dancers and the practice of tipping musicians to sustain the duration of a *horo* or to request a specific tune. It is common for musicians to trade solos throughout the performance of a melody, each contributing to the final shape of the piece. When I interviewed him in 1992, Papazov described this style of wedding music as "*balkanski dzhaz*" (Balkan jazz), pointing to its ethnically amalgamative nature and roots in Western popular culture.

Throughout the 1980s, wedding music emerged as a powerful, meaningful, grassroots alternative to the music of professional, state-sponsored folk ensembles, which the general public associated largely with socialist culture and whose music was broadcast continuously on Bulgarian radio and television. Wedding orchestras became exceedingly popular with people of all class, political, and ethnic backgrounds, despite a concerted effort by the Bulgarian government to eradicate this music (see below). As a vital component of all social celebrations connected with the lifecycle rites of contemporary Bulgarians — especially soldier send-offs and weddings — *svatbarska muzika* represented a spontaneous element occurring in association with — but extrinsic to — the prescriptions of the state ritual system.[3]

The importance of this wedding music to Bulgarian social life is reflected in the fact that wedding musicians were paid outrageously high sums of money for their services. Bands were engaged well before an event. Fees were arranged through contracts and were supplemented by tips. Within the command economy of the socialist state, *svatbarski orkestri* operated on the basis of market principles in which the most talented musicians were paid the highest amounts of money (D. Kaufman 1990: 30). The economic incentive provided by wedding music appealed to instrumentalists working in all spheres of *narodna kultura* (folk/national culture) in the late 1980s, as consumer goods grew scarce and many families experienced financial hardships. For many state folk ensemble instrumentalists, weary of stereotypical compositions for folk orchestra, the performance of wedding music provided a lucrative and stimulating supplement to their daily work (see Buchanan 1995). An instrumentalist who earned roughly 300 *leva* per month in 1990, could make the equivalent of a month's salary (or more) by playing one weekend wedding (Buchanan 1991: 324; see also Silverman 1989: 155). Participation in wedding orchestras was not limited therefore to minority or non-state-sponsored musicians, but the music's association with ethnic groups deemed extrinsic to Bulgarian culture remained problematic for cultural policy makers.

The Mythology of Ivo Papazov

As the country's most sought after and highly paid performer of wedding music, clarinetist Ivo Papazov personifies for many Bulgarians the creative vitality associated with this genre. Papazov was born in 1952 in Kŭrdzhali, Thrace, a small urban center in the Rhodope mountains of south-central Bulgaria located near the point where the Bulgarian, Turkish, and Greek borders meet. His family is of mixed Turkish-Rom ancestry. His paternal relatives were Turkish-speaking *zurla* (zurna) players and blacksmiths from what is now northern Greece, the region once called Rumelia (Papazov 1992a).[4] His father and great-grandfather also played clarinet, and he describes his great-grandfather as one of the founders of the Bulgarian clarinet style (Papazov 1992b). In his youth Papazov learned both instruments (in addition to *gaida* and accordion), but admitted that as a small boy he found the *zurla* too heavy to hold and preferred the clarinet (Papazov 1992a).

Papazov says that the popularity of his band grew slowly. Trakiya's members began by performing only on Sundays for weddings, and then increased their bookings to include name days, christenings, births of children, and soldier send-offs. With time, the demand for Papazov's music has increased to the point that Trakiya now plays every day of the week and is booked two or three years in advance (Papazov 1992a). Papazov possesses a proverbial status among Bulgarians of all ages. Two films have been made about him (Bakalov 1992: 186). His significance as a cultural symbol is illustrated by anecdotes and legends that attest to and explain the mastery of his playing.

Papazov's predilection for the clarinet is explained by his mother, who maintains that Ivo's umbilical cord was tied with a piece of string taken from his father's instrument[5] (Sŭrnev 1988: 23).[6] Indeed, Papazov's playing is so acclaimed that the clarinet, as a symbol of a financially and artistically successful career, is now the basis of new ritual practices. One source reports that when a boy is born in the town of Shumen, he is given a clarinet instead of gifts of money. If he shows an interest in playing it after three or four years, then it is said that he will become a musician. If not, then he will pursue other work (Bakalov 1992: 184).

Papazov himself tells several stories about his popularity with both Bulgarians and foreigners. He recounts, for example, how a Finn came to listen to Trakiya perform for half an hour, and ended up staying two days; how two Americans followed the band from wedding to wedding for a week without bathing or shaving; and how a Greek spent eleven days in a hotel in the nearby town of Haskovo on the off chance that he might catch the band at a wedding (Sŭrnev 1988: 23). In one instance, a Bulgarian couple who had engaged Papazov to play at their wedding approached him three times about moving the nuptials forward, but he was unavailable for the dates they suggested. He recommended other musicians to them, but they declined changing bands categorically. Later he learned that the bride was pregnant, and that she decided to abort her child rather than to wed on an earlier date when Papazov could not perform (Sŭrnev 1988: 23).

Such weddings cost a fortune to host, because if Papazov performs, hundreds of uninvited guests are likely to appear (Papazov 1994: 26). He estimates that 2,500 people usually attend such events (Papazov 1992b). Additionally, wedding bands are expensive. Between 1988 and 1990, when a good monthly wage totaled 450–500 *leva,* wedding bands earned 1,000–

5,000 *leva* per engagement, depending upon the reputation of the group (Buchanan 1991: 521). Yet these high costs do not dissuade Papazov's fans. One man invited Trakiya to perform for his son's wedding in Istanbul. Papazov was unable to travel to Turkey, so the father — at considerable expense — moved the wedding to Bulgaria (Sŭrnev 1988: 23).

I recount these tales because they express both the importance of wedding music to Bulgarian life and the centrality of Papazov to its performance. What they do not divulge are the difficulties faced by wedding musicians: the exhaustion experienced from playing continuously at a two-day wedding celebration, aggravated by constant traveling from job to job, and the persecution encountered at the hands of state authorities.

Wedding Music and Minority Rights

The relationship between wedding orchestras, the Bulgarian public, and the state is historically embedded within a disturbing framework of ethnic discrimination and minority rights abuses. Like the older *chalgadzhii* from which they derive, many wedding orchestras consist of musicians of minority heritage, especially ethnic Turks and Roma, which constitute the country's largest ethnic groups (Tomova and Bogoev 1992: 1). For many years the administrative and academic sectors refused to recognize wedding music as a legitimate form of Bulgarian music for reasons that illustrate the gross contradictions inherent in socialist cultural policy. Wedding music's syncretic repertoire and ties to urban life disqualified it as "pure" *narodna muzika*, despite the fact that urban songs and melodies were a prestigious and popular folklore genre throughout the twentieth century (D. Kaufman 1990: 26). Although it made use of *moderni* instruments and represented a "more contemporary" development, one "closer to the European" for the Bulgarian intelligentsia, *svatbarska muzika* did not fit within the tradition of symphonic orchestral music heralded by cultural authorities as the main model for musical development from the mid-1800s to the present day (D. Kaufman 1990: 26; Buchanan 1991, 1995). Instead, administrators perceived wedding music as associated with negative social values: minority and lower-class society, decadent urban lifestyles, and "oriental" (largely Ottoman Turkish) cultural influences (Buchanan 1991: 521–22). Because wedding orchestras thrived outside the sphere of state-sponsored folklore, they were perceived as an uncontrollable phenomenon that threatened the domination of state musical culture and the livelihood of musicians employed within professional folk ensembles (Buchanan 1995).

In an attempt to deter the spread of *svatbarski orkestri,* the government excluded wedding musicians from the social amenities guaranteed by the state (D. Kaufman 1990: 30; Buchanan 1991: 538). Wedding musicians not already employed by the state were ineligible for pensions or social security. They were given no health insurance and were refused the right to hospitalization if seriously ill. The state taxed musicians' earnings heavily. In addition, they were prohibited from joining any professional union (such as the Bulgarian Composer's Union), one of the avenues to a successful career (Buchanan 1991: 281–83). Such practices effectively stripped wedding musicians of their rights as citizens, and compelled them to seek exorbitant performance fees as a means of ensuring their financial security.

The crusade against wedding music climaxed between 1984 and 1989 in conjunction with former premier Todor Zhivkov's policy of monoethnic nationalism, which denied the existence of minority groups in Bulgarian culture. By 1984, leading scholars on music and folklore published articles describing wedding music as "anti-national," "of doubtful Bulgarian origin," and "devoid of artistic value" (N. Kaufman 1984: 26; Todorov 1985: 31). They accused wedding orchestras of contaminating *narodna muzika* with foreign, oriental elements — modal qualities, microtones, musical motifs, timbres, and aggressive, virtuosic improvisatory passages that they associated with Turkish culture and the music of Muslim Gypsies (see Silverman 1989: 156). This attitude was rooted in xenophobic racism, conceptual ambiguity regarding the bounds of collective Bulgarian identity, and an underlying preoccupation with cultural purity, authenticity, and national unity (Buchanan 1991: 522).

This stance decried the cosmopolitanism that was the very essence of wedding music and ignored the long local history of such music. Particularly at issue were the vibrato style employed by vocalists, which state-trained folk ensemble vocalists viewed as lacking finesse; the *zurna*-like timbre of the clarinet, which one journalist characterized as evoking "blood memories" linked to the former Ottoman presence; and *chalga* (Ruskov 1987: 2). In 1988 I was told that *chalga* was the Turkish term for "music," and that while at its most innocuous, *chalga* referred simply to the art of instrumental improvisation, it was usually employed as a "coarse, ugly word" to describe the playing style of urban Rom musicians (Buchanan 1991: 525). For cultural authorities, the improvisatory aspect of wedding music was impossible to predict or legislate. For wedding musicians, *chalga* carried overtones of artistic freedom.

Papazov, for example, indicates that he prefers to play weddings rather than concerts, because of the unrestricted playing time that weddings afford (Papazov 1992b). He says he closes his eyes when he plays so that nothing matters to him except the music (Papazov 1992b; 1994: 23). He views his folk-jazz fusion style as a medium through which to improvise freely — a technique he learned by listening to recordings of Charlie Parker and Benny Goodman (Papazov 1992a). Perhaps most telling is his comment, "I can eat the same dish twenty times, but I can't play one and the same thing twice" (quoted in Papazov 1994). Likewise, Papazov's colleague Teodosi Spasov, a *kaval* player renowed for his own innovative style of folk jazz, maintains that "improvisation is the means through which he [the musician] achieves the free flight of his artistic fantasy. Improvisation is that which separates free artistic souls from the whole terrestrial globe."[7]

Papazov therefore perceives some of the qualities of *svatbarska muzika* deemed objectionable by cultural bureaucrats as positive attributes. For example, while administrators decry the music's oriental characteristics, Papazov considers the Near East as the wellspring of Bulgarian music and a source of its originality. This reveals an interesting dialectic between wedding musicians and the cultural administration: the social values attached to the origin of wedding music by each group are at odds. In 1992, when one of my students asked Papazov how he would describe his musical style, he replied, "one-third jazz, the rest other Balkan elements, as well as Turkish and oriental influence" (1992a). He added that the oriental elements appear especially in the improvisatory segments of wedding music, in which the manipulation of clarinet timbre plays an important role, in the vibrato style of Strandzha, and the use of modes akin to the Turkish *makam* system (Buchanan 1991: 555).[8] While the "professors," Papazov maintained, lectured against such orientalisms because they were "not authentic," he posited that Bulgarian music actually arose in the Orient, and said that he actively incorporates such elements to enrich the Bulgarian repertoire — to make it "fresher" and "newer" (1992a).

The official outcry against wedding orchestras in the mid-1980s dovetailed with the implementation of Zhivkov's "regeneration process," the horrific campaign of ethnic assimilation that banned the practices and symbols of Muslim and Turkish culture and forced citizens bearing Turkish or Muslim names to change them to official Bulgarian alternatives, sometimes at gunpoint (Tomova and Bogoev 1992: 11).[9] The details of this campaign have been well documented elsewhere.[10] Basically, it is one of a series of ideological programs launched against the Turkish, Pomak (Muslim Bulgarians), and Rom minorities in Bulgaria since the 1940s. These programs banned the speaking of Turkish in public; listening to Turkish news broadcasts; producing or importing Turkish periodicals, literature, or artistic works; wearing distinctive Turkish apparel; practicing Muslim rites such as circumcision; and teaching the Koran. Ethnic Turks were not allowed to join the Communist Party, their marriages and births went unregistered, and they were unable to use banks or receive state monies (such as pensions) unless all parties had Bulgarian names (Helsinki Watch 1986: 15–16). In essence, such edicts transformed members of minority groups into noncitizens if they refused to assimilate.

In terms of music, Zhivkov's assimilation campaign carried serious implications not only for musicians but also for average citizens. In the mid-1980s, authorities banned the performance and consumption of Rom, Turkish, Greek, and Serbian music (see Zang 1991: 12, 40–41, 49). They proscribed the *zurla* as well as the popular, somewhat sensuous, Turkish-derived Rom dance form *kyuchek* from public performance at restaurants, weddings, festivals, and other social gatherings (Silverman 1986: 55–58, 1989: 146–48; Buchanan 1991: 538–39). Those found listening to Turkish radio or music cassettes were subject to fines or imprisonment as well as confiscation of the radio or cassette player (Poulton 1991: 137; Tomova and Bogoev 1992: 9). One informant told me that in Ruse, a city located in northeastern Bulgaria on the Romanian border, it was rumored that the Bulgarian militia confiscated cassettes of Serbian music from private homes (Buchanan 1991: 538–39). Likewise, a Bulgarian-Turkish construction worker traveling to work with her colleagues in a truck near the city of

Shumen reported to Helsinki Watch that when the vehicle was stopped and searched by the Bulgarian militia, "the driver of the truck, who was holding a cassette of Turkish music, was beaten and asked: 'Why do you listen to that music?' " (Zang 1989: 11).

To try to co-opt and control the performance of wedding music, cultural authorities designed the Stambolovo festival, an annual national competition adjudicated by government officials, state folk ensemble directors, composers, ethnographers, folklorists, and ethnomusicologists whose opinions frequently reproduced or molded cultural policy.[11] The first of these festivals was held in 1985 in the town of Stambolovo (located near Haskovo in the southern Rhodopes), an area with a large minority population. Preliminary competitions were held at local and regional levels. *Direktsia "Muzika,"* one of the primary state directorates overseeing musical activity, developed strict rules regarding what groups could perform at the festival (unadulterated regional musical styles), from which area of the country (the region from which the band came), in what manner (on a concert podium), and for how long (fifteen- to twenty-minute sets) (D. Kaufman 1990: 30). As Carol Silverman has noted, although a few hundred groups entered the competition, the jury opted not to award first prize because "no one played 'pure' Bulgarian music" (Silverman 1989: 156). Further, this festival, like all of the Stambolovo competitions, was followed by a mandatory lecture in which musicologists and folklorists decried the corruption of *narodna muzika* by "foreign" stylistic elements (Silverman 1989: 156; Dzhidzhev 1991). The goal of this and subsequent festivals was to augment the "professional skill" of the orchestras in terms of harmonization, form, and the maintenance of a "pure Bulgarian style" (N. Kaufman 1987: 79; Buchanan 1991: 546). The cultural administration's concern with stamping out any association between minority culture and wedding music is reflected in the fact that festival organizers rechristened *svatbarski orkestri* "instrumental groups for the performance of Bulgarian *narodna muzika.*" Such festivals also served to identify wedding bands and their members for cultural and political authorities. And as cult events attended by thousands of people (an estimated 30,000 in 1988), the festivals provided a good opportunity for the cultural administration to instill its ideology of musical style — apparent in the requirements for festival participation and adjudication standards — into the public taste.

Following Stambolovo '86, Balkanton issued a double LP (Balkanton BHA 12181/82) presenting the prize-winning bands, including that of Ivo Papazov. Rather than live recordings from the festival, this album featured the bands performing symphonic arrangements of their work created by conservatory-trained composers of state folk ensemble repertoire. According to the jacket notes, these "discreet professional" arrangements "enhanced" and "refined" the band's original music, resulting in a product deemed more sophisticated, legitimate, and socially valuable by the cultural administration. This tendency to rewrite Bulgarian music according to the canons of the classical symphony orchestra, a propensity clearly evident in the repertoires of state folk ensembles, demonstrated the administration's effort to incorporate wedding music into a more acceptable Western European cultural mold (Buchanan 1995). When I asked one wedding instrumentalist why the cultural bureaucracy insisted on repackaging wedding music in this manner before disseminating it through the mass media, he snapped, "because we think that when a composer arranges something, he is like a god!" (Buchanan 1991: 549). Indeed, in 1992, when I asked Papazov the same question, he replied with disgust, "These [arrangements] are not my work," explaining that the album's final form was not his choice (Papazov 1992a).[12] Unfortunately, because wedding musicians were denied access to the state mass media and concertizing system, such recordings were the only way for them to release their material via the state recording industry and a strong incentive for their participation in the Stambolovo festival.

Papazov purports that by 1987, *svatbarski* and restaurant bands were required to perform 50 percent Bulgarian music and 50 percent Russian music — no other Balkan musical styles were allowed (Papazov 1992a). Local representatives of the Committee for Culture visited restaurants and other establishments where bands played to be sure that they were not deviating from their officially approved repertory lists, an offense punishable by fines amounting to as much as a month's salary (Buchanan 1991: 539). This supervision and the huge number of attendees prompted families to hold weddings at unlikely locations such as tobacco factories or barns (Coleman 1988; Buchanan 1991: 539). Despite these prohibitions, Trakiya continued to perform wedding music because this was what the people wanted (Papazov 1992a). As a result, in 1987 Papazov and his entire band were arrested while playing for a wedding near Papazov's home. They were

imprisoned for twenty-five days for speaking Turkish in public and pro-
pagandizing Turkish music. According to Papazov, because no law existed
under which to arraign them officially for these offenses, they were charged
with hooliganism (Papazov 1992a). This event, while clearly linked to the
ethnic assimilation campaign, should also be understood within the context
of the state's desire to control *all* forms of music-making. Cultural administrators (and some ensemble musicians) resented the large sums of money
earned by wedding musicians, whose rights to citizenship were made ques-
tionable by their ethnic heritage and whose livelihoods depended on a musical practice that authorities deemed illegitimate and even illegal (Buchanan
1991: 538, 596). Monitoring such groups through taxes, fines, and festivals
was one means for authorities to take a percentage of the musicians' profits.

Historical Patterns and Cultural Tropes

As the leading performer of wedding music and hence a prominent symbol
of minority culture, Papazov was a highly visible target for state policy. The
state's reaction against wedding music and the culture of ethnic Turks in
general is deeply seated not only in the history and political policies of the
Bulgarian socialist regime but in the very psyche of ethnic Bulgarians. It is
an emotional response rooted in a fear of (Turkish) political Islam that is
kept alive in all types of expressive culture, including songs, legends, literature, scholarship, metaphors, and racial slurs. The basis of this response
revolves around four concepts that have become nearly synonymous in the
perceptions of most ethnic Bulgarians: Ottomanism/Turkism, Islam, orientalism, and to some extent, rurality. In this section I show briefly how these
concepts might be viewed as an historically embedded cultural trope that
continued to pattern Bulgarian political and cultural policy throughout the
transition period. I do this by examining perceptions of the Islamic presence
in Bulgarian society as they appear in historical and ethnographic scholarship, song texts, ideological discourse, literature, and film. My aim is not to
dispute Bulgarian claims of Ottoman oppression, many of which are well
documented, but to demonstrate how profoundly they have permeated Bulgarian national awareness and sensibilities. It is in this context that the
nature and significance of wedding music must be interpreted.

Islam and Islamic Conversion

Four different Muslim groups reside in Bulgaria: ethnic Turks, who arrived with the Ottoman conquest in the 1300s and who have retained Turkish language and customs; Pomaks, defined most frequently as Bulgarian Slavs who converted to Islam during Ottoman rule but who continue to speak Bulgarian; Muslim Roma, found throughout the country; and Tatars, who settled in Bulgaria during the mid-1800s as refugees fleeing from Russian tsarist expansion in the Caucasus (Crampton 1990: 43–44). Bulgarian political and cultural ideology tends to lump these four groups together as "Turks" because they all practice Islam (Poulton 1991: 123–26; Tomova and Bogoev 1992: 2).

A raging debate exists regarding the manner in which Pomaks adopted the Muslim faith. While many non-Bulgarian studies contend that most Pomaks converted to Islam voluntarily and individually during the sixteenth and seventeenth centuries as a means of either avoiding the *jizya* tax exacted from non-Muslims by the Ottoman regime or improving their legal status, Bulgarian scholarship insists that "the Pomaks were forced to convert en masse through unprecedented terror and torture" to the extent that this perception "has become part of the national consciousness of the Bulgarian people" (Silverman 1984: 612–13; see also Karpat 1990: 4; Todorova 1996: 38). Such writings paint Ottoman rule as imposed domination by "cruel religious fanatics" responsible for the forcible transformation of Bulgarian communities into Islamic colonies politically and culturally allied with the Ottoman Empire and its successor state, Turkey (Tomova and Bogoev 1992: 8; Todorova in press: 47–48). It is no accident, for example, that ethnic Bulgarians refer colloquially to the period of Ottoman rule as the *tursko robstvo* (Turkish enslavement). The extent to which this conflation patterns the thinking of ethnic Bulgarians is revealed in the expression *poturchvam se* (to turn into a Turk), often used in song texts to signify conversion to Islam.

Music, Conversion, and Cultural Purity

The image of Ottoman Turks as bloodthirsty converters is perpetuated musically in *haiduk* songs that extol the deeds (and often deaths) of Bulgarian

guerrilla fighters, called *haidutsi,* who secreted themselves in mountain
recesses to fight for Bulgaria's liberation. In particular, slow-moving, improvisatory, heavily ornamented ballads (*bavni pesni*) from the Strandzha
and Rhodope areas lament the pain of Ottoman rule, the mandatory blood
tax that supported the Ottoman Janissary corps, incidents of forced conversion to Islam, the rape of women, the cruelty of criminal punishment, and
the pilfering of villages (Buchanan 1991: 39–43). Many such texts exist;
they figure prominently in folk song collections (*sbornitsi*) produced by the
Bulgarian Institute for Musicology (see Gorov 1983: 163–221).

The song that I have transliterated and translated below, for example, is
one variant in a larger corpus of ballads that describes the fate of Golden
Mara, who is raped and dragged away for a life of servitude by a band of
marauding Ottoman Janissaries after they persuade her, through trickery, to
open the doors or gates of her home. Such songs are described by Bulgarians
as *tezhki* (heavy) because their ponderous style captures the emotional
weight of oppression, and *zaplakveni* (weeping), which describes their character (Buchanan 1991: 51–53).

Altŭn Mara	*Golden Mara*
"Mari, maro, mari,	"*Mara, maro, mari,*[13]
Yaltŭn Maro,	Golden Maro,
Mŭri, maro, mari,	*Mŭri, maro, mari,*
Yaltŭn Maro, Maro,	Golden Maro, Maro,
Stani, Maro, mari,	Get up, Maro, *mari,*
Otvori ni.	Open up [the door] for us.
Ni sme doshli, doshli, Maro,	We have come Maro,
Da te klanim, Maro,	To pay homage to you, Maro,
Da te klanim, altŭn Maro."	To pay homage to you, Golden Maro."
Maro, mari.	Maro, *mari.*
Stanala e altŭn Mara.	Golden Mara got up.
Otvorila chemshi porti.	She opened the gates of boxwood.
Vleznali sa godezhari.	*Godezhari* came in.
Vzeli sa altŭn Mara.	They took Golden Mara.
"Mari, maro, mari,	"*Mari, maro, mari,*
Yaltŭn Maro, maro,	Golden Maro, Maro,

Stani, Maro, mari.	Get up, Maro, *mari*,
Otvori ni, altŭn Mara, altŭn."	Open up [the door] for us, Golden Mara."

This version of "Golden Mara" appears on the recording *Le mystère des voix bulgares, Volume III* (Fontana/Polygram 846 626–4) under the title "The Rape of Golden Mara" and is performed by the women's choir of Plovdiv's state folk ensemble, Trakiya, in an arrangement by Georgi Minchev.[14] When I listened to this piece together with Stefan Mutafchiev, a well-known Bulgarian composer and the ensemble's director, he indicated that Mara apparently witnesses the slaughter of her family before being taken away to the Sultan (Buchanan 1991: 403). Mara is to be married; members of the groom's engagement party — the *godezhari* — have come to pay their respects. According to Mutafchiev, Mara opens the door expecting to see the cherished guests whose arrival her family has been awaiting. Instead, she finds Turkish soldiers. Mutafchiev was quick to point out that these soldiers were not officers or even first- or second-class regulars, but wandering brigades of fourth-class soldiers — hooligans, really — who went about the countryside causing trouble. Despite the fact that Minchev's text does not explicitly take the story to its terrifying conclusion, the history of the event is alluded to in the harmonic tension that the composer artfully develops within the piece. Released in 1990, the inclusion of "Golden Mara" on this recording exemplifies not only the nature of such songs, but their longevity.[15]

The presence of Muslims in contemporary Bulgaria was thus an anomaly explained through conversion (Todorova in press: 35). One justification for Zhivkov's assimilationist policies was that ethnic Turks were really descendants of Bulgarians — "reborn Bulgarian Muslims" (Helsinki Watch 1986: 9, 17; Poulton 1991: 123–26, 132). Political leaders avowed that any Turks living in Bulgaria had moved to Turkey between 1949 and 1951 or from 1969 to 1979 in conjunction with the Turco-Bulgarian Agreement on Partial Emigration, and that any remaining Turkish minority was therefore "fictitious" (Helsinki Watch 1986: 17; Eminov 1990: 209, 215; Poulton 1991: 121, 131). The Bulgarian press maintained that name changes among the ethnic Turks occurred voluntarily and resulted from "a resurgence of Bulgarian identity among Bulgarian Muslims," or requests by Bulgarian Muslims themselves for new, ethnic Bulgarian identities (Helsinki Watch 1986:

9; Eminov 1990: 205, 208; Poulton 1991: 130–31). Underlying the monoethnic ideology was an obsession with constructing a genetically, culturally,
and musically pure society that would fuel Bulgarian national unity and
ward off the encroachment of Islamic fundamentalism posited in theoretical
Turkish imperialist ambitions (Eminov 1990: 217; Todorova in press: 48,
54). As Gerald Creed (1990: 14) notes, these objectives cast Bulgarian
nationalism as a backward-looking struggle against and survival of Ottoman
rule, rather than as a force leading to the country's future achievements.

Bulgarian ethnography, for instance, has historically treated Pomak culture as Slavic (Silverman 1984: 613). Bulgarian ethnomusicologists claim
that "Turkish music did not even leave any traces in the songs of the Bulgarian Mahommedans [*sic*]" (Katsarova 1954: 202). The inability of Turkish elements to penetrate any type of Bulgarian music is a conviction voiced
frequently by scholars and nonscholars alike. In July 1994, when I spoke
with a *kavaldzhid* (kaval player) who grew up in a Strandzha village about
his early life, he emphasized that although this village bordered on Turkey,
there was no Turkish influence in its music. Raina Katsarova (1954: 202)
similarly describes Bulgarian folksong as "pure and untouched by Turkish
influence," "a shield [protecting] the spiritual freedom of the Bulgarian
people," and "though frequently threatened . . . wholly unshaken both in its
music and in its language."

Rurality and the Ideology of Orientalism

The conflation of Ottoman, Turkish, and Islamic is framed in an orientalist
discourse that extends to Arab, Persian, and Byzantine influences; is located
geographically (for ethnic Bulgarians) in Turkey; and is manifest in the
lifeways and cultural expressions of Bulgarian Muslims (see Todorova in
press). This discourse splits the European continent into that (southeastern)
territory which fell under the Ottoman Empire and those (northwestern)
lands which did not (Bakić-Hayden 1992: 3).[16] For ethnic Bulgarians this
split holds enormous historical, philosophical, economic, and political implications that pertain directly to their identity and worldview. They perceive the Ottoman presence as hindering the spread of the European Renaissance throughout the Balkan peninsula and as inducing a lifestyle of
pastoralism, agrarianism, "regionalism, parochialism, familialism and clan

orientation" (Todorova in press: 55). Further, it inspired "indifference to the European technology, activities and values which secured the steady development of the capitalistic mode of production" (Todorova in press: 52, 54–55; see also Buchanan 1991: 39–40; Bakić-Hayden 1992: 3–4). Ottomanism/Islam, in short, impeded Bulgarian technological and industrial progress (Todorova in press: 54).

Many of these same negative stereotypes characterize rural Bulgarian life throughout the socialist period and beyond (Creed 1993). They represent not only a part of the socialist ideology for constructing an industrialized Bulgaria, but an ideological move away from Ottoman Islam. Bulgaria's Muslim populations, located principally in rural villages of border areas such as Haskovo, Razgrad, Varna, Burgas, and Kŭrdzhali, bear the burden of this legacy (Tomova and Bogoev 1992: 2–3).

The Time of Parting: *Literary Film as Metaphoric Discourse*

In 1988 the release of the two-part epic film *Vreme Razdelno (Time of Parting)* focused the public's attention on the increasingly multidimensional and volatile nature of the "national question." In many ways the film's narrative invokes history and folklore to construct a metaphor of the Bulgarian national consciousness. In addition, viewer responses to and reviews of the film drew significant parallels between the film's contents and contemporary events, illustrating the extent to which the philosophy explored above still pertains to how ethnic Bulgarians make sense of their world.

Vreme Razdelno, based on the book by Anton Donchev, portrays the conversion of a Christian Bulgarian village to Islam by Turkish Janissaries during the seventeenth century.[17] The film is in two parts: "Zaplakhata" ("The Threat") and "Nasilieto" ("The Coercion"), reflecting the narrative's structure. The Janissaries initially try to convince the villagers to adopt Islam through peaceful persuasion. When this fails, they hold the town's notables captive, executing them by grisly methods and raping the village's maidens (some of whom commit suicide) in an effort to make the people convert. A rebellion by the townspeople eventually overthrows the invaders.

The drama's axial point is the wedding of Manol — the hero of the story and a symbolic representation of all things Bulgarian — to Elitsa (see Naidenova 1988; Staikova 1988). The marriage, however, is never completed, for as the townspeople dance the wedding *horo* around the wedding musicians (here the local bagpipers, as was traditional in pre-twentieth-century village life), the Turks — following their leader Karaibrahim — stealthily infiltrate the celebration. With a chop of his arm, Karaibrahim breaks through the *horo* circle, separating the linked hands of the community. Advancing to the wedding musicians, he shoots a hole in the *gaida*'s bag, silencing it. At this point the village's leaders are captured, the maidens are divided among the Ottoman troops, and Karaibrahim takes Elitsa for himself. Later, in one of the plot's many twists, we learn that Karaibrahim is the son of the man who raised the orphaned Manol, and that Elitsa is actually his sister.

The response to this film was overwhelmingly positive. My friends described it as "very well done," having "made a big impression" on them, and "deep." Other viewers termed it a "very Bulgarian film" and said it presented the "history of our people [with] such plausibility" that the audience was watching, in effect, "the tragedy of its forbearers" ("Vreme Razdelno" 1988). One critic likewise characterized it as "an authentic situation, [one that] deeply wounded our national unity" (Naidenova 1988).

The historical accuracy of the film's source, however, is disputed by at least one Turkish scholar, who asserts that in the 1960s

the Bulgarian government went so far as to ask an upcoming party member with literary ambitions, Anton Donchev, to write a novel to back the historian's contention that the Pomaks were forcibly Islamized. Donchev wrote the novel, *Vreme Razdelno* (*Time of parting*), in just 144 days after he had supposedly spent two years living among the Pomaks. He was awarded the Dimitrov Prize in literature, given only to "remarkable creative work," and this novel was translated into western European languages. (Karpat 1990: 6)

In this scholar's eyes, Donchev's book was thus part of a campaign to produce nationalist, historical documentation justifying the claim that the Pomaks have Slavic blood.[18]

Whether or not *Vreme Razdelno* actually was written as a propaganda document, the film version clearly resonated with the ideologies and events that inspired the political transition. The fundamental issue of the narrative is choice: the voluntary selection of one's faith, way of life, and belief system (Naidenova 1988; Stoyanov 1988). Choice implies divorcing prior ways or maintaining them—in this case, embracing a new and foreign lifestyle or sustaining the purity of the preexisting community. Such a choice depends upon one's morality and values, and upon one's definition of honor, freedom, and truth (Stoyanov 1988).

Karaibrahim's puncture of the bagpipe is an important dramatic climax because it marks the point in the narrative when the townspeople must make a choice leading to either conversion or death. It is at this moment that the Ottoman Turks advance into the most intimate territory of Bulgarian society—the Christian wedding ritual that allows the regeneration of the Bulgarian community. Here Karaibrahim—ripped from the social fabric of the village as a child in payment for the blood tax, and replaced by Manol in his native family—returns to take his revenge. As a personification of the *tursko robstvo,* Karaibrahim breaks the wedding circle-dance, a symbol of community unity, and silences the bagpipe, its facilitator. This is, in effect, the *razdelie,* the time of parting, the division of the Bulgarian community into two populations—the Bulgarian Mohammedans and the Slavic Bulgarian Christians—that Bulgarians now perceive as the Ottoman legacy.

The release of this film in the late 1980s, at the height of the "regeneration process," encouraged the Bulgarian public to view the entire Muslim population as Slavs turned into Turks—"ours" turned into "theirs." Manol is the hero of the story because he retains his faith—and thus the community's purity—unto death. Just as Karaibrahim is portrayed as a Bulgarian gone bad, so too had the cultural and political administration depicted *svatbarska muzika* as Bulgarian music polluted by Turkish orientalism. While the decision to play or listen to this music at weddings, soldier send-offs, and baptisms—those celebrations that give a community life—represented on one level an alignment with minority culture, at a more basic level it signified choosing an alternative to socialism at a time when that political system was in crisis (Stoyanov 1988). In this regard the film operated as a "mediascape"—an "image-centered, narrative-based account" constructed from "strips of reality" whose script, formulated from "imagined lives," not only justified the ideological past but provided a metaphorical proto-narrative upon which to build the future (Appadurai 1990: 9). It heralded a "time of transition" in which political choice and social identity (at all levels) would become crucial, interwoven factors. As one reviewer (Kostova 1988: 12) put it:

This film has something to tell us today: every forced, [super]imposed doctrine is doomed: Has a "time of parting" come when not only your fate and mine is being decided, but [one in which] the fate of the community, the family, the nation, human-kind, [and] identity must find its place[?] . . . Freedom, power, roots. After it has grabbed our souls and held them captive with its powerful historical and moral impact, the ballad-like film epic *"Vreme Razdelno"* will cause us to think about these and many other things.

Transition and the Transnational Marketing of Wedding Music

Amidst the climate of glasnost and mounting international criticism regard-ing the treatment of Bulgarian minorities, scholars who had previously lambasted wedding music looked for ways to justify its existence within Bulgaria's borders by positing historical and stylistic connections between traditional village music and wedding music. They cited the flexible struc-ture of the performances, the interchange of soloists, and the music's im-provisatory nature as having much in common with the traditional per-formance of *horo*s (D. Kaufman 1986, 1989; N. Kaufman 1987, 1989; Dzhidzhev 1987; Buchanan 1991: 552–54). While the general preoccupa-tion with the music's purity continued, one scholar recently described its incorporation and variation of new musical material — a process he terms *intonatsionna vseyadnost* (intonational omnivorousness) — as "giving life" to *svatbarska muzika* to the same extent that traditional musicians construct *horo*s by improvising on traditional motives or phrases called *persenkove* or *kolena* (Buchanan 1991: 556–57; Dzhidzhev 1991: 83–84; Rice 1994: 64–67). Likewise, Dimitrina Kaufman — always a staunch supporter of wed-ding orchestras — argues in a recent, pointed critique of socialist policy toward these groups, that the regimentation, concert format, and calls for "regional purity" introduced by the Stambolovo festivals went against both the international eclecticism that defined the music's style and its service-oriented relationship with the contemporary wedding rite (D. Kaufman 1990: 31).

A factor that contributed to the reversal of scholarly opinion was the visit of British impresario Joe Boyd of Hannibal Records to Bulgaria in 1987, during which he heard Ivo Papazov perform at a wedding and expressed an interest in organizing a concert tour for him in Europe and North America (Punkin 1988: 8). However, as Papazov pointed out to me, he and his band were not given the right to travel outside the country until 1989 (Papazov 1992a). The government refused to issue visas to the band's members, and in mid-August 1987, Boyd instead arranged a tour of the state-sponsored group Balkana to England and Scotland.

In 1988, Boyd returned to Bulgaria, where he again voiced his appreciation for Papazov's wedding music style. In January and April his positive descriptions of wedding music as contemporary *narodna muzika* were published in the Bulgarian press, together with Papazov's picture, but the government's prior stance remained firm (Punkin 1988a and 1988b).

In 1987 and 1988 the successful transatlantic tours of major Bulgarian state-sponsored folk ensemble groups and the subsequent international acclaim voiced for recordings such as the Nonesuch *Le mystère des voix bulgares* series, the Hannibal Records releases of Balkana and Trio Bŭlgarka, and the Japanese JVC recordings of the Women's Choir of the State Ensemble for Folk Songs and Dances "Filip Kutev" convinced the cultural administration of the hard currency opportunities presented by marketing contemporary forms of Bulgarian music as voices of the past. But to market Papazov abroad as a representative of *narodna muzika* meant officially admitting to the historical existence, popularity, and vitality of minority culture within Bulgaria, and of minority musicians as bearers of Bulgarian national tradition.

The summer months of 1989 witnessed the large-scale, often forced exodus of 370,000 ethnic Turks and Muslims from within Bulgaria's borders, which precipitated Zhivkov's fall from grace on 10 November of the same year (Zang 1989; Karpat 1990; Buchanan 1991: 39–58; Poulton 1991; Tomova and Bogoev 1992). Some sources suggested that Zhivkov's ouster was due at least in part to his nationalities policy. Indeed, in January 1990, in a continuing attempt to convince citizens that they represented the democratic path of the future, members of the Bulgarian Socialist Party (formerly the Bulgarian Communist Party) televised slogans like "Division — The Biggest Felony of Zhivkov," blaming their former leader for the country's disunity and disassociating themselves from the assimilation campaign in which they all had participated (Buchanan 1991: 129).

It was in this context that Boyd, together with Hannibal Records/Rykodisc, finally sponsored Trakiya's tour of Europe and North America to support the band's first Western record release, *Orpheus Ascending* (Hannibal Records HNCD 1346). On 25 September 1989, Bulgarian Radio broadcast a telephone interview with Papazov while he was touring the U.S., to inform the Bulgarian public how, in the words of the announcer, "*bŭlgarska narodna muzika* was being received in America" (Buchanan 1991: 554). This official recognition of a musician and musical style formerly branded a public menace as in fact representative of Bulgarian tradition illustrated the extent to which the attraction of American dollars and transcontinental renown, together with internal and international pressure to reinstate the civil rights of Bulgarian minorities, reshaped cultural policy toward wedding music. I suspect that the impresario activities of Joe Boyd and the public acclaim voiced for wedding music by prominent jazz artists like David Sanborn — whose NBC-TV *Night Music* program showcased Papazov — served as important catalysts in this process (see also Coleman 1988; Pareles 1989).

That Ivo Papazov felt comfortable openly discussing what he claimed was the "oriental" basis of *svatbarska muzika,* his own ethnic heritage, and the problems he faced as a wedding music performer with students and faculty at the University of Texas at Austin in May 1992 was for me an extraordinary marker of the political transition.[19] The purpose of his tours was not to make money, he said, for he was already extremely wealthy, but to popularize the music he loved and to show others what it represents.[20] Wedding musicians, historically both lauded and denigrated by Bulgarian society at large, were now, he explained, "gaining more respect," because they had "created a revolution," and "people were grateful" (Papazov 1992a).

In his playing he was striving, Papazov claimed, not simply for the coexistence of Bulgarian traditional music with characteristics of jazz, but for a complete fusion of Balkan musics with Western free jazz. While most wedding bands linearly juxtaposed multiple themes and styles, resulting in a musical collage, Papazov aimed for an integration that would produce a new musical genre (see Buchanan 1991: 558–60). Both *Orpheus Ascending* and his 1991 release, aptly titled *Balkanology* (Hannibal Records HNCD 1363), accentuate different aspects of this fusion. *Orpheus Ascending* emphasizes soulful improvisation; Papazov says he created this record with the musician in mind. *Balkanology* — which features Turkish, Rom, Romanian, Bulgarian, and Macedonian dance tunes — illustrates the international character of his repertoire and desire to appeal to all of Bulgaria's ethnic groups (Papazov 1992a). The inclusion of Turkish and Rom styles on the second recording is particularly significant as a symbol of the changing political climate surrounding its release.

Papazov's words reveal that the power of music to invoke simultaneously multiple sociocultural identities is a key to understanding some important facets of the political transition. Papazov's description of his wedding music as "*balkanski dzhaz*" is significant because it shows that he is struggling to create a musical style that supersedes his local senses of identity as a member of the ethnic Turkish and Rom subculture within Bulgaria, as a citizen of the Bulgarian nation, and as a representative of the Balkans. His stylistic aspirations bridge these affiliations with Western musical idioms, creating an emblematic musical pastiche positioned squarely in the political economy of transnational popular culture. Just as post-socialist Bulgaria is, in the words of journalist Slavenka Drakulić, a nation "struggling to be born," struggling to define its image within the environment of shifting world power relations, so Papazov's music engenders this process (Drakulić 1990).

While his search for a satisfactory Balkan jazz style dates at least from his performance on the recording *Plovdiv: Folk Jazz Band* (Balkanton BTA 11859), released circa 1988, Papazov intimated in 1992 that both of his recent records were already outdated in terms of his personal stylistic development and the degree of fusion he hoped to achieve (1992a). In a 1994 interview with the Bulgarian magazine *Folk Panair* he again emphasized his desire for a complete melding of styles, criticizing other bands who attempt to create folk jazz by simply slapping seventh chords on top of styles that "don't coincide" (Papazov 1994: 26).

Yet the wedding music public does not always understand Papazov's emerging style. In the autumn of 1988, at a special Sofia concert showcasing the 1986 and 1988 Stambolovo laureates, Papazov and bands emulating him were booed by the crowd for playing too much eclectic jazz and not enough *chalga*. "Why don't you play music?!" a man venomously screamed at Papazov, indicating that he could not identify with Trakiya's changing style. Another man commented that Papazov no longer played his "own music."

In both cases what was meant by "music" was *chalga* and *kyuchek*—it was these wedding music idioms that people applauded wildly at both the Stambolovo festival and a subsequent concert in Sofia, and which some termed *"tsigansko-bŭlgarska muzika"* (Rom-Bulgarian music) and a *"dzham sesiya"* (jam session) (Buchanan 1991: 557–60). At Stambolovo '88 some listeners danced *kyuchek* during appropriate moments of the bands' performances, despite immediate police reprisals. Because these styles stand for minority culture, when Papazov put them in a more radical, free jazz context, he extended the limits of his own identity to points that some listeners could not appreciate.

Wedding Music in Post-Zhivkovian Bulgaria

As I write the conclusion to this article from the vantage point of Sofia during July 1994, it seems to me that Trakiya's continued exploration of jazz also demonstrates an effort to formulate a trademark style within an emergent Bulgarian musical economy that is based upon market incentives. The effects of privatization can be seen in the rapid growth of a music industry that now boasts more than fifteen active recording studios; new stores owned by private entrepreneurs featuring stereo equipment, musical instruments, and a diverse variety of cassettes and compact discs; and an assortment of new radio stations with programming geared specifically to different musical tastes. Bulgarian consumers can now tune in to a wide array of musical traditions; Anglo-American and European pop, Serbian, Macedonian, Greek, and Rom music are all readily available. While the rivalry between wedding bands under socialism promoted their professionalization and prompted their continual search for new material, and hence a personal musical style, in the 1990s this competition has been intensified by the ample supply of music marketed by the mass media and entertainment industry and by an economy that is making it increasingly difficult for families to afford the high fees charged by wedding bands (D. Kaufman 1990: 31).

The search among wedding musicians for a unique musical profile embodies the political transition from socialism to a more democratic society. It is precisely the intensely emotional, syncretic, and virtuosic jazz-like improvisation of wedding music that was always absent from the music of state folk ensembles. Wedding music still functions primarily in oral tradition. The improvisation is spontaneous and soloistic; almost every wedding band is constructed around the playing of one individual who, like Papazov, is usually the best technician in the group (Buchanan 1991: 556). Wedding music showcases the individual as music-maker, in sharp contrast to the collective performance of folk ensembles. In this regard *svatbarski orkestri* may be perceived as vehicles of democratization, for through them individual creative voices were heard over the collective voice of socialist cultural policy. What wedding musicians present is an alternative musical cartography and an "epistemology of multiplicity" that is "caught in the webs" of Bulgaria's borders (Gómez-Peña 1988: 129–30). I believe that this is what Papazov meant when he said that wedding musicians "created a revolution."

While *svatbarski orkestri* stood counter to state folk ensembles during the 1970s and (especially) 1980s, it now seems that they may replace these socialist monoliths altogether. Not only have folk ensembles become far too expensive to market effectively, they are icons of socialist ideology that, like the names of streets and monuments to heroes of the revolution, many would like to eradicate. Professional instrumentalists presently or formerly attached to the remaining ensembles are seeking other forms of employment to supplement their low incomes. Most have established their own chamber groups with the desire to concertize at home and abroad. All of these groups utilize *narodna muzika* as their basis, but perform it in combination with stylistic idioms of urban and popular culture, like disco rhythms and jazz harmonies. Some of these musicians played with wedding orchestras during the late 1980s, or are currently so engaged. I view the present proliferation of neotraditional instrumental groups as an extension of wedding music performance and an adjunct of economic privatization. The hybridization of Bulgarian traditional music with other Balkan or popular idioms, once largely the domain of *svatbarski orkestri,* is practiced now by everyone.

The search for new musical styles within the myriad newly established instrumental groups has fractured the preexisting urban wedding-music scene and is reconfiguring it on a regional basis. The Thracian style perpetuated by most wedding orchestras before 1990 has been joined by two other, derivative, regional musical idioms: Dobrudzhan wedding music, associated with the northeastern area of Bulgaria bordering on Romania; and *avtorski Makedonski pesni* (composed Macedonian songs), associated with the Pirin-Macedonia area of southwestern Bulgaria, which put old urban Macedonian songs dating from the early twentieth century in a wedding-music frame.[21]

The reasons for the development of these new musical styles are both economic and political. Briefly, the growth and popularity of the new urban Macedonian style is connected to the rise of big business in Pirin and the cultivation of a regional Macedonian political identity. The emergence of a Dobrudzhan wedding music style may be linked directly to the spiraling inflation plaguing Bulgaria's economy. As one of my informants explained, Dobrudzha, because of its agricultural wealth, is one of the few regions in Bulgaria that can still host large weddings, which in turn support a number of wedding orchestras. Top bands throughout the country now demand exorbitant fees — so high, in fact, that when approached by a Sofia resident to play for a wedding, Papazov says he "categorically turn[s] him down." "I can't take his soul from him," remarks Papazov, "tomorrow he won't have anything to eat" (Papazov 1994: 26).

I suspect that the decline in large weddings, the divestiture of the state music industry, and the elimination of travel restrictions together will direct the energies of wedding musicians toward the concert podium, the recording studio, and tours. Dobrudzha, Thrace, and Pirin, for example, have already developed festival-competitions for instrumental groups, modeled on the Stambolovo event. Some of these new festivals have a dual focus: regional instrumental groups compete in one category and groups playing *balkanski folklor* in another (see Petkov 1994). Recordings of the festival performers are produced and marketed by the fledgling record firms. This trend illustrates that — given the fragmentation of Bulgarian politics and the absence of a convincing, overarching sense of political nationalism — regional self-awareness is becoming an important feature of Bulgarian identity. This regional identification is expressed in the music sphere through regional styling, but in a context that also recognizes Bulgaria's complex relationship to other Balkan peoples. As Michael Fischer indicates, it is these "inter-references, the interweaving of cultural threads from different arenas, that give ethnicity its phoenix-like capacities for reinvigoration and reinspiration," and which allow for the "textured sense" of one's identity (Fischer 1986: 230).

Since 1990, regional self-awareness has also grown among Bulgaria's Muslim populations, but here it is politicized in the platform of the Movement for Rights and Freedoms Party (DPS). This party helped secure the rights of minorities guaranteed by the Bulgarian constitution of 13 July 1991, and continues to lobby actively on their behalf. The consolidation of minority groups under the DPS banner, however, has prompted a backlash against their demands (see Tomova and Bogoev 1992: 12–13). This backlash is apparent in the current debates over which language soldiers and their officers should speak in military regiments comprised predominantly of ethnic Turks or Roma, and over the position of the Turkish language in schools that have a high percentage of minority children.

Underlying this debate is the Ottoman complex. As one friend passionately explained, the DPS "is a *movement* (*dvizhenie*), not a party," with "pretensions toward another country" (cf. Kaplan 1993: 262–63). She added convincingly that she believed the DPS aimed to join with the Islamic fundamentalists on the rise in Turkey, once again depicting "Islam as the handmaiden of Turkish bourgeois nationalism and religious fanaticism" (Eminov 1990: 217).

Perhaps this fear of Islam rationalizes the continued preoccupation of the Bulgarian administration with the ethnogenesis of Pomaks, apparent in an experiment proposed by Professor Georgi Petkov of Stara Zagora to trace the ancestry of a select population through an examination of genetic markings (Grudev 1994). That such a study has, in the opinion of one doctor interviewed on the Bulgarian national news, "no medical value" should surprise no one (Bulgarian National Television, channel 1, 8 July 1994). What these examples do elucidate is the persistent play of ethnicity in the construction of post-socialist Bulgaria.

The primary issue underlying the Eastern European political transitions is the transformation and reassertion of social identities in the political and economic spheres of culture. It is people's identities — albeit porous and composite — that are ultimately in transition. This flux includes the realignment of individual and collective social alliances within an immensely complicated arena of power relations that link local cultures to international forces. In Bulgaria, the practice of *svatbarska muzika* was a portent of the transition and is an indexical symbol of its intricacy. Within the sphere of Bulgarian culture, wedding musicians continue to serve as agents or vehicles of the transition by invoking myriad sociocultural affiliations through the varied stylistic components of their music.

Notes

I wish to dedicate this essay to Frank Magne.

Research was supported by the International Research and Exchanges Board (1988), the Fulbright-Hays Foundation (1989–1990), the University of Texas Graduate School (1990–1991), and the National Endowment for the Humanities (1994). I am indebted also to the Musical Sector of the Bulgarian Institute for Art Studies for allowing me access to secondary sources housed in the Institute's library. None of these organizations is responsible for the views expressed by the author.

1. As illustrated in the writings of Ljerka Rasmussen and Mirjana Laušević in this volume, nationalism predicated upon politicized ethnicity, perceptions of orientalism, and cultural purity are also manifest in some current Serbian, Bosnian, and Macedonian musical styles (see also Rasmussen 1991). Interestingly, Martin Stokes (1992b) points to many of the same factors in his discussion of *arabesk* and the Turkish state.

2. Bakalov (1992: 7, 182) estimates the number of wedding orchestras in Bulgaria as "over 2500." My own sense is that this figure is a bit high.

3. Bulgarian males are required to complete two years of military service upon finishing high school. Initially at least, they are allowed little contact with their families. This period has become a kind of rite of passage marking a young man's passage into adulthood. The days immediately prior to a boy's departure are quite sorrowful, and a band is usually hired to play music for his send-off. A man who comes from a musical family described to me, for example, how his male relatives played clarinet and sang in the car all the way to the military installation, while his mother cried.

4. The *zurla* is a raucous, double-reed instrument that Bulgarians associate with Turkey and the Muslim Gypsy population of Macedonia. It is generally played in pairs in which one instrumentalist sustains a drone. The combination of two *zurli* with a *tŭpan,* a double-headed frame drum, constitutes one of the most typical idioms for the performance of Balkan wedding music.

5. Bulgarian musicians frequently wrap string around the joints of clarinets and *kaval*s so that they will fit together snugly.

6. Some of Sŭrnev 1988 is reprinted in Bakalov (1992: 188–90).

7. Program notes, jazz improvisation concert, 28 June 1994, Sofia. The similarity be-

tween Spasov's philosophy and that expressed by Soviet jazz musicians similarly oppressed by their government, such as the Ganelin Trio and Sergei Kuryokhin, is striking (see Buchanan 1985: 109–15).

8. Papazov named several *makamlar* in this discussion, illustrating his knowledge of Turkish music theory.

9. Ivo Papazov, for example, was christened Ibrahim Hapasov.

10. On the persecution of Bulgarian minorities, see Helsinki Watch 1986; Silverman 1985, 1989; Zang 1989, 1991; Eminov 1990; Karpat 1990; Şimşir 1990; Poulton 1991; and Tomova and Bogoev 1992. It is important to interpret the name-changing campaign in the larger context of Bulgarian society, in which even ethnic Bulgarians were required to select their children's names from a governmentally approved register. When prohibitions against the use of other names by minority groups were lifted in 1990, some of my Bulgarian friends viewed this as the ascription of special privileges to minorities. Freedom of choice in naming was not guaranteed for all Bulgarian citizens until ratification of the July 1991 constitution.

11. For fuller descriptions of the Stambolovo festivals, see Silverman (1989), Buchanan (1991: 541–50), and Rice (1994: 250–55).

12. Another important facet of such recordings is that because Bulgarian copyright laws didn't recognize performers' rights, the arranger and recording label (i.e., the state) probably received most of the proceeds from this release.

13. It is common for Bulgarian songs to include interjections like *mari* to fill out the text. In this case, *maro, mari,* and *mŭri* are also adaptations of Mara's name.

14. I am indebted to Lauren Brody for her help in transcribing this text.

15. For alternative versions of this text, see Madzharov (1983: 224) and the liner notes to *Le mystère des voix bulgares, Volume III,* which present a slightly different translation than my own.

16. See also Stokes (1992b) for an interesting parallel in Turkey that supports Bakić-Hayden's thesis of "nesting orientalisms" (Bakić-Hayden 1992: 4).

17. For an excellent English translation of this novel, see Donchev (1968).

18. Part of the government's justification for both the Bulgarianization of the Pomak population and Donchev's book was a liturgical manuscript dating from 1660 that was written by a Bulgarian priest named Methodii Draginov. Karpat contends that the manuscript was probably spurious (Karpat 1990: 7).

19. To fully appreciate the weight of this event, the reader must understand that eliciting information from my friends and colleagues about Bulgarian government policy toward minorities or *svatbarska muzika* was nearly impossible before 1990 and was usually accomplished in an atmosphere of secrecy.

20. Some of my folk orchestra colleagues assert that Papazov makes so much money within Bulgaria that he in fact loses money when on tour.

21. On the significance of Thrace, see Buchanan (1991: 59–67, 520).

Discography

Ivo Papasov and His Bulgarian Wedding Band: Orpheus Ascending. Produced by Joe Boyd and Rumyana Tzintzarska, liner notes by Joe Boyd. Hannibal Records HNCD 1346, p/c 1989.

Ivo Papasov and His Orchestra: Balkanology. Produced by Joe Boyd, liner notes by Carol Silverman. Hannibal Records HNCD 1363, p/c 1991 by Rykodisc.

Le mystère des voix bulgares, Volume III. Produced by Marcel Cellier, liner notes by Marcel Cellier. Recordings made by Radio Sofia and Marcel Cellier during the period 1985–1989. Fontana/Polygram 846 626-4, p1990 Disques Cellier. Features Choir Trakia, Choir RTB, Choir Rodopi-Smolyan, Choir Tolbuhin.

Plovdiv: Folk Jazz Band. With the participation of "White, Green and Red," Ivo Papazov, and Petŭr Ralchev. Balkanton BTA 11859, purchased in 1988.

Stambolovo '86. Features the bands Trakiya, Mladost, Horo, Kanarite, and Orfei. Balkanton BHA 12181/82, p1986.

Stambolovo '88, Volumes 1 and 2. Balkanton BHMC 7331/32, p1988.

Music and Marginality: Roma *(Gypsies) of Bulgaria*

and Macedonia

In an effort to counter the tendency of scholars studying politics to marginalize music and other expressive arts, this volume illustrates how music is constitutive of politics. If music were indeed so marginal, why, then, was folk music censored in Khomeini's Iran, why were Turkish and Rom[1] musics prohibited in socialist Bulgaria, why was epic poetry censored in socialist Central Asia, why was Western rock music severely regulated in every socialist nation, and why is music being ethnically cleansed in the former Yugoslavia (Laušević 1994; Petrović 1994)? It is clear that music is not merely derivative of politics, not merely a reflection of politics — it is political. Music shapes politics and economics and social life as well as being shaped by them. Moreover, music is often part of a cultural milieu that displays specific social values, values that may represent the existing hegemony, counter it, or subvert it. Socialist and post-socialist Eastern Europe provides a rich arena for examining the role of music in creating and reinforcing ideology as well as contesting ideology.

The case of Balkan Roma (Gypsies) is illuminating for an analysis of music and politics because of the paradox that Roma are powerless politically and powerful musically.[2] During the socialist period Roma were marginalized not only in the realm of state-sponsored politics but also in the realm of state-sponsored folk music. Yet even during this period Roma continued to exert a profound influence on unofficial musics; they continued to be professional musicians in the private realm, playing for non-Rom as well as Rom audiences at village and town events, such as weddings, birth celebrations, soldier send-off celebrations, circumcisions, and baptisms. Moreover, Roma have shaped major Balkan musical genres, such as wedding music in Bulgaria (Silverman 1988; Bakalov 1992; Buchanan and Rice

in this volume), *čalgija* music in Macedonia,[3] and *musica lăutareasca* in
Romania.[4] These genres have been intertwined with popular music, the
recording and cassette industries, and other forms of media dissemination
that highlight their economic importance (Rasmussen 1991). Using a cultural studies framework, this essay examines Roma in Bulgaria and Macedonia from the 1970s to the 1990s, tracing the relationship among politics,
economics, and musical culture. Bulgaria and Macedonia are useful to compare because Bulgaria had one of the most centralized forms of state socialism, whereas Macedonia had one of the least centralized.

Roma: History

Linguistic evidence reveals that Roma are originally from northern India
and that they migrated westward sometime between 800 and 950 A.D.,
arriving in the Balkans in the fourteenth century, some settling and others
remaining nomadic (Soulis 1961: 152, 163). Romany, the Rom language, is
descended from Sanskrit and closely related to Hindi. Today Romany exists
in many dialects, reflecting the paths of Rom dispersion (Hancock 1987: 7–
10; Liégeois 1986: 34–38). In the Balkans, Roma have been professional
musicians for over five hundred years. They have been indispensable sup-
pliers of diverse services to non-Roma, including music, entertainment,
fortune-telling, metalworking, horse dealing, woodworking, sieve making,
basket weaving, comb making, and seasonal agricultural work. Many of
these trades required nomadism. Roma are extremely adaptable in the area
of occupations, thus music is often combined with other trades due to economic necessity. The professional music niche, primarily male and instrumental but often vocal, requires Rom to know expertly the coterritorial
repertoire and to interact with it in a creative manner. Although the vast
majority of Balkan Roma are sedentary today, they do travel for musical
jobs; this, plus a lively pan-Balkan trade in cassettes, has given them the
opportunity to enlarge their repertoire and enhance their multimusical as
well as their multilingual abilities.

Initial curiosity about Roma by European peoples and rulers quickly
gave way to hatred and discrimination in virtually every European region, a
legacy that has continued through the present. In the Romanian principali-

ties of Wallachia and Moldavia, Roma were slaves from the fourteenth to the nineteenth centuries, owned by noblemen, landowners, monasteries, and the state. Slavery was abolished in 1864, but patterns of exploitation have continued (Hancock 1987; Crowe and Kolsti 1991). In other countries, Roma were viewed as outcasts, intruders, and threats, probably because of their dark skin, their association with invading Moslems, and their foreign ways. They are the quintessential "Other" for European peoples. Despite their small numbers, they inspired fear and mistrust and were expelled from many European territories. In some places, bounties were paid for their capture, dead or alive, and repressive measures included confiscation of property and children, forced labor, prison sentences, whipping, branding, and other forms of physical mutilation.

Assimilation was attempted in the eighteenth century in the Austro-Hungarian Empire during the reign of Maria Theresa and her son Joseph II by outlawing Romany; Rom music, dress, and nomadism; and banning traditional Rom occupations. In the twentieth century, persecution escalated with the Nazi rise to power. Between 1933 and 1945 Roma faced an extermination campaign, which is only now being historically investigated. Over 600,000 were murdered, representing between one-fourth and one-fifth of their total population (Liégeois 1986: 87–141; Hancock 1987; Crowe and Kolsti 1991).

In the socialist countries of Eastern Europe, assimilationist campaigns were carried out among Roma to settle them, force them to become socialist workers, and to prohibit their culture. The Bulgarian government instituted one of the most brutal campaigns, whereas Yugoslavia was much more haphazard, disorganized, and inefficient. In Bulgaria, by the mid-1970s, Roma were settled and some forced to relocate, extended families were broken up, and state jobs were assigned. The ethnic category Rom and *Tsigan* (derogatory designation for Rom) was abolished, and the government claimed that all Roma had been assimilated. By the 1980s, Muslim Rom clothing was outlawed, Muslim Roma were forced to change their names to Slavic ones, and Rom music and language were prohibited (Silverman 1986; Cartner 1991).

In Bulgaria in the post-socialist period there has been a rise in anti-Rom sentiment and an alarming outbreak of violent incidents against Roma, including mob attacks, burnings of homes, and police brutality (Cartner

1991, 1993; Bulgarian Helsinki Committee 1993). Segregation in housing, education, and the army still continues. Unemployment rates are highest among Roma, with discrimination in jobs and biased press coverage adding to this problem. Modest gains have been made, however, such as the introduction of some elementary school language classes in Romany, the offering of scholarships for promising high school students, the organization of the Human Rights Project for legal defense, the publishing of a Rom newspaper, and the formation of many Rom political organizations, clubs, and unions. One of the biggest problems of political mobilization is the disunity among the many Rom organizations (Marushiakova and Popov 1993).

Unlike Bulgaria, the former Yugoslavia was hailed by many authors for treating its Roma better than any other Eastern European country (Puxon 1973: 4, 18–19; Poulton 1989: 29, 1993).[5] Indeed, perhaps because Yugoslavia had the largest population of Roma in Europe, plus having a few extremely large population concentrations (in Niš, Belgrade, and Skopje), the government did pay some attention to Roma.[6] In the early 1970s, the ethnic designation *tsigan* disappeared from print, radio, television, and official documents, and the designation Rom was substituted. Of course, in practice, the derogatory appellation *tsigan* continued to be used, but this official change signaled some goodwill on the part of the government. In the 1980s, Romany-language radio programs were introduced in Serbia, and a few hours of Romany language teaching were introduced in the primary grades in Kosovo and in Tetovo, a city in Macedonia. By 1990, Macedonian Roma also had a weekly thirty-minute television show.

As early as 1948, the Roma of Macedonia began to organize politically and culturally. They obtained seats on the Skopje town council and formed their own association, Phralipe (Brotherhood). During the socialist era, Rom social and cultural organizations — such as soccer teams, boxing clubs, drama clubs, and music and dance ensembles — proliferated in Skopje. The amateur folk music ensemble, also called Phralipe, traveled throughout Europe to rave reviews. Regarding music, it is important to note that the 1970s also represented the first success of Roma in the world of professional non-Rom commercial recording (see below and Silverman forthcoming). Some Rom singers and instrumentalists became well-known performers, achieving fame in both Rom and non-Rom circles.

Since the formation of the independent Former Yugoslav Republic of

Macedonia in 1991 (henceforth known as Macedonia), Roma have been mobilized into two Rom political parties, and have achieved the status of "nationality."[7] In spite of suffering more discrimination than any other ethnic group, Roma have increased their visibility in the political life of the country; unlike Bulgarian Roma, Macedonian Roma appear more organized and unified in political life. This increased politicization of Roma plus their increased economic vulnerability in the post-socialist atmosphere of scapegoating has made the Rom profession of music especially important as a viable economic niche. Moreover, Rom expressive culture, especially music, can be explored as a barometer of identity issues in this time of transition.

Cultural Studies and Folk Music

The cultural studies literature[8] can be very useful for scholars of Rom music (and indeed all music) because of its concern for the production and consumption of culture (Lave, Duguid, and Fernandez 1992). Whereas works in cultural studies have dealt mainly with the United States and Britain, it is fruitful to apply cultural studies modes of analysis to Eastern Europe. Although the class analysis of British society offered by the Centre for Contemporary Cultural Studies does not apply to Eastern Europe, the notions of class and race do help us explore the extreme marginalization of Roma in virtually every realm except music and certain crafts. Also, the notion of a dominant political ideology and resistance to it applies well to Rom music in relation to pre-1989 socialism. Furthermore, the issues of cultural property, the ownership of knowledge of group creativity, and the control of artistic expression are central to Eastern Europe ideological systems.

Ethnomusicology and folklore studies, like cultural studies, have tended to focus on the culture of subordinate groups, but unlike cultural studies they do so not because the groups are subordinate but because their culture is traditional or artistic. Early folk music studies focused on aesthetics and creativity rather than on power differentials; they were primarily about the culture within folk groups, not about domination, resistance, and conflict among groups.[9] Thus until recently, studies of Rom music focused on style and repertoire and ignored the marginal position of Roma. This is true of many folk music studies and also of early folklore and ethnicity studies, and is derived in part from an acceptance of the bounded culture concept. The ethnicity literature before Barth (1969), for example, focused on cultural forms within the bounded units called ethnic groups rather than on the problematic nature of identity in those groups and the boundaries between them.[10]

In discussing Rom music, the relationship between marginalization, commerce, and expression needs to be fleshed out. In this light, I find Gilroy's analysis of the music of Blacks in Britain and across the Black Atlantic very relevant. Gilroy points out that for oppressed and marginalized people, expressive culture is a zone of negotiation, of working out the nature and limits of that oppression; it may be a zone of resisting oppression and resisting stereotypification or of cashing in on or reappropriating stereotypes (Gilroy 1993; Abrahams 1992). Similarly, Scott analyzes the hidden and public transcripts and performances of oppressed peoples (1990). Rom music, like Black music, deals with marginalization in multiple ways; for the in-group it may be a marker of celebrating Rom ethnicity; it may also, however, be a commodity to be sold to non-Roma. Thus, I am led to reject Gojković's (1986) dichotomy between in-group and out-group Rom repertoires because I find it too absolutist, even though it might be accurate in some locales. Gojković posits two bounded cultural groups: the first, Roma who play a certain repertoire for themselves; and the second, non-Roma, whose different repertoire is played for them by Roma for money. This model omits the many ways in which Rom music is part of a wider economic and cultural matrix that includes non-Roma. Eschewing a model based on bounded groups, I see a more complex web of musical associations embedded in the realm of commercially available popular and folk music, with which both Rom and non-Roma interact. Like Black music in the English-speaking world of the Atlantic, Rom music of the Balkans has been a particularly important element in the traffic of popular and commercially mediated musics at least since World War II and possibly earlier. For example, Rom stylistic elements — such as the *čoček* rhythm,[11] emotional quality of singing, and instrumental improvisation — have been appropriated into Serbian, Bosnian, Albanian, Bulgarian, and Macedonian popular forms as markers of an "eastern, oriental style" (Rasmussen 1991). The fact that Rom music shares many of these stylistic markers with Turkish music does not make them any less Rom in my estimation, since I am not seeking origins or essences, but it may highlight the fact that for non-Roma, Rom stylistic elements of music performances are coded as positive whereas Turkish stylistic elements are more problematic. This is due to the overwhelmingly negative association of the Ottoman legacy. In fact, most Balkan non-Roma do value Rom musical abilities while simultaneously discriminating against them as a people; the Black music analogy is obvious.

Music, Mobilization, and Resistance: Bulgaria

Music mobilizes both for official purposes and for subversive purposes, be they socialist or capitalist, democratic or totalitarian, nationalist or internationalist. The French Revolution, the American Revolution, the Russian Revolution, and the Breton and Catalonian separatist movements, have all produced songs of mobilization, and patriotic songs are part of the repertoire of every democratic as well as totalitarian nation. During the nineteenth-century period of nation building in Eastern Europe, the collection of folk songs was an important part of defining the nation (Halpern and Hammel 1969). Today in Bosnia, all three sides in the war have constructed their own nationalist music and cleansed the media of the enemies' musics (Lauševic 1994; Petrović 1994). This reminds us that one group's orthodoxy is another group's counterculture and that no philosophy is exempt from ideology. Eastern European researchers tend to see socialism as official state ideology in every context, forgetting that in other parts of the world and at other times — for example, in Latin America — socialism can be oppositional and countercultural.

In Eastern Europe it is certainly striking how socialist governments supported certain kinds of folklore for certain reasons. Lenin embraced folklore as an expression of the working class; Izaly Zemtsovsky speaks of the Soviet policy on paper of exalting folklore as "the foundation of socialist thought . . . the source of all that was best in culture" (1993). But what they actually supported was not what people sang, wore, or narrated but rather a selected, centralized, government-sanctioned version of folklore labeled "authentic." In Bulgaria, the government poured huge amounts of money into the amateur folk music movement through village music collectives and through festivals. Festivals promoted a monoethnic image of the state and fostered a static view of the peasant past. The government also sponsored professional ensembles and folk music schools, both of which promoted a unified national style, which displayed the modernization of the nation's folklore through elaborate choral and instrumental arrangements and staged choreography. Musical policy in Bulgaria displayed an official discourse of legitimation — that is, folklore in the service of building the socialist nation (Buchanan 1991; Silverman 1989; Rice 1994). In both spheres, festivals and ensembles, the music of minority ethnicities was censored and repressed, as were their languages, costume, and many of their professions.

There never existed, for example, a Bulgarian village folklore collective composed of Roma, nor did folklore scholars acknowledge that Roma have their own folklore. Bulgarian folklore collectives that performed at folk festivals were required to cleanse their music of all Rom and all Muslim elements as part of an effort to preserve "pure, authentic" Bulgarian folklore. Remember that Roma were legislated out of existence as an ethnic group in Bulgaria in the 1970s by being officially absorbed (and hopefully assimilated) into the group "Bulgarians" (Silverman 1986). Of course, discrimination and prejudice against Roma continued, both in state and local contexts (Cartner 1991). The only time Roma performed at folk festivals were as instrumentalists for Slavic Bulgarian groups or offstage in unofficial settings such as restaurants. On stage, they were required to perform "pure" Bulgarian music, defined as being without any "foreign" influence. A striking example of this policy was the 1985 decision of the Communist Party to ban the *zurna* (keyless oboe) from the Pirin Folk Festival because it was "foreign." This instrument is played only by Rom men and is the most typical instrument for dance music in the Pirin region. The *zurna* had also been excluded from government-sponsored folk music schools from their inception in the 1960s. Instead of *zurna,* the government organizers at the festival substituted *svirki* (flutes), which are shepherds' instruments and are very soft in volume. Audiences failed to show up at the stages where dances were performed, and if they did, they found the dancing boring and uninspired without the loud *zurna* accompaniment. Although banned on the official stages, Rom *zurna* players turned up anyway and played for dancing for tips in a meadow above the festival site, until the police chased them away.

This example shows how Rom musicians and non-Roma who hired them

operated outside and in opposition to the socialist system of musical management; audiences and performers experimented in the interstices of official culture. Another example is wedding music, a phenomenon in which
Rom musicians played a leading role.[12] Wedding music emerged in the
1970s as a countercultural, mass youth movement complete with superstars
and inflated prices. In Bulgaria, wedding music — with its loudness, electric
amplification, Western instruments, daring speed and technique, rock and
jazz influences, and eclectic borrowings from film, classical, and pop music — epitomized youth culture even more than rock music. The fact that it
was associated with Roma, who didn't officially exist in the socialist Bulgaria of the 1980s, made it doubly subversive.

The popularity of wedding music illustrates the often ignored point that
in Bulgaria the socialist period was not a stagnant era, either musically (Rice
1994) or economically (Creed 1992). Rather it was an extremely dynamic
period when cracks in the socialist system appeared regularly, especially in
the 1980s. For example, at the same time the government condemned wedding music as decadent and censored it from the state recording industry, it
allowed a second economy of wedding cassette duplication to flourish. This
upholds Verdery's assertion that the socialist economy needed the black
market to fill in its shortcomings (1991b: 423). Thus, we need to rethink and
reconceptualize the simplistic comparative dichotomy of socialist/post-
socialist. At the same time, we also need to recognize that profound changes
occurred in 1989, especially in the realm of public expression.

In the 1980s, wedding music was not only about being antisocialist;
it was equally and, for some, more about Westernization, youth alienation, urbanization, and free-market economics. Musical changes are never
merely products of pro- or antigovernment ideology but also interact with
other spheres of life. Thus, in socialist Bulgaria, wedding music was a viable
niche in the second economy, especially for Roma, who had few options in
employment. It was, moreover, a youth audience movement that successfully bridged urban and rural contexts. At the mega-concerts of the mid-
1980s, which hastened the government acceptance of and attempt to regulate wedding music, one could see urban and village, Bulgarian and Rom
youth side by side, both consumed by the frenzy of fandom. These youth
had rejected both the "authentic" folk music of festivals as irrelevant to
modern life, and ensemble music as too formulaic, too predictable, and too

allied with state mandates. At that time, some folklorists began to write of the stagnation in state-sponsored folklore due to the "transition to modernity" (Kokareškov 1986). It is not surprising that both Rom and non-Rom youth were attracted to wedding music for its unpredictability; thriving on technology and change, wedding music epitomized modernity.

In many ways, wedding music is still associated with newness and openness in contemporary Bulgaria, although the economic structuring of its performance has changed greatly. A few wedding bands have recently introduced computer technology into musical composition and performance.[13] During the heyday of wedding music, the early 1980s, villagers could afford to hire famous bands for rituals that lasted two to three days and could afford to spend six months' salary for one event. At that time wedding music was a persecuted, unofficial, free-market niche in a socialist economy. Ironically, now, since 1989, when the free market reigns, wedding musicians are suffering financially, because villagers no longer have the money to pay for live music. Some families now opt for recorded music and a small number of guests; most families settle for an abbreviated ritual — for example, a one-evening wedding, baptism, etc. The only families that regularly put on relatively large events with live music are Roma and Turks, not because these groups can afford them more (in fact, the opposite is true — they are the poorest), but because in these groups, music and dance are part of everyday life and have a significant role in displaying status.

Currently wedding musicians are hired not by the day, as in the pre-1989 period, but rather by the hour, and the average event requires six hours of performance. Because each event is only one evening long, musicians must play more weddings per week in order to make a decent income. This is more stressful and involves more driving and hence more money spent on gasoline, which is very expensive.[14] Yet, comparatively speaking, wedding musicians are lucky, because at least they have profitable work. In one day a famous musician can make the equivalent of a week's work in a factory. Their work, however, is seasonal, and during the winter many musicians are idle. With the current economic crisis, unemployment has reached 90 percent in many Rom neighborhoods, and music remains one of the few viable trades.

An important current concern of the more popular professional musicians is the question of the ownership of music, piracy, and authors' rights.

The less well known groups do not care as much, because no one is trying to disseminate their music illegally. This was also a concern in the socialist period, but no one could do anything about it. During the socialist period, wedding music and other types of Rom music, such as songs in Romany and music played on *zurna,* were disseminated illegally or semilegally through privately duplicated cassettes (Peičeva and Dimov 1994). As far back as the 1970s, fans would record the performance of a good band at an event and pass around the cassettes to friends. In the 1980s, private entrepreneurs and employees of semilegal duplicating studios began to do the same in order to sell the tapes at inflated prices, again without permission. During this time, there was virtually no concern with composers' or authors' rights in the realm of wedding music, a fact that greatly angered wedding musicians. This was in stark contrast to the rigidly controlled system of authors' rights for *obrabotki,* government-sponsored arrangements of folk music written by conservatory-trained, non-Rom composers, who usually were not performers. Every time an *obrabotka* was played by an ensemble or was reprinted in a publication, the composer received royalties.

Since 1989 there has been a proliferation of small cassette and CD production companies — such as Payner, Unison Stars, and Lazarov Records — who distribute through shops and open market outlets. When producing a tape, they typically pay a fairly large fee to the musicians plus a small royalty fee (*avtorsko pravo*) for every cassette they sell. According to many professional musicians, these companies underreport the number of cassettes they sell in order to pay less royalties; thus the musicians feel cheated by them. In addition, some of these companies now sponsor private folk festivals and one also sponsors a radio station, which plays its products almost exclusively.[15]

According to many musicians, it turns out that the free market is not so "free" after all. This nicely illustrates the emergence of hegemony — not the socialist kind based on a central state control, but the capitalist kind based on market control. As Vesa Kurkela writes: "the way is open to another global system which is probably more powerful than the Soviet model ever was and can be a real threat to local cultural identity" (1993: 81). With the post-1989 shift to the free market, a commodification of music has taken place: music is viable only if it can sell cassettes or fill concert or festival halls. Of course, this process of music being absorbed into global capitalism has not occurred overnight — back in the socialist 1980s, Ivo Papazov was recording and touring for Hannibal, a Western label, and the Bulgarian Women's Choir was recording and touring for Nonesuch/Elektra. But the penetration of capitalism into local settings since 1989 has had a profound effect on the making and selling of music for wedding musicians. With the economy in decline and people hurting for money,[16] competition has increased; Roma and other wedding musicians are seeking fresh ways to be unique and creative. The recent proliferation of Romany songs and new styles of Rom music is in part an attempt to attract larger audiences; it is also an expression of the public emergence and display of Rom identity.

Songs in the Romany language have always been especially important for Bulgarian Roma because of the immediate manner in which Roma identify with them and because of the many years they were suppressed.[17] During the early socialist period (1944–1960s) a number of Romany songs were released on record by the state company Balkanton and there briefly existed a state theater for music and drama, *Roma,* whose musical director was Jasár Malikov (Peičeva 1994b). By the 1970s, however, Romany language songs (like Rom dance music, *kjučesti*) were prohibited from all concerts, restaurants, and media, and the Romany language itself was banned. Romany songs, like the language, were nevertheless illegally sung at family events, and sometimes the performers or sponsoring families were fined.

Since 1989 there has been a surge in the popularity of Romany songs. This is tied to the recent emergence of a public, political Rom identity, which can be seen in recent organization of Rom parties, unions, confederations (Marushiakova and Popov 1993). In 1990 I attended the first concert in Bulgaria since the 1970s in which Romany songs and music were performed. The Sofia audience consisted mainly of Roma, who were clearly moved to hear their language in public. In 1993, Anželo Malikov, son of Jašar Malikov, tried to organize a new Musical Theater Roma, but it disbanded in 1994 due to lack of government and private funding. According to recent interviews with Malikov, his vision of the theater is to present "pure," "authentic" Rom music and songs. He feels that wedding music utilizes Rom musical elements in a narrow, Thracian style:[18] "Take Ivo Papazov, for example. He plays Turkish and Rom music, but he plays everything in a Thracian style. . . . Wherever you go in the countryside, Rom music is played in Thracian style" (Peičeva 1994a: 17). While Malikov may be correct that some *kjučetsi* have Thracian stylistic features (such as staccato, repeated-note patterns), in others Turkish or Rom elements (such as legato, wide-range melodies) clearly predominate. What is a bit ironic in Malikov's comments is his adoption of the precise terminology ("pure," "authentic") that was used to exclude Roma from the realm of supposedly pure and authentic Bulgarian music in socialist times; this terminology was also used in the nineteenth century by collectors wishing to record the true spirit of the folk in the service of nation-building. Rejecting the terminology of authenticity, I would emphasize that Rom music has always interacted with coterritorial musics and both influences those musics and is influenced by them (Silverman forthcoming).[19]

Two post-1989 influences on Bulgarian Rom songs are rap and flamenco, the former coming from Western rock music and the latter from the Spanish Gitano[20] group Gipsy Kings. Rap music from the West began to be circulated illegally in the 1980s, and by the 1990s it had attracted a wide youth audience. Perhaps the first Rom group to use a rap style was Gypsy Aver, which means "the other Gypsy friend"; the group was formerly called Tato Nilaj, which means "hot summer." The group probably changed its name because of the recent fame of the Gipsy Kings; one wonders if either group realizes that the term "Gypsy" is taken to be negative by Roma in English-speaking countries. Gypsy Aver produced the cassette *Gypsy Rap* in 1993 and won first prize for it at the Stara Zagora Festival (see below). On this cassette, Gypsy Aver performs a rap remake of "Čaj Šukarije," the song which in the 1960s first introduced non-Rom audiences in Yugoslavia to Rom music. Sung by Esma Redzhepova, it made her famous and initiated an era of commercial success of Rom music in Yugoslavia (see below). The song thus has a long history and has been rerecorded a number of times. Gypsy Aver's rap version retains the Romany text about a beautiful girl but is actually a synthesis between a typical *kjuček* style and the typical rap meter and word phrasing. The Romany words sung in rap phrasing are a wonderful reminder of global trends in music. As Mark Slobin (1992) points out, it is important to analyze the relationship between "micromusics" and global "superculture." Micromusics do not, of course, all sound the same in spite of being influenced by global commercial trends. The local combines with the global in ever-changing ways.

The Bulgarian public was exposed to pop/flamenco style[21] via the Gipsy Kings, who forged a pop/flamenco style in the late 1980s. They have made a few tours to Bulgaria since 1989, and their cassettes are widely available. In Bulgaria, Roma as well as non-Roma flocked to see them, and all their concerts were sold out. After their tour, Rom musicians started to experiment with flamenco-type rhythms and hand-clapping simulations in *kjučetsi*. The result is multilayered rhythm that sounds Balkan as well as Gitano, with Romany words. The pan-European Rom connection is political as well as musical, for at precisely the time the Gypsy Kings were visiting Bulgaria, Rom activists were visiting other European countries for the first time to learn about political organizing.

An important manifestation of the emergence of an organized, public, Rom musical face was the first Festival of Rom Music and Song, which took place in Stara Zagora in June 1993.[22] Financed in part by the government and in part by the private recording company Payner, this festival and its successors in 1994 and 1995 have served as an impetus for Roma to write new songs and compose new *kyučetsi*. Substantial cash prizes were awarded in several categories, such as best song, best group, best vocalist, and best instrumentalist.[23]

Anyone listening to contemporary Bulgarian Rom music, whether vocal or instrumental, will be struck by the incorporation of many stylistic elements of rock music, such as use of electric guitars, electric bass, synthesizers, and drum sets, heavy bass lines sometimes doing intricate improvisations, and slow 2/4 songs. This trend began in wedding music in the 1970s but has accelerated in the post-1989 period because of greater access to the many genres of Western rock (such as rap; see above). Rock-influenced Rom music is very popular now, having the connotation of modernity, urbanity, and Westernness. In fact, rock music itself is enjoying a burst of popularity among contemporary youth (Ramet 1994). This phenomenon was illustrated at a Rom wedding in a Thracian village in August 1994. At 3 A.M., after four hours of dancing *kyučetsi* played by the Rom wedding band Trakija, led by Ivo Papazov, the assembled teenagers brought out their own sound system, set up a disco, and danced to rock music until dawn. I was also struck by the creative way in which they incorporated stylistic dance elements from *kjučetsi,* such as shoulder shakes and hip movements, into their disco dancing. Rock music has continued to influence wedding music since its inception in the 1970s, but in the 1990s the heavy metal sound made its appearance in Rom music.[24] However, it is important to note that musical styles also travel in the opposite direction, from Roma to non-Roma.

Rom music has been conceptualized by many scholars and lay people as taking elements from other cultures, not as giving (Silverman forthcoming). This simplistic generalization proves to be wrong on many counts, because the trafficking of styles goes in two directions, if not more. For example, in Bulgaria, the Rom form *kjuček* has been played by non-Rom wedding bands for non-Roma since the 1980s in spite of prohibition because they too enjoy hearing and dancing to at least one *kjuček* at a celebration, especially when the male guests are drunk. While it is beyond the scope of this essay to analyze how Bulgarians feel when dancing *kjuček* like Roma, the point is that every wedding band has to know at least one *kjuček* melody. In addition, in the 1980s rock bands needed to know one *pravo horo* (a 6/8 basic dance found in every region of Bulgaria) in wedding style. Today, rock bands in Bulgaria are experimenting with the *kjuček* rhythm in many of their pieces.[25] *Kjuček* is definitely becoming more mainstream. A *kjuček* in rock style played by Roma for Roma sounds surprisingly similar to a rock song in *kjuček* style played by Bulgarians for Bulgarians. As I mentioned earlier, this borrowing of Rom styles is not unique to Bulgaria, but can also be seen in Kosovo, Serbia, Bosnia, and Macedonia.

Music and Identity: Macedonia

Turning to Macedonia, one immediately notices a different picture of socialism and hence of Rom music during the socialist period. As a republic of Yugoslavia until 1991, Macedonia had a form of decentralized socialism that revolved around worker self-management, open borders, and a small capitalist sector. There were no state-run folk music schools as in Bulgaria, only one professional dance ensemble, and fewer professional musicians hired at Radio Skopje. As in Bulgaria, however, there was a state-sponsored recording industry and a system of amateur collectives or ensembles (KUD, Kulturno Umetničko Društvo) that performed at government-sponsored folk festivals. In addition, a specific style of village instrumental folk music

(labeled *izvorno,* from "the source"), created by radio performer and producer Pece Atanasovski in the 1960s, came to represent "authentic" village
music. *Izvorno* music is produced on village instruments such as *gaida*
(goatskin bagpipe), *kaval* (end-blown flute), and *tambura* (fretted, plucked,
long-necked lute), which Roma do not usually play in Macedonia. The only
role Roma have in *izvorno* music is as players of the *tapan* (two-headed
drum), an accompanying role. In Bulgaria, on the other hand, Roma play
village instruments professionally, both in villages for celebrations and also
in the state-supported radio orchestras. In fact, some of the best Bulgarian
instrumentalists on *gaida, kaval, tambura,* and *gudulka* (vertically held
bowed lute) have been Roma, assuring them a visible place in village professional music.[26]

How did Macedonian Roma operate within the socialist sphere of music?
Minimally, but there was a presence. On the level of the amateur ensembles,
there were Rom KUDs as early as 1967, such as Phralipe of Skopje (although in the beginning they performed only Macedonian dances), and by
the 1970s Rom groups regularly participated in Macedonian festivals at
Bitola and Ohrid. Dunin reports that Serbia held republic-wide Reviews of
Rom Cultural Accomplishments in the 1970s (1977: 14). With KUDs the
problems were more financial than ideological, because government funding was minimal. At Radio Skopje, a number of Roma were hired as *surla*
(Macedonian word for zurna) and *tapan* players, and as players of clarinet,
ud (plucked, short-necked, fretless lute), *kanun* (plucked zither), and violin
in the *čalgija* division, but they were clearly in subordinate positions financially as well as in terms of decision making (Seeman 1990b). During the
socialist period Radio Skopje rarely broadcast music identified as Rom, but
the Radio did regularly broadcast Macedonian music performed by Roma.
As mentioned earlier, weekly Romany music and news programs were
introduced in the late 1980s, and in 1990 a weekly Romany television show
with news and music was introduced. In short, exclusion and discrimination
existed in socialist-sponsored music contexts, but it was nowhere near the
exclusion and discrimination that Roma experienced in Bulgaria.

It was in the realm of cassette production in which the state companies
were most liberal in issuing Rom music. In the 1970s a number of 45 rpm
records were released by Jugoton, and in the 1980s hundreds of cassettes
were issued by state companies such as Jugoton, RTB (Radio Television

Beograd), and Diskoton (Sarajevo). These were quickly purchased by Rom as well as non-Rom fans. In the late 1960s and early 1970s Stevo Teodosievski, a Macedonian accordionist, promoted the young Rom singer Esma Redžepova and the clarinetist Medo Čun to non-Rom audiences in concerts all over Yugoslavia. He later married Esma and they moved to Serbia to avoid the discrimination against Roma at Radio Skopje. Simultaneously in other parts of Yugoslavia, Rom singers such as Šaban Bajramović forged a commercially viable niche in the recording industry by appealing to the tastes of non-Roma and Roma alike (Rasmussen 1991).

In Macedonia, socialist cultural policy was never very efficiently organized, so very little policing was done of the private realm, unlike the situation in Bulgaria. The Rom *surla* and *tapan* tradition in Macedonia, for example, though never disseminated widely by radio and record, was nevertheless a visible, legal, and unharassed niche for Roma during the entire socialist period; this is in stark contrast to Bulgaria, where the *surla* was outlawed in 1984. In Macedonia, *surla* and *tapan* players found work at Macedonian, Turkish, Torbeš (Slavic-speaking Muslims), Albanian, and Rom events (Rice 1982), as well as in KUDs and at Radio Skopje. *Surla* and *tapan* remain important musical instruments for the Rom community because they are deemed necessary for certain ritual events, such as the henna ceremony for the bride, processions in the wedding and circumcision ceremonies, and the slaughtering of lamb and greeting of the guests on Erdelez (St. George's Day). *Surla* and *tapan* players, who typically are Rom everywhere in the Balkans, learn to play from male family members. In Šuto Orizari alone (a Rom settlement outside of Skopje that has a population of 40,000), there are nine families of *surla* and *tapan* players. In Rom communities, *surla* and *tapan* ensembles coexist with modern amplified bands because of the former's role in ritual and its symbolic association with Rom identity. This is illustrated by the use of *surla/tapan* music for political events, such as the press conference of the first Macedonian Rom political party (Silverman 1995).

Like Bulgaria, Macedonia experienced a technological revolution in the 1970s, and thus unamplified *čalgija* music began to be replaced by amplified bands of Western instruments (Seeman 1990b). Stylistically, Rom music in Macedonia as well as in Bulgaria and Serbia has been open to many influences from folk and popular music. In Bulgaria, for example, wedding music incorporates motifs from film, cartoon, and classical music in addition to rock music (Silverman 1988). Macedonian Rom music has also been influenced by rock music and has incorporated non-Balkan tunes. In Macedonia in 1990 the Brazilian pop song "Lambada" was made into a *čoček* and became an instant hit.[27] Also popular in 1990 in Macedonia was a *čoček* version of the theme song from the Indian film *The Cobra,* known as *Sapeskiri* (snake). In the post-socialist period, rap *čočetsi* and flamenco-style *chochetsi* were created in Macedonia even earlier than in Bulgaria.[28]

It is clear that the trafficking in musical styles does not proceed only in one direction. By the 1980s, Rom stylistic elements such as *čoček* rhythm and improvisational instrumental breaks had found a secure place in the popular genre of urban, youth-oriented, pan-Macedonian folk music.[29] Songs such as "Kamenite Pagjat" in the Macedonian language in *čoček* rhythm are very popular at events for Macedonians, illustrating the adoption of musical styles by Macedonians from Roma. Recent dance innovations also illustrate this direction of change. The most common folk dance now done by city youth is a line dance whose step pattern was adopted from Roma. At a 1994 gathering of Macedonians and Roma in Berlin, I observed that Macedonians under the age of 50 danced the Rom step pattern, while those older than 50 danced a village-based step pattern. Roma danced solo *čoček* in the center.

Rom innovation is not simply a matter of adoption in one direction or another, but also of creating new performances by trafficking in the styles, languages, and rhythms of the entire Balkan region. For example, Macedonian Rom singer Muharem Serbezovski commercialized the practice of taking popular Turkish folk songs and translating them into Serbian, giving them an upbeat Rom flair and recording them on Yugoslav labels for sale to Rom and non-Rom Yugoslavs.[30] Bulgarians have done this to a lesser degree; instead, Bulgarian Roma have been extremely influenced by Turkish instrumental styles, especially the clarinetist Mustafa Kandirali. Because of the open borders of socialist Yugoslavia, Macedonian Roma were able to travel much more easily than were Bulgarian Roma. As a result, famous Macedonian Rom musicians and singers were frequently hired for Rom or Macedonian events in Western Europe, or they themselves sought work abroad. The singer Dzhansever, for example, lived in Germany for years, and the clarinetist Tunan currently lives in Germany. During the socialist period, Bulgarian musicians were rarely permitted to travel, and even now there are few emigrant Bulgarian Rom communities in Western Europe to hire them.

The dissemination of Macedonian Rom music through the mass media has been boosted recently by the formation of independent Rom radio stations. In Bulgaria, such a phenomenon is totally absent, although Rom music may now be heard occasionally on regular music shows. In Skopje, two stations operate from Shuto Orizari; they broadcast not only Rom music but also advertisements and greetings in the Romany language twenty-four hours a day (Silverman 1996). Another boost to the visibility of Rom music was the organization of a festival of Rom music in Skopje in 1993; Šutka Fest included groups from Albania, Bulgaria, Romania, Serbia, and Italy as well as Macedonia. Thousands of people attended, two cassettes and a videotape were released, and a second festival was held in 1994. Clearly, Rom music festivals in Bulgaria and Macedonia (and many other European countries) serve as a forum for the display of ethnic identity and artistry, political organization, and the economic viability of music as a commercial commodity.

Conclusion

An examination of Balkan Rom music illuminates the interaction of the local and the global. Both the socialist and post-socialist periods reveal how various hegemonies, be they state policy or global capitalism, have penetrated musical realms. Roma have at times resisted these ideologies and at times used them for their own creativity and survival. Recently, Slobin found Appadurai's discussion of the term "global cultural economy" to be limiting because of its omission of the level of the nation-state. Slobin writes: "He is admittedly ambivalent about the relationship between the nation-state and global patterning, preferring to talk about deterritorialization and the decline of central authority rather than take on the precise interplay of state and populace. He is equally reticent to set out the dynamics of state and commercial forces in any given society" (1992: 12). Balkan Roma in Bulgaria and Macedonia have indeed interacted with global musical trends, both during and after socialism; but in order to analyze these interactions, the arena of the nation-state must be considered. In Bulgaria, socialist policy tried to obliterate Rom musical identity, and Roma responded with countercultural musics that subverted the dominant ideology. In post-socialist Bulgaria, Rom music no longer has the constraints of socialist ideology but rather has the constraints of a capitalist economy. In Macedonia, where the level of centralized socialist management was fairly minimal, Rom music continues to serve as a visible identity marker both in local contexts and in the recent realm of Rom activist politics.

Notes

Fieldwork for this article was supported by the International Research and Exchanges Board.

1. The term "Rom" (adjective and singular noun, plural "Roma") is used throughout this essay because it is the most widespread ethnonym employed by members of this ethnic group. "Gypsy" is a derogatory term used by outsiders, which mistakenly implies Egyptian origin.

2. Similar observations can be made about Blacks in specific places and historical periods. See discussion of Gilroy 1991 and 1993 below.

3. *Čalgija* is an urban-based genre heavily influenced by Turkish music. For a detailed treatment, see Seeman (1990).

4. *Musica lăutareasca* refers to urban Rom music of the southern regions of Romania (Radulescu 1984; Beissinger 1991).

5. However, this comparison is nothing to boast about, considering the deplorable assimilationist measures of other Eastern European socialist governments (Silverman 1986; Crowe and Kolsti 1991) and the fact that Roma are still the most oppressed group in Yugoslavia (Whitman 1994: 13).

6. In 1973, Puxon estimated that in Yugoslavia there were 200 Roma in the professions — working as doctors, lawyers, engineers, etc. — a figure double that of 1953. He claimed that more than 50 percent of Rom wage earners were industrial and municipal workers, 20 percent were farmers who owned their own land, and the rest were self-employed artisans and traders (Puxon 1973: 18).

7. According to the 1991 census, there are 54,000 Roma in Macedonia. Rom groups, however, claim there are actually 220,000 (Whitman 1994). From 1981 to 1991, the official political status of Roma in Yugoslavia was that of "nationality." Yugoslavia had a three-level system: the "nations" of Yugoslavia were Croatians, Serbs, Slovenians, Bosnians, and Macedonians; the "nationalities" included Turks, Albanians, and Hungarians; the rest were "other nationalities and ethnic groups," such as Vlachs and Jews. In practice,

however, most of the republics, which had their own constitutions, considered the Roma to be an "ethnic group." Thus in the 1981 Macedonian census, Roma were still considered an ethnic group (Poulton 1989: 29, 1993: 42). This designation is one of the factors that mobilized Macedonian Roma to political action in the 1980s. For a detailed treatment of political mobilization of Macedonian Roma, see Silverman (1995) and Puxon (1993).

8. I am referring primarily to the work at the Centre for Contemporary Cultural Studies at Birmingham, England, in the 1960s and 1970s and the subsequent studies by American and European scholars. For an overview, see the collection edited by Grossberg, Nelson, and Treichler (1992).

9. For a cogent summary of this argument, see Abrahams (1993: 389–93).

10. For example, cultural studies defines culture quite differently than did early folklorists, ethnomusicologists, and anthropologists. As John Fiske writes:

The term "culture" used in the phrase "cultural studies" is neither aesthetic nor humanist in emphasis, but political. Culture is not conceived of as the aesthetic ideals of form and beauty to be found in great art, nor in more humanist terms as the voice of the "human spirit" that transcends the boundaries of time and nation to speak to a hypothetical universal man (the gender is deliberate — women play little or no role in this conception of culture). Culture is not, then, the aesthetic products of the human spirit acting as a bulwark against the tide of grubby industrial materialism and vulgarity, but rather a way of living within an industrial society that encompasses all the meanings of that social experience. (1987: 254)

To be fair, earlier folk music studies have also questioned the entire project of universal humanism and the judging of art as high or great, but they have tended to do so more in aesthetic terms than in social, political, or economic terms. Moreover, the issue of the economic "commerce" of folklore forms has been slighted in part because commerce was seen as a contaminating force by Richard Dorson, one of the founders of American academic folklore (Abrahams 1993: 395). Recently there has been a flowering of sophisticated works such as those of Gilroy (1991, 1993), Abrahams (1992), Erlmann (1991), and Waterman (1990), which have analyzed the politics and economics of music. These works have shown that folk, subcultural, and elite (in fact, all) musical products are always tied to power, to claims of legitimacy, and to ideology and its representation in symbolic forms.

11. *Čoček* is in duple meter subdivided 3+3+2. The Bulgarian form of this word is *kjuček,* plural *kjučetsi.* The word *čoček* is also used for a solo dance form that uses hip movements and is associated with women (Dunin 1973, 1977, 1985).

12. The ethnic composition of wedding bands vary. Some, such as the Vievska Grupa from the Rhodopes, are composed totally of non-Roma and play mostly non-Rom Bulgarian music. Even they, however, are required to play a few *kjučetsi,* because non-Roma also dance *kjuček,* mostly when they are a little drunk. At the other extreme, bands such as Brestovica from Pazardzhik and Gypsy Aver from Sofia are composed exclusively of Roma and play both Rom *kjučetsi* and Bulgarian music, depending on the audience. The

majority of bands, such as Mladost from Haskovo, Trakija from Stara Zagora, Orfei from Plovdiv, and Kozarite from Yambol are composed of both Roma and non-Roma and play a mixed repertoire. The repertoire depends both on the context and also on the ability and the proclivity of the individual musician. For example, Ivan Milev, arguably the most famous accordian player in Bulgaria, is a Bulgarian who feels he does not excel in Rom music and thus he rarely plays *kjučetsi*. He does, however, regularly hire Roma for his band. On the other hand, Orfei is lead by Georgi Janev, a Bulgarian violinist who excels in *kjučetsi*. Thus, in wedding music there is a lively exchange of styles between Roma and non-Rom musicians.

13. For example, the band Orfei, based in Plovdiv, regularly performs with a computerized synthesizer. Their new version of the *kjuček* "Anadol" features computer-synthesized backup, which imitates electric guitar, drums, and synthesizer. To this they have added their live accordionist (Petur Ralčev), clarinetist (Orlin Pamukov), and violinist (Georgi Janev). Even though the package was recorded for eventual release on CD, they use it for live performances; however, when playing live, the drummer (Payčo) and guitar player (Nikolai Todorov) often play along with the computer, adding another layer of texture.

14. Orfei, based in Plovdiv, had the following fairly typical weekly performance schedule in summer 1994: Thursday — drive to Sofia (two hours each way), play six hours, return at 4 A.M., sleep six hours; Friday — drive to a village near Vratsa (five hours each way), play seven hours, return at 7 A.M., sleep three hours; Saturday — drive to Stara Zagora (90 minutes each way), play six hours, return at 3 A.M., sleep six hours; Sunday — drive to Dimitrovgrad (90 minutes each way), play seven hours, return 4 A.M., sleep six hours; Monday, Tuesday, and Wednesday — no work.

15. The company Payner, based in Dimitrovgrad, sponsored the Trakija folk festival of wedding music held in Dimitrovgrad in summer 1994; at this festival, Payner required the participating wedding bands to be taped for a concert cassette. The band Orfei refused to "sign on" because they wanted to produce their own cassette. But in producing one's own cassette one faces enormous obstacles in taping, marketing, and distribution. Although Orfei recorded its master tape digitally in a very sophisticated studio owned by its leader Georgi Janev, it has yet to produce cassettes because of the difficulty of distribution.

16. Inflation has steadily increased in Bulgaria since 1990 (see Engelbrekt 1993).

17. Romany was not heard on television, radio, or state recordings from the 1970s until 1990. Even in socialist Macedonia, where it was permissible to use the Romany language, Roma greeted the first Romany-language film, *Dom Za Vešanje* (made in 1988), as a welcome sign.

18. Much of wedding music is heavily influenced by Thracian music. Malkiov believes that wedding music does not represent the breadth of style of older Rom songs.

19. For discussion of the interaction between Jewish music and coterritorial musics, see Slobin (1982).

20. The Gitanos are a subgroup of Roma who live in Spain and are known for flamenco music. The Gipsy Kings are actually from France.

21. The Hungarian Rom group Fracilor also performs a Rom tune in Spanish flamenco style. Katalin Kovalscik claims that flamenco music was used by Hungarian Roma even before the Gypsy Kings began to tour (personal communication).

22. For a similar phenomenon of organizing politically as well as musically, see the work of Ursula Hemetek on the Austrian Roma (1994).

23. Payner released a cassette of the festival winners, which includes Tato Nilaj (now Gypsy Aver) from Sofia, Kristali from Montana, Kitka from Sliven, and Lira from Stara Zagora. Cash prizes are also awarded in festivals for wedding music but not for "folk" festivals.

24. For example, the 1994 cassettes of the bands Kozarevska Grupa and Brestovica and the cassette from the 1993 Rom festivals in Stara Zagora all contain *kjučetsi* influenced by heavy metal.

25. The most popular folk/rock band in Bulgaria, Kristal from Yambol, plays a form of disco rock/*kjuček*. Kristal's many imitators disseminate this style to rock music audiences.

26. See Rice (1994: 93–94) for comparison of the roles of a Rom and Bulgarian *gaida* player in a Bulgarian village.

27. Pettan (1992) reports the popularity of this melody in many variants among Rom performers in Kosovo.

28. A pioneer innovator is Dzhansever, a popular female Rom singer from Skopje, whose repertoire includes "O Romane Chave Najšužiye" ("The Beautiful Rom Child"), a rap song in Romany, and "Vogi Tharel" ("My Heart Burns"), a flamenco-style song in Romany. Her songs are sung by many other Rom performers in Macedonia and in surrounding areas; for example, the Bulgarian wedding band of Osman Žekov and Kostadinkova Žekova includes one of her trademark songs, "Kemano Bašal" ("Violin, Play"), on their 1993 cassette.

29. This is also true in Serbia.

30. A partial list of Turkish songs that have been translated into Serbian and recorded by Roma includes "Emina," "Sine Moj," "Bože, Bože," and "Mastika." Usnja Redžepova has also pioneered in translating and adapting Rom and Turkish songs into Serbian.

Change as Confirmation of Continuity As

Experienced by Russian Molokans

Bitter cold (−30 Celsius), a dark stairway all covered with ice and without handrails, long strips of old wallpaper and plaster of all imaginable colors peeling from the walls, no light and almost no heat inside of the house — outside, as far as my eyes can see in this December's twilight hour, a beautiful and electrifying view of icy lace on trees and, in the distance, wooded hills, all deeply under snow. About thirty young Molokans live in this old country squire's house, which probably has not been repaired for a hundred years. They came here about three months ago, in the fall of 1992. Most of them are young men, a few came with their families; all others left children, wives, and parents beyond the Caucasus mountains till they can build places for them to live.

These Molokans migrated to the village of Slobodka (in Tula province, about 250 miles south of Moscow) from the Caucasus, where, in contrast to the Baltics, the local government did not officially encourage Russian out-migration. They migrated out of fear that their lives and those of their wives, children, and parents would be lost in the civil war that had surrounded their villages in Georgia, Armenia, and Azerbaijan.

When one powerful elder, Mr. Timofei Shchetinkin, the *presviter* (presbyter, minister) of an influential church in the Stavropol area (in South Russia), found out about the difficulties his fellow Molokans were having in the new settlement, he gathered a group of the most experienced singers and brought them to Slobodka to help the new settlers. It was an expensive, long, and exhausting journey. It would have been much easier for him and the singers, none of them young, just to send the money that was so sorely needed in Slobodka. However, the elder decided that a visit by the singers would be a more effective contribution. They brought with them a few

Bibles and songbooks, a gift from American Brothers, Molokans from San Francisco. When they came to Slobodka, a full *sobranie* (Molokan communal worship) was held, the first since the young Molokans had migrated there. The head of the district administration, the key person in local politics and new economic policies, no doubt a devout communist in the past, accepted an invitation to the *sobranie* and sat in the place of honor, next to the elder *presviter* and Mr. Tikunov, the young leader of the Slobodka group.[1] During the service, the district administrator even made a speech and a personal donation to the needs of the community. Also present in the room were four other outsiders (two photographers and two scholars, myself included), all invited and welcomed guests. Molokans are very private people and just the presence of any outsider, not to mention the presence of a video camera and a head politician, could not have been taken lightly. Certainly, the situation revealed the impact of new times in Russia.

Being there throughout this tense and emotional *sobranie*, I discerned an experience of tremendous magnitude and consequence. What was the significance of this visit by the elder singers? To have a proper *sobranie*, there must be experts (i.e., individuals specially trained within the community) officiating for various components of the *sobranie:* a *presviter* and his helper; *besedniki* (singular *besednik*), who read and interpret the Bible during *besedy* (singular *beseda;* literally, a conversation, talk), an oratory form or a special sermon modeled as a situated rhetorical discourse; *skazateli* (singular *skazatel'*), readers or announcers who call out scriptural passages before they are lined out to the melody of a *posalom* (plural *posalmy,* psalms);[2] and the *pevtsy* (singular *pevets*, singer). Why was it that all the people selected by the *presviter*, although they could perform functions of other officiants during the *sobranie*, were first of all good singers and not simply other elders? Why didn't he select sophisticated *besedniki*, theorists of Molokanism or knowledgeable construction workers, whose help was so much needed? What would be the impact of this visit on the future of the young group?

The Molokans are members of a religious sect that has existed in Russia in one form or another for more than 200 years. Because of their beliefs, they have always lived as social and religious outsiders, most of the time ostracized by the mainstream society. Molokan communities, spread all over the world, appear to have certain cognitive, social, and cultural similarities and even consistency. This seemingly coherent universe emerges from a discordant chorus of discrete personal experiences and individual reflections on various aspects of Molokanism — from history, religious, and cultural issues to matters of family and private life. Personal experiences and opinions, contrasting and complementing each other, usually are vigorously verbalized and debated within the community.

Individual interpretations and communal perspectives on Molokanism are completely interdependent, if not altogether inseparable; entwined, they constitute a multidimensional spiritual and earthly continuum. The inner tension within this dynamic complexity may have been largely responsible for the perpetuation and survival of this egalitarian community. Reflecting individual concerns of valued members of the community, a continual process of constructing negotiated meaning[3] takes place. This continual dialogue between individual experiences and practical needs on the one hand and traditional interpretations handed down from generation to generation on the other, secures a certain flexibility of communal awareness and enables gradual adjustments of communal attitudes to the perpetually changing challenges of the environment. In this process, alternatives offered by the nonvalued members probably would be simply disregarded by the Molokan community, but the requests and concerns of its valued members must be recognized in order to perpetuate their status and needs. During the *sobranie* in Slobodka, which occurred at a turning point in the community's history, this process was amplified, allowing an observer to discern at least one way in which the construction of negotiated meaning takes place.

Some History and Ways of the Molokans

The Spiritual Christians Molokans, as they identify themselves, are one of the many peasant alliances that represented religious dissent in rural eighteenth-century Russia.[4] Like the Dukhobors (Spirit Fighters), a sect from which the Molokans branched out circa the 1760s, they were seeking religious freedom from the Russian Orthodox church and economic independence from state-imposed poverty by establishing a self-governing brotherhood of equal men. To this day, Molokans consider communal energy, both spiritual and human, much more powerful than individual.

The Molokans as a group are little known even to specialists in Russian culture. Therefore, I will profile certain facets of their worldview and beliefs that I consider indispensable for the present essay, because they help to identify a conceptual universe within which their singing functions and of which it is an integral part.[5]

Molokanism is a peculiar amalgamation of the Old and New Testaments and, at the same time, of peasant faith and folk beliefs characteristic of Russian villagers.[6] Links with Russian mystics, Western sectarian Protestants, and Judaic practices are also evident. Essentially, all religious and cultural junctions notwithstanding, Molokanism is a Christian movement that grew out of traditional values and cultural models of Russian peasantry, although it evolved into unique forms. As the Molokans' favorite expression goes: "We live and sing by the spirit and by the mind." This expression provides a good insight for understanding the Molokan spiritual and cultural universe as being simultaneously deeply mystical and thoroughly rationalistic.

Like other earlier sectarians, the Molokans abandoned the Russian Orthodox Church altogether. They rejected the church's rituals, most holidays, and all material sacraments of the Orthodoxy, including the cross and icons. They also rejected the church's hierarchy and paid clergy, as they seek direct contact with God. During the *sobranie,* every participant should contribute to building up the communal spiritual power according to his or her gift to enact a specific component of the service, *beseda, skazyvanie,* singing a psalm or reciting a prayer. All Molokans whom I met, without exception, insisted that they believe only in internal spiritual aspects of Christianity, accepting only the symbolic essence of religious sacraments. Salvation is in the faith alone, they said, not in the church's ritualistic celebration of sacraments made as "objects of human artistry." The ultimate enlightenment, according to Molokan elders, comes through experiences incomprehensible to the senses and logic. One is to seek it not in the material world but only in the spiritual world within, through communal worship "in spirit and truth." At the same time, personal wealth is desirable, in contrast to the Russian Orthodox doctrine. The material aspects of Molokans' earthly life, perhaps in an effort to build an independent and self-sufficient community and also in preparation for the millennium of Christ's kingdom on earth, has to be of good quality.[7]

For their resentment of the Orthodox church, the Molokans were outlawed by the mainstream society and severely repressed throughout their history in Russia. In the 1830s the government removed them from Central Russia, the main lands of Russian peasantry, to the Transcaucasus and the Caucasus mountains. After their exemption from military service expired and petitions to renew it were denied, they migrated farther south, some to the land that later fell under Turkish jurisdiction. Thousands of Molokans, in search of quality land, "better life," and religious freedom, ended up in Persia, Iran, Turkey, North America, Australia, and other parts of the world. Many Molokans (those in the Jumpers and Maximists denominations only) insisted that their migration out of Russia was led by the prophesies. The largest Molokan community, however, still lives in Russia.

At present, there are three main denominations of the Molokan sect: the Steadfast, who supposedly preserved the original doctrine and order; the Jumpers, who later began to accept the manifestation of the Holy Spirit in prophecy and physical form (i.e., jumping); and the Maximists, who formed during the late nineteenth century and accepted the teachings of new prophet-leaders, mainly those of Maxim Rudometkin.[8] Mr. Shchetinkin and his *pevtsy*, as well as the majority of the young settlers in Slobodka, belong to the Steadfast denomination.

Competing interpretations of Molokanism, both on the individual and the denominational levels, are a constant source of inner tension and challenge. Combined with separatism, historically strong among the Molokans, the controversy over individual opinion splits the community into small factions. Each elder disapproves the liberty exercised by other congregations in maintaining denominational teachings. One may even say that this fragmentation weakens the movement at large. At the same time, the construction of negotiated meaning through a continual dialogue between varied interpretations of the doctrine secures the perpetuation of the sect, providing a channel for innovation and adjustment to new social and cultural conditions. In this respect, the situation in the Slobodka group is not unusual. What sets it apart from the established Molokan communities in Russia is the divergent backgrounds within the group, as the members all come from different churches and different places in the Caucasus area.

Throughout their history, the Molokans have lived in strong confrontation to the mainstream society, in conscientious religious, social, cultural, and often ethnic opposition to the *ne nashi* (those who are not we) or, in

Bakhtin's term, the Others. As one Molokan elder explained, they praise "the living in the world without being a part of it." Not unlike the situation in other closed confessional groups, Molokan culture is self-sufficient — that is to say, the preservation and maintenance of their spiritual life is secured from within. Except for one printed book, the Bible, Molokan *sobranie* needs no props or other material objects produced outside of the community.

Like any other closed group, in order to perpetuate their faith and culture, the Molokans have to draw boundaries that differentiate them from the Others. These boundaries are closed to the *ne nashi* and have to be learned as part of the experience of being a Molokan. Their singing is one such demarcation. Actually, their whole order of life separates them from the *ne nashi*. They call this order Molokan *zakon* (literally, the law), a distinct and self-sufficient maintenance system responsible for the perpetuation, stability, and well-being of the brotherhood. The *zakon* governs not only cultural and social institutions, the code of conduct, structure of the religious rite, and the *sobranie,* but also relationships between man and God, world-view, values, personal relations, etc. A complex and well-structured order regulates almost all spheres of Molokan spiritual and everyday life. As in many other closed communities, this self-imposed discipline functions through a system of restrictions and prohibitions. Molokan *zakon* is considered "too strict and exacting" by many. At the same time, it must be open-ended to be able to tolerate the diversity of interpretations and internal tensions. Disputes among its competing interpretations are themselves an essential means of perpetuating the Molokan *zakon.* The *sobranie* in Slobodka can serve as an illustration of the inner dynamics of this most vital process.

For the Molokans, not unlike other evangelicals, the Bible has become not only the theological base of their beliefs, but also a lens through which they perceive, interpret, and evaluate everyday life. Driven by the aspiration to comprehend the inner sense of life, they find in the Bible a suitable analogy or metaphor for practically any need. Their approach to the Bible, it appears, is metaphorical rather than literary. Analogy and metaphor as major instruments of the Molokan world outlook are noticeable on every level, from an explanation of their origins and name to an interpretation of religious doctrine and the way they express themselves in everyday life. This is particularly noticeable in *besedy,* during which a *besednik* reads a passage from the Bible and pursues his interpretation of the passage in connection with daily life. Events that happened in the community, examples from the speaker's personal life, his own observations, thoughts and assumptions — all examined and validated by parallels and analogies from the Bible — become the instruments of the *besednik*'s discourse. Molokan *besedy* show a great variety of local schools and individual styles of folk hermeneutics. Many *besedniki* build their discourses on the highest level of oratory. The majority of Molokans (particularly men and the *besedniki* specifically) are experienced speakers who develop skills and the art of expressing thoughts verbally through continuous practicing of discourse. Not only in rhetorical situations structured by ritual but also through countless private disputes, Molokans are perpetually negotiating and redefining the meaning of certain notions or actions. Speech, both ritualized and ordinary, and the expressive means of the *besedy,* as well as their formal configurations, are topics for sociolinguistic investigation and are beyond the scope of this essay. However, the Molokans' strong tradition and long history of practicing discourse must be emphasized here because the meaning and significance of the *sobranie* in Slobodka cannot be interpreted outside of this context.

The Power of Molokan Singing

Understanding the high status of verbal expression and the power of the word reinforced by the ritual and communal participation is also important for conceptualizing Molokan singing. Stripped of the effects of bright and solemn costumes, icons and frescos on the walls, lighting of candles and incense — all widely used by the Orthodox ritual — the Molokan *sobranie* takes place within bare white walls in rooms furnished with backless wooden benches; religious books on top of a modest table covered with white cloth are the only props.[9] As Molokanism rejected all visual attributes of the Orthodox religious service, forms of verbal and nonverbal communication through sound assimilated some of the functions and energy that flowed through other channels of the ritual.

A variety of aural forms is used during the *sobranie.* They are all based on the scripture — that is, on "God's word" — but their symbolic powers differ. In the words of one Molokan elder, "God's word is sonic," and its power, it seems, does not rely on the meaning of the word alone. The power of "the sonic word," one can note, increases within the sonic continuum of spoken-read-sermonized-recited-sung-prayed verbal manifestations, which we will call *modalities* (Crystal 1976). Each modality has a distinct para-linguistic profile (tempo, loudness, intensity, voice quality, pitch contour, duration, etc.), and this sonic profile, one can speculate, is one of the decisive factors in determining the power of the sacred word. The sung modality occupies a remarkably high point in this continuum.

Beseda (consisting of spoken, read, and sermonized modalities) and a ceremonial psalm singing (consisting of recited/chanted and sung modalities) make up a cycle that is repeated several times during the first part of the *sobranie.* The *beseda,* like the entire *sobranie,* is intended to praise the Lord, but it addresses directly the people present: "Dear brothers and sisters," as articulated during every *beseda.* While the *beseda* is meant to communicate with people and to effect their understanding of the spiritual truth as well as to address the immediate concerns of the community's ordinary life, singing is considered a channel of direct communication with God. The second half of the *sobranie,* the communal prayer proper, includes only sung and prayed modalities of the word. "Singing is the same as a prayer, only more emotional," asserts the head *pevets* of the Shchetinkin's group.

Singing as the source of spiritual power is a characteristic rhetoric of all Molokans: "singing is to melt the heart, then the heart opens itself to God"; "through singing goes the same spiritual road that brings one to pray"; "singing reveals the word of God to man." (One cannot fail to notice how tightly the singing and the word are bound in the Molokans' own expressions.) The image of Heaven, according to the Molokan cognitive world, is impregnated with singing: "Those Molokans who have merited Heaven sing. They do not work there, they do not eat there, they only sing." The Molokans identify Molokanism "as a singing religion" (Samarin 1975: 66–67) and think of themselves as "Christians who sing the psalms" (O'Brien-Rothe 1989: 1).

Singing during the *sobranie* is in itself an act of "divine inspiration," and the Spirit dictates a particular *posalom* or song to be sung. Thus, the Molokans sing "by the spirit." At the same time, they also sing "by the mind." The Molokans have developed a huge repertory of psalms (virtually hundreds), but only a few would be suitable for any one occasion. Psalms are divided into several categories, each corresponding to a specific communicative intention. There are psalms to console, to beseech, to thank; there are psalms for funerals, weddings, house warmings, etc. Moreover, each psalm has to correspond to the subject of the discussion during the *sobranie.* Choosing a psalm proper for the occasion is crucial, and it is left to the experts, the *pevtsy.*

Singing as a symbolic act that triggers an enormous collective experience has been long recognized in many religions. It is important that the symbol be realized as such. Not infrequently, however, the details and aesthetic quality of the ritual singing have little significance for the participants; they pave and adorn the road for more essential experiences and aspects of participation. In Molokan practice, however, "good" singing is crucial. They even have a special concept, *khoroshii pevets,* translated by American Molokans as "a quality singer." In the words of one Molokan leader, "singing during the *sobranie* can either stifle or raise everything," and a "poor" performance might prevent reaching a spiritual state in which communication with God becomes possible. Because singing has the power of evoking the Spirit, experienced leaders engage singing as a medium to facilitate "working of the Spirit" and experiencing the presence of the divine during the service. Moreover, the Spirit cannot reveal itself to humans without singing.

The act of communication with the divine has different forms among the Jumpers and the Steadfast. The Jumpers employ both psalms and spiritual songs, the only two categories of Molokan ecclesiastical repertoire. Psalms are sung to scriptural prose texts directly, the melodies being very intricate and long; the tempo is usually slow and syllables are prolonged by elaborate melismata. Texts of the spiritual songs are composed as rhymed poems that interpret the scripture. The tempo is faster than in psalms; songs are syllabic, with melodies most often based on repetitions of short phrases. The Steadfast Molokans, however, if they sing songs at all, allow them only after the *sobranie* proper is ended. This distinction is important rhetorically in interdenominational polemics. During the *sobranie* in Slobodka, as we discuss later, the meaning of this argument was forcefully renegotiated by the leader of the young group.

During the *sobranie* of the Jumpers, appropriate singing and working of the spirit bring changes in the physical behavior of the congregation, the jumping. The spiritual life of the Steadfast Molokans is less discernible visually, but for them as well singing gradually intensifies during the service. In both denominations, the communal prayer, the climax of the service, is a complex sonic whole. It consists of a prayer recited by the *presviter* (or another man of his choice) and, simultaneously, individual petitions to the Lord. These petitions, at least in Molokan communities residing in Russia, are often expressed in a form coinciding with village laments or keening, in which singing and recitation are mixed with tears and sobs, sometimes even wails. Such an application of Russian laments has not been previously reported in literature. As during other village rituals that use simultaneous laments (funerals, weddings), all participants employ the same melodic pattern, although each renders it differently.[10] Similarly to village laments, Molokan individual prayers during the *sobranie* are on the border of musical, paramusical, and paralinguistic expression. The application of laments during the communal prayer becomes more comprehensible conceptually if one keeps in mind that lamenting, not unlike a true prayer, brings a cathartic feeling of relief (Mazo 1994b).

The *Sobranie* in Slobodka

We shall now examine how these main aspects of the Molokan service were worked through in the *sobranie* in Slobodka.

Normally, no recording is allowed during the *sobranie,* although religious psalms and songs can be recorded at other times and places. This is to say that sanctity does not reside in the song itself but rather in the context of its performance. Russian Molokans will often ascribe failure and trouble in life to some fault in singing during the *sobranie.*[11] Previously I was lucky and several times was allowed to make tape recordings during the *sobranie,* but I was never permitted to photograph. Permission to film the first *sobranie* of the new settlement in Slobodka appeared to signal meaningful changes. The elders who organized the trip actually welcomed an opportunity to film their visit and willingly ignored the presence of the cameras and bright lights.

The Molokan *sobranie* is supposed to be shaped by the "golden thread," a continual idea or a concept that unites its components into a coherent web and regulates the topic of the *besedy,* psalms, and prayers. In Slobodka, the "golden thread" was dictated by the overall goal set by the *presviter:* to persuade the young people to believe in God and make them accept Molokanism as "a guiding star" in their ordinary life. Raised within the Soviet social system, the young people were brought up in atheist schools; many carry the scars of the former Soviet society and are used to drinking, smoking, and swearing — all unacceptable to Molokan doctrine. Shchetinkin's message was "Dear children! Believe in God and accept Molokanism — it will bring a solution to your daily problems and reduce your suffering." This in itself is not a typical "golden thread" of a *sobranie* in a traditional Molokan community. Reinforcements of beliefs and persuasion toward a certain meaning of life and God's word are common, but there is not much need of missionary rhetoric during an assembly of brothers in faith, unless some nonregular members of the congregation are present. Missionary rhetoric and teaching the basics of how to be a Molokan are carried on largely in different social settings, but the *sobranie* in Slobodka, by necessity, condensed the functions of several social institutions. At the same time, as much as the *sobranie* in Slobodka was a unique form of religious discourse, Shchetinkin's rhetoric and the way he employed the persuasive power of the word are similar to those employed by the leaders of other new diaspora communities, even with entirely different religions, social, and ethnic background (compare, for example, Palinkas 1989 on Chinese immigrant churches in the United States).

The Slobodka situation not only predetermined the "golden thread" chosen by the *presviter,* but also justified deviation from the usual symmetry and the temporal balance between the *besedy* and singing. As an experienced leader, Shchetinkin knew well the power of the *besedy* to persuade the new settlers and to control their social behavior. He allowed almost 90 percent of the first part of the *sobranie* to be spent in these verbal sermons. This asymmetry, improper for other occasions, seemed to have been conscientiously implemented by Shchetinkin. In the second part, his prayer was also long and, in addition to its obvious purpose, seemed to embody a covert didactic underpinning: to teach the young people how to pray. When the *sobranie* was over — as though to compensate for the imbalance of the *sobranie* created by overwhelmingly long *besedy* and to satisfy the psychological need for catharsis and relief of much accumulated anxiety, pressure, and fear — young people asked the *presviter* to repeat the prayer once again.

An even more profound negotiation on behalf of the needs of the Slobodka group took place in the middle of the first part of the *sobranie*, when its young leader, Mr. Victor Tikunov, requested that the elders should sing songs and not psalms during the *besedy*, because, he reasoned, psalms are too complex to grasp. The following translation provides a good insight into the rhetoric of this powerful negotiation. Tikunov said:

We have lost the communal life, and we want it back. We do want to return to the spirituality that we lost, and we see our hope in your visit. But we don't want just the ritual. What we want is a dialogue. As you want our work not to be in vain before God, we want your work not be in vain and bring the results. [To achieve it], please sing more melodious and simple songs, because we want your singing to reach us.

After a long silence, Shchetinkin responded: "God, help us to sing and you to hear." Then, after singing a psalm appropriate for the preceding *beseda*, he addressed his *pevtsy*, asking them to honor the request. He himself helped to sing two songs, "Molitva materi" ("Mother's prayer") and "Liubeznye deti" ("Dear children"), both based on popular Soviet melodies.[12] Both songs are about children's appropriate behavior and parents' compassion for children, so both carried a message corresponding to the "golden thread" of the *sobranie*. The *presviter* thus responded to Tikunov's request and found a compromise by allowing singing songs during the *sobranie*, although not instead of but in addition to "conventional" psalms.

This was a negotiation of the symbolic meaning of one of the most fundamental procedures in the communal rite. The request to sing songs instead of psalms was not a result of ignorance of the Molokan *zakon*, because Tikunov comes from a very "strict" Molokan family. In addition, he himself has already achieved a high status as a knowledgeable and a sophisticated thinker and speaker. But the social dynamics of the situation (the young community's alienation from traditional life, inability to learn by experience, and lack of elders, experts, and teachers) called for this adjustment; otherwise, as Tikunov explained, the perpetuation of the entire rite is endangered. In other words, the young group wanted to accept Molokanism but had to do it in their own way. The response of the wise *presviter* seemed amazing to me at the time because what he was asked to do appeared as something inconceivable in any other situation. It could not possibly have taken place at any of the Steadfast Molokan *sobranie* I had previously attended. In addition, the request seemed to contradict one of the *presviter*'s goals — that is, to teach the young the Molokan *zakon.*

The incident in Slobodka shows the complexity and dynamics of the Molokan *sobranie* as a living entity. It illustrates one way that changes are negotiated by the valued members of the community: readjustments are introduced by finding a compromise between the traditional and the new.

Building a New Diaspora Community in Post-Soviet Russia

The experience of the Slobodka group is also revealing when viewed in the larger context of cultural strategies espoused by small diaspora communities. Among many factors controlling the cultural survival of a new diaspora community, the number of people in the group and the sufficiency of their singing repertoire are important, if not crucial. Any small cultural enclave develops in a unique way, and often a single factor can change its practices (singing practices included) drastically. The visit of experienced singers to the Slobodka settlement can become such a single factor, at least for its spiritual life and singing practices. The enormous intensity throughout this *sobranie,* felt by everyone present, makes one think that this experience will not be easily forgotten.

Young Molokans in the Slobodka settlement came from different places in which Molokan communal life was well established. All of them had previously experienced a *sobranie,* although to a greatly varied degree. Many were familiar with the complex and well-developed terminology for the experiences essential for Molokan spiritual life, including singing and its performance practices. They were able to follow the psalms and some even attempted to sing along with the elder singers. Several young people knew a spiritual song or two, but songs, as mentioned earlier, are not sufficient to fulfill the symbolic purpose of singing during Molokan *sobranie.* Thus, only after the arrival of the qualified singers did a "proper" communal prayer become possible. When Molokanism started, in the eighteenth century, the founders considered it their first duty to build into the *zakon* vital institutions that support singing and forms of its maintenance. Today the necessity of such institutions is sustained in the Slobodka settlement. Young people welcomed the singers, they listened with immense concentration, they were willing to fast and to work hard to learn the singing they needed.

From observations during this service, it appears that even though the Slobodka Molokans cannot sing a single psalm today, they may have a future as a Molokan community. What these young people understand is the essence and the power of singing as a channel for transcendent communication. It means that no matter what borrowings, influences, and changes might occur, the singing tradition as a symbolic and artistic whole has a chance to endure there. As the years go by, it will probably web its various musical encounters in a unique way, as is the case with singing traditions of every other diaspora community. Tikunov's aim as the leader of the Slobodka group is to be able to reenact the main spiritual rite, the *sobranie,* as a whole, even though some important components will have to be renegotiated or even sacrificed. This strategy is characteristic of Molokan communities the world over. As far as I know, they do not select a certain section of the ritual to perpetuate, but rather aim to preserve it in its entirety. Russian Old Believers and Dukhobors living in North America seem to have similar strategies.

Even though this essay focuses on the Molokans living in Russia, some parallels with American Molokans are hard to avoid. Regardless of the differences in living conditions and historical ways during the last century, Molokans in both countries undergo a similar period in their spiritual development. In both, they make a serious effort to preserve the essence of Molokanism and to retain the younger generations. In both, Molokanism is in danger; the threat comes from the dynamics of contemporary life itself. The causes of this danger are different in Russia and the United States. In the United States the threat comes first of all from the loss of the language and ethnic identity, and also from the social standing of the group as a marginal community. Children of American Molokans want, most of all, to be like all others. In the former Soviet Union, Molokanism, as any other religious movement, was under ideological repressions. Today, however, the situation in Russia has changed significantly.

With the new freedoms, the Molokans in Russia can practice their religion freely. As the necessity to search for one's own roots is growing fast in the former Soviet society, Molokans are gaining the respect and even admiration of their fellow Russians for having been able to maintain their faith and preserve their history continuously throughout the Soviet era. Nobody ridicules Molokan men for their long beards and rope-like belts or women for their shawls and dresses anymore. Nobody laughs at their singing processions during funerals and weddings. The attention of scholars to the Molokan culture also has played a positive role. What separates and differentiates the Molokans from their neighbors now acquires a positive value in the eyes of the others as well. In new Russia, the Molokans' carefully guarded self-identity once again asserts its powerful role in their survival as a community.

Two major changes in Molokan communities in Russia are manifested clearly through the *sobranie* described here: first, it is possible to practice Molokanism openly; and second, in a related development, it is possible to reestablish contact with their historical brothers living in the United States. The renewed contact began with an inflow of religious books (virtually thousands of copies of the Bible and the songbook) and was soon followed by a steady, two-way traffic of people related by blood and then by the visits of leaders. With the opening of archives in Russia, Mr. Edward Samarin, a prominent leader of the American Steadfast Molokans, unearthed about a thousand documents (letters, photographs, etc.) collected by a renowned scholar, Vladimir Bonch-Bruevich, which had been inaccessible to scholars and the public during the Soviet years.[13]

Both similarities and differences among people separated for several generations are profound. The renewed contacts have had a deep impact on both communities. In particular, the Molokans living in Russia have been confronted by new concepts based on a sharply dissimilar American way of life. These meetings have not always been smooth; different attitudes toward their faith and way of living have not always been greeted favorably and have generated friction and disapproval. But as has become obvious over the last few years, particularly during two All-Molokan congresses, they have a way of working around the differences and have accepted certain changes. Inherited skills in negotiating the meaning of their legacy have been invaluable during these meetings. An ability to sing together, for example, regardless of all stylistic differences, highlights every meeting, and a cassette with psalms and songs recorded from the "quality singers" is the best gift.

In 1991 and 1992, two All-Molokan international congresses took place in Russia to pronounce the unity and firmness of the movement all over the world (the first All-Molokan Congress took place in 1905). There were *presviters* and other members of the communities that had not known about each other until that time. After long and controversial debates, an all-Molokan *presviter* was elected. The great difficulties with which this was accomplished are telling: Molokans have no experience in such elections, and the idea of a church hierarchy itself is foreign to their teachings. Traditionally, the regionalism and independence of small local communities/ churches have been the Molokans' characteristic mark. Local variations in singing schools have played an important role in these regional distinctions. Mr. Shchetinkin, eventually elected as the all-Molokan *presviter,* was asked to establish connections between various communities, facilitate their mutual support, and, particularly, promote Molokanism and teach young people who have grown up as Soviet citizens how to become responsible Molokans. Legitimizing the authority of his new position became an important issue for him. His visit with the Slobodka group was one step toward this multifaceted goal. He did it with the help of the tradition he knew best, that of his own church. The young people in Slobodka made several tapes during this visit, with the intent to learn psalms and songs.

The Slobodka Molokans' relocation to Russia is just a small part of the general demographic process taking place in Russia today: between 500,000 (according to an official 1992 figure of the Migration Service of the Russian Federation) and 2 million (unofficial figure) ethnic Russians have fled into Russia from former Soviet republics.[14] In a peculiar twist of fate, since the degeneration of the Soviet empire, these Russians have found themselves in a situation in which they must fight for survival. Needless to say, the situation is one of immense complexity for all Russian refugees.

Perhaps the Molokans' worldview and their historical past may actually help them to survive in this situation. The Slobodka group, for instance, may have a better chance than those ethnic Russians who do not belong to any confessional group outside the main Orthodox religion. For two centuries, their sociopolitical and economic circumstances and their ethical and moral code have forced the Molokans to take charge of their own lives, to develop excellent entrepreneurial skills, and to be independent and strong, both spiritually and physically, in order to withstand the pressure from the surrounding dominant mentality. So, today, despite the tragedy and unhappiness of the present conditions, despite a bleak existence, Slobodka Molokans understand that their arrival might be a blessing in disguise for the area into which they have moved. Hopefully, they will bring new vitality to places that for some time have been under strong economic pressure for survival. The local authorities understand this as well and actually welcome them (hence, the presence of the local administration during the *sobranie* in Slobodka). This is an unusual situation in the history of any confessional community in Russia. They are used to hiding and running away. Previously, the Molokans have chosen (and often have forced to select) the conditions of conscientious isolation, no matter where they lived — in Russia, Turkey, Australia, China, Brazil, or the United States.

Throughout the history of Russian confessional groups, the relativity of their living space has become a factor of cultural conservation. For any culture, a space change — that is, the process of migration — is like taking a plant out of its soil, but for several Russian confessional groups (Old Believers, Dukhobors, Molokans) it has also been a factor that stimulates the preservation of culture wherever the groups settle. Throughout their numerous migrations over the last two centuries, Molokans have been capable of balancing the preservation of the old and creation of the new. Their stability has been maintained through flexible readjustments and keeping a balance with the ever-changing natural and cultural environment. Their singing is an example of their capability for readjustment. Molokans welcome an opportunity to borrow a melody and make any tune they like into their own spiritual song. All-time song hits (e.g., "Korobochka," "Kogda b imel zlatye gory," "Oi tsvetet kalina," "Na zakate khodit paren"), ironically including songs from Soviet films, have left traces in the Molokan repertoire (some Molokan elders in Russia still forbid watching the television and going to the movies). Now, one can also hear the melodies of "Amazing Grace," "The Last Rose of Summer," "Clementine," "Red River Valley," and "Battle Hymn of the Republic," learned from their American brothers. A diaspora culture often operates as a continuum between the present and the communal memory of the past. Among the Molokans, it is usually singing that first fills in the continuum: the traditional melody of a psalm assures continuity with the past, while composing and learning new songs link history to the present. The construction of negotiated meaning in the

Slobodka community also involves songs that have been called to connect the past and the present.

The inner dynamics of Molokanism are constructive and destructive simultaneously. Molokan culture contains seemingly opposing tendencies. As Molokan common rhetoric asserts, the community as a whole is oriented toward history and tradition. Historical events that happened years ago are recounted continuously; what happened to their forefathers is relevant directly to the present: "We live and pray exactly as our forefathers did." Usually, new features are introduced slowly and imperceptibly. At the same time, the community is open to anything from the outside world that can be useful for future prosperity, both spiritual and economic. There are always some individuals, both in Russia and the United States, who are "twenty years ahead of all others in the community," as one Molokan leader put it. These Molokan explorers were among the first Russian villagers to buy personal cars and refrigerators, to use tape recorders to record singing, etc., while some other Molokans in Russia still reject any use of tape recorders and television to this day. It is perhaps not by chance that the majority of Molokans were quick to test and explore the new political and economic freedoms in the new Russia. It is perhaps also not a coincidence that many Molokans love the American way of living, with its dynamic necessity to make choices constantly and quickly, inclination for personal prosperity, and respect for professional skills. Yet, the Molokan community as a whole can be described as one with a centric orientation: quickly responding to modern advantages, the community is tightly closed to outsiders. Today, as always, the oppositions "we/not we" and "ours/not ours" reveal themselves clearly and strongly. Molokans have almost no friends from the outside. The Molokans do not invite people from the outside to their gatherings; their beautiful and powerful singing is not known even to their neighbors. A combination of the openness and hermitage of the Molokan community helps to ensure the preservation of the culture; at the same time, it threatens the very existence of the sect.

How will the changes brought by new social, political, and economic conditions in Russia affect the survival of Molokanism, Molokan culture, and their singing in particular? Will the Slobodka group, for instance, learn how to sing from the tapes they made during the visit by the elder singers? Will they prefer to recreate and perpetuate the singing of their own churches back home in the Caucasus? Will they be able to maintain the balance between the old and the new forms of singing, one of the major factors that has assured their existence as Molokans? Only the future will tell, but now, for the first time in Molokan history, these processes can be documented.

The changes in the political situation in Russia are so tremendous that it has become a common practice to draw direct parallels between political and cultural paradigms. Because of my personal background (I lived in Russia before 1979, and I cannot pretend to be entirely objective), I find it difficult to agree with the notion that in Russian expressive cultures, "the stagnation" paradigm of the Brezhnev times has been replaced with "the reform" paradigm of the Gorbachev perestroika times. There was no stagnation in the inner spiritual and artistic creativity during the 1960s and 1970s. If anything, these aspects of societal life grew creatively intense under political pressure, presaging dramatic social changes. It is true that under the political and social reforms of perestroika, several confessional communities in Russia (Molokans, Dukhobors, and Old Believers, particularly) went through some drastic changes. At the same time, it is also true, one can argue, that the inner dynamics of their spiritual life have not changed much.

Postscript

Long after the completion of this essay, in the summer of 1994, I had the occasion to visit the Slobodka Molokan community once again, now without the group of elders led by Shchetinkin from the Stavropol area. It appears that during the interim period, the younger generation had managed to learn two or three of the psalms from the tapes made of the Shchetinkin group's singing in Slobodka two years earlier. They also learned a couple of psalms from tapes recorded "at home." Young Molokans expressed some frustration at not having had the benefit of the continuous support of the elders. Learning from tapes, they said, is so much harder than learning from a living singer. Learning the psalms at all, however inadequately, still afforded them the possibility of conducting a *sobranie,* thus getting closer to the essence of their being Molokans.

Shchetinkin himself exhibited a remarkable ability to modify long-held attitudes. In 1995 he eagerly accepted an invitation to his group to participate in the Russian-American program "Russian Roots, American Branches: Music in Two Worlds" at the American Folklife Festival, organized by the Smithsonian Institution. On the way to Washington, D.C., the group first went to San Francisco, where they spent about a month in the homes and the church of San Francisco Molokans. The stay had a tremendous effect on both groups, but particularly on Shchetinkin's. Eventually both groups came to the festival in Washington, where they lived for two weeks, singing in public twice every day, publicly discussing issues of their identity, talking about changes and continuities in their life, and sharing the joy of singing together with their American brothers.

Notes

Field data for this article were collected since 1989 in Russia and the United States as part of a research project on cognate cultures. The project focuses on cultural continuities and transformations under different social, cultural, and ecological conditions. It has been supported by the Office of Folklife and Cultural Studies of the Smithsonian Institution, the Russian Ministry of Culture, and the Research Center for Studies on Russian Folklore in Moscow. After two initiatory field trips (1989 in Russia and 1990 in the U.S.), I invited Dr. Serafima Nikitina, a linguist from the Institute of Language Studies at the Russian Academy of Sciences, to join the project, and at present we are working on a joint article on musical and verbal components of Molokan culture. Leonid Filimonov and Alexander Goriachev, both from the Laboratory for Visual Anthropology at Moscow State University, joined our team to film documentary footage during the 1992 fieldwork in the village of Slobodka. I am indebted to Ohio State University graduate students, members of my seminars on Russian music, for being a responsive and stimulating audience for several sections of the article. I am particularly indebted to Kathy Gruber, Vladimir Marchenkov, and Margaret Bdzil for transcribing and translating parts of field interviews, and to Todd Harvey, Olga Velichkina, Deborah Andrus, and Deborah Wilson for transcribing some songs and psalms. Special thanks to Edward Samarin for comments.

1. Mr. Shchetinkin, Mr. Tikunov, and Mr. Samarin permitted me to use their names. Other Molokans asked that their names not be used in print; throughout this essay, statements and expressions recorded from them during field interviews are cited in quotation marks but without attribution.

2. Molokan *posalmy* can be sung to any part of the scripture, not only to the texts from the book of Psalms.

3. The term "construction of negotiated meaning" is borrowed from social cognitive theory (e.g., Flower 1994).

4. "Molokan" is not the original name of the sect of Spiritual Christians. According to one of the leaders of Molokanism, the movement began from "a soft blowing of God's breath" — that is, from the Holy Spirit (Berokoff 1966: 23). Three major interpretations of the origins of their name (all in current circulation) are connected with the Russian word *moloko* (milk). According to the first version, their teachings are based on the literal reading of the Bible, that is, on spiritual milk; the second dwells on their defiance of the Russian Orthodox Church's prohibition against consuming milk (among other non-vegetarian products) during weekly fasts on Wednesdays and Fridays, as well as during the longer fasts; a third version links their name with the river Molochnye Vody ("milky waters") along which they lived in the eighteenth century. For English sources on Molokan history, see Dunn (1983), Klibanov (1982), Moore (1973), or Young (1932).

5. No observer has failed to notice the power and importance of singing in the Molokan communities. However, only two publications, as far as I know, contain specific studies of Molokan singing. In 1911, Lineva was the first to record phonographically and publish transcriptions of Molokan psalms (Lineva 1911). The next study, by the American ethnomusicologist Linda O'Brien-Rothe, appeared only in 1989. This was the first serious effort to comprehend the phenomenon of Molokan singing, although it concentrated primarily on Molokan songs, not psalms (O'Brien-Rothe 1989).

6. Molokans look and speak like Russian peasants. They widely use charms similar to those in circulation all over rural Russia. Ties between village folksong and Molokan psalms and songs are unmistakable, although Molokan singing practices have evolved into unique and intricate forms. Perhaps even more importantly, the Molokan understanding of religion as a syncretic entity with no compartmentalization between life and faith is close to other peasant communities in Russia. Traditionally, the spiritual life of Russian villagers, unlike that of their contemporary city-dwellers, has been not a separate sphere of activities but very much a part of "secular" life itself (Mazo 1991). However, while many Russian peasants have had a rather limited knowledge of Christianity as a religious doctrine — knowing it mostly from icons and the so-called *dukhovnye stikhi* (spiritual verses), songs based on biblical and apocryphal stories — every Molokan has some clear knowledge of Molokan doctrine and the Bible.

7. The concept of the new millennium, analogous to that of other Russian sectarians and Western prophetic Protestants of the seventeenth to eighteenth centuries, is not equally strong among different Molokan denominations, but all believe that as a chosen people, they will be taken into God's Kingdom on Earth.

8. In American settlements, there has been a radically new development over the last few years: a small Reform group has adopted English as their liturgical language. The very existence of this group has generated immense antagonism from other Molokans, who insist that those who abolish the Russian language cannot claim to be Molokans any longer. The members of the Reform church have been disavowed even by their own parents (Mazo forthcoming).

9. The ceremonial table is called *prestol* (a throne and also the altar in Russian Ortho-doxy). As used by the Molokans, the word *prestol* refers primarily to the community's spiritual leadership, a group of men who, during the *sobranie,* sit *pri stole* — that is, occupy the first row at the ceremonial table.

10. In many areas of rural Russia, lamenting, or crying with words and melody, is not only a symbolic component of a ritual but also a conventional form of individual expression of frustration, grief, unhappiness, and similar psychological and emotional states. Laments are always improvised; these improvisations are based on strict patterns determined by each local tradition. While each lament is unique, the local tradition regulates formal and idiomatic aspects of both melody and words, as well as the lamenter's body movement and the role, placement, and even the volume of sobbing and wailing (Mazo 1994a).

11. In 1989, my friendly host did not allow me to record during his son's wedding and insisted on "arresting" my tape recorder "just in case," saying that if his son's married life went wrong, he would never forgive himself and would blame himself for allowing the ceremony to be recorded.

12. The second song is an adaptation of "Oi tsvetet kalina' " a hit tune by Isaac Dun-aevsky from the popular 1949 film *Kubanskie Kazaki.* More research is needed to identify the origins of the first melody. Both are adjusted, however, to melodic and harmonic idioms characteristic of the group.

13. Bonch-Bruevich (1908–1916) was compiler and editor of a multivolume publication of materials and documents on the history of Russian sectarians and Old Believers. Volume 8, dedicated to the Molokans, was to have appeared in print just before the October Revolution, but it has never been published.

14. Figures provided by Lydia Grafova, co-chair of the Russian Civilian Assistance Committee in her report at the Kennan Institute for Advanced Studies, Washington, D.C., on 1 December 1992.

Works Cited

Abrahams, Roger. 1992. *Singing the Master: The Emergence of African American Culture in the Plantation South.* New York: Pantheon.

——. 1993. After New Perspectives: Folklore Study in the Late Twentieth Century. *Western Folklore* 52(2–4):379–400.

Anastasijević, Bratislav. 1988. O Zloupotrebi narodne muzike. *Kultura* 80–81:147–56.

Anderson, Benedict. 1991. *Imagined Communities: Reflections on the Origin and Spread of Nationalism.* Rev. ed. London: Verso.

Appadurai, Arjun. 1990. Disjuncture and Difference in the Global Cultural Economy. *Public Culture* 2(2):1–24.

——. 1991. Global Ethnoscapes: Notes and Queries for a Transnational Anthropology. In *Recapturing Anthropology,* ed. Richard G. Fox, 191–210. Santa Fe: School of American Research.

Armstrong, John A. 1980. *Ukrainian Nationalism.* Littleton, Colo.: Ukrainian Academic Press.

Aves, J., P. Duncan, and G. A. Hoskins, eds. 1992. *The Road to Post-Communism: Independent Political Movements in the Soviet Union, 1985–1991.* London: Pinter.

Bahry, Romana. 1994. Rock Culture and Rock Music in Ukraine. In *Rocking the State: Rock Music and Politics in Eastern Europe and Russia,* ed. Sabrina Petra Ramet. Boulder, Colo.: Westview.

Bakalov, Todor. 1992. *Svatbarskite orkestri: Maistori na narodnata muzika, Tom II.* Sofia: Muzika.

Bakić-Hayden, Milica, and Robert M. Hayden. Orientalist Variations on the Theme "Balkans": Symbolic Geography in Recent Yugoslav Cultural Politics. *Slavic Review* 51(1):1–15.

Balzer, Marjorie Mandelstam. 1994. From Ethnicity to Nationalism: Turmoil in the Russian Mini-Empire. In Millar and Wolchik, 56–88.

Banac, I. 1986. *The National Question in Yugoslavia: Origins, History, Politics.* Ithaca: Cornell University Press.

Barth, Fredrik. 1969. *Ethnic Groups and Boundaries.* Oslo: Universitetsforlaget.

Bartók, Béla. 1981 [1931]. *Hungarian Folk Music.* Albany: State University of New York Press.

Baumann, Zygmunt. 1992. *Intimations of Postmodernity.* London: Routledge.

Beck, Sándor. 1991. Interview. Budapest, Hungary.

Beissinger, Margaret. 1991. *The Art of the Lautar: The Epic Tradition in Romania.* New York: Garland.

Bencze, Mrs. László (Judit Mező). 1981. Hangszeres népzenei együttesek a Hajdúságban [Instrumental folk music ensembles in Hajdúság]. In Széll, 41–51.

Benjamin, Walter. 1968. *Illuminations: Essays and Reflections.* New York: Schocken.

Berokoff, J., trans. 1966. *Selections from "The Book of Spirit and Life."* Whittier, Calif.: Stockton Trade Press.

Billington, James. 1966. *The Icon and the Axe: An Interpretive History of Russian Culture.* New York: Alfred A. Knopf.

Bloch, Maurice. 1989. *Feudal Society.* London: Routledge.

Blödli dal. 1987. *Magyar Nemzet,* 16 May.

Boiko Martin. 1994. Latvian Ethnomusicology: Past and Present. *Yearbook of Traditional Music* 26:47–65.

Bonch-Bruevich, Vladimir. 1908–16. *Materialy k istorii i izucheniiu russkogo sektanstva i staroobriachestva.* St. Petersburg: n.p.

Bošnjaković, Mata. 1984. Neka zapažanja uz diskografsku produkciju "lakih žanrova" u nas. In *Diskografija u SR Hrvatskoj. Studije i documenti X,* 99–103. Zagreb: Zavod za kulturu Hrvatske.

Both, Erzsébet. 1981. Muzsikás évtized [The decade of Muzsikás]. In Széll, 23–30.

Bourdieu, Pierre. 1984 [1979]. *Distinction: A Social Critique of the Judgement of Taste.* London: Routledge and Kegan Paul.

Buchanan, Donna A. 1985. Musical Change and Ideological Revision: Creation and Concepts of Contemporary Soviet Popular Music. Unpublished master's thesis, University of Texas at Austin.

——. 1991. The Bulgarian Folk Orchestra: Cultural Performance, Symbol, and the Construction of National Identity in Socialist Bulgaria. Ph.D. dissertation, University of Texas at Austin.

——. 1995. Metaphors of Power, Metaphors of Truth: The Politics of Music Professionalism in Bulgarian Folk Orchestras. *Ethnomusicology* 39(3):381–416.

Bukharin, Nikolai Ivanovich. 1925. *Historical Materialism: A System of Sociology.* New York: International Publishers.

Bulgarian Helsinki Committee. 1993. *Human Rights in Bulgaria in 1993* (report). Sofia: Bulgarian Helsinki Committee.

Burg, Steven L. 1983. The Political Integration of Yugoslavia's Muslims: Determinants of Success and Failure, *Carl Beck Papers in Russian and East European Studies,* No. 203. Pittsburgh: University of Pittsburgh.

Burke, Peter. 1978. *Popular Culture in Early Modern Europe.* New York: New York University Press.

Cartner, Holly. 1991. *Destroying Ethnic Identity: The Gypsies of Bulgaria.* New York: Helsinki Watch.

———. 1993. Bulgaria: Police Violence Against Gypsies. *Helsinki Watch Report* 5(5):1–14.

Cohen, Lenard J. 1992. Regime Transition in a Disintegrating Yugoslavia: The Law-of-Rule vs. the Rule-of-Law, *Carl Beck Papers in Russian and East European Studies,* No. 908. Pittsburgh: University of Pittsburgh.

Coleman, Nick. 1988. Bulgarian Rhapsody. *Time Out,* 13 April, 12.

Crampton, R. J. 1990. The Turks in Bulgaria, 1878–1944. In *The Turks of Bulgaria: The History, Culture and Political Fate of a Minority,* ed. Kemal H. Karpat, 203–22. Istanbul: Isis Press.

Creed, Gerald W. 1990. The Bases of Bulgaria's Ethnic Policies. *Anthropology of East Europe Review* 9(2):12–17.

———. 1992. *Economic Development under Socialism: A Bulgarian Village on the Eve of Transition.* Ph.D. dissertation, City University of New York.

———. 1993. Rural-Urban Oppositions in the Bulgarian Political Transition. *Südosteuropa* 42(6):369–82.

Crowe, David, and John Kolsti. 1991. *The Gypsies of Eastern Europe.* Armonk, N.Y.: M. E. Sharpe.

Crystal, David. 1976. Nonsegmental Phonology in Religious Modalities. In *Language in Religious Practice,* ed. W. Samarian, 17–23. Rowley Mass.: Newbury House.

Csók, Ferenc. 1991. Interview. Molványhidpuszta, Hungary.

Csorba, Zoltán. 1988. Lakodalom az egész világ. *Békés Megyei Népújság,* 13 parts, 11–25 January. (Originally published in *Magyar Szo.*)

Czekanowska, Anna, ed. 1996a. *Dziedzictwo europejskie a polska kultura muzycyna w dobie przemian.* Krakow: Musica Iagellonica.

———. 1996b. Muzyka ludowa dzisiaj: Trudnosci Interpretacji. In Czekanowska 1996a, 407–25.

Dahlig, Piotr. 1996. Do badan nad funkcjonowaniem tradycji muzycznej przesiedlencow: Przyklad repatriantow z Bosni. In Czekanowska 1996a, 285–327.

Deak, Frantisek. 1975. Russian Mass Spectacles. *Drama Review* 19(2):7–22.

Décsi, Ágnes. 1987. Lesz-e saját csipkés kiombinétunk? *Magyar Ifjúság,* 9 January.

Dobszay, László. 1984. *Magyar zenetörténet* [A history of Hungarian music]. Budapest: Gondolat.

———. 1993. *A History of Hungarian Music.* Budapest: Corvina.

Donchev, Anton. 1968. *Time of Parting.* Translated from Bulgarian by Marguerite Alexieva. New York: William Morrow.

Dragičević-Šešić, Milena. 1989. Novokomponovana narodna muzika u postmodernom kontekstu. *Quorum* 3(26):608–21.

Drakulić, Slavenka. 1990. Bulgaria's Opposition: Struggling to Be Born. *Nation,* 28 May, 735–37.

D. Szabó, Ede. 1986. Kombiné, kombiné, csipkés kombiné. *Magyar Ifjúság,* 26 December.

Dunin, Elsie. 1973. Cocek as a Ritual Dance Among Gypsy Women. *Makedonski Folklor* 6(12):193–97.

———. 1977. The Newest Changes in Rom Dance (Serbia and Macedonia). *Journal of the Association of Graduate Dance Ethnologists, University of California, Los Angeles,* 1:12–17.

———. 1985. Dance Change in the Context of the Gypsy St. George's Day, Skopje, Yugoslavia, 1967–1977. In *Papers from the Fourth and Fifth Annual Meetings, Gypsy Lore Society, North American Chapter,* ed. J. Grumet, 110–20. New York: Gypsy Lore Society, North American chapter.

Dunn, Ethel, ed. 1983. *The Molokan Heritage Collection, Vol. 1: Reprints of Articles and Translations.* Berkeley, Calif.: Highgate Road Social Science Research Station.

Dzhidzhev, Todor. 1987. Problemi na orkestrite za narodna muzika. *Muzikalni horizonti* 10:38–42.

———. 1991. Cherti na stiloviya oblikna reditsa süvremenni instrumentalni grupi za bulgarska narodna muzika. [Lecture read following Stambolovo III.] *Bulgarski folklor* 17(4):82–84.

Eminov, Ali. 1990. There are No Turks in Bulgaria: Rewriting History by Administrative Fiat. In *The Turks of Bulgaria: The History, Culture and Political Fate of a Minority,* ed. Kemal H. Karpat, 203–22. Istanbul: Isis Press.

Encyclopedia of Islam. 1934. London: Luzac & Co.

Engelbrekt, Kjell. 1993. Bulgaria: the Weakening of Postcommunist Illusions. *RFE/RL Research Report* 2(1):78–83.

Erlmann, Veit. 1991. *African Stars: Studies in Black South African Performance.* Chicago: University of Chicago Press.

Fehér, Ferenc, Agnes Heller, and György Márkus. 1983. *Dictatorship over Needs.* Oxford: Basil Blackwell.

Feldman, L. C., R. Senjković, and I. Prica, eds. 1993. Poetics of Resistance. In *Fear, Death, and Resistance (An Ethnography of War: Croatia 1991–1992),* 1–4. Zagreb: Institute of Ethnology and Folklore Research.

Fischer, Michael. 1986. Ethnicity and the Post-Modern Arts of Memory. In *Writing Culture: The Poetics and Politics of Ethnography,* ed. James Clifford and George E. Marcus, 194–233. Berkeley: University of California Press.

Fiske, John. 1987. British Cultural Studies and Television. In *Channels of Discourse: Television and Contemporary Criticism,* ed. Robert Allen. Chapel Hill: University of North Carolina Press.

Fitzpatrick, Sheila. 1976. Culture and Politics under Stalin: A Reappraisal. *Slavic Review* 35:211–31.

Flower, Linda. 1994. *The Construction of Negotiated Meaning: A Social Cognitive Theory of Writing.* Carbondale: Southern Illinois University Press.

Fodor, Lajos. 1987. Lakodalmas Rock. *Esti Hirlap,* 2 March.

Foster, George. 1965. Peasant Society and the Image of Limited Good. *American Anthropologist* 67(6):293–315.

Foucault, Michel. 1980. *Power/Knowledge: Selected Interviews and Other Writings, 1972–1977,* ed. Colin Gordon. New York: Pantheon.

Frasunkiewicz, Dorota. 1994. Świadomość Polaków na Białorusi a kształt repertuaru muzycznego. In Czekanowska 1996a, 327–70.

Frigyesi, Judit. 1989. Béla Bartók and Hungarian Nationalism: The Development of Bartók's Social and Political Ideas at the Turn of the Century (1899–1903). Ph.D. dissertation, University of Pennsylvania.

———. 1994. Béla Bartók and the Concept of Nation and *Volk* in Hungary. *Musical Quarterly* 78(2):255–87.

Gilroy, Paul. 1991. *"There Ain't No Black in the Union Jack": The Cultural Politics of Race and Nation.* Chicago: University of Chicago.

———. 1993. *The Black Atlantic: Modernity and Double Consciousness.* Cambridge: Harvard University Press.

Gojkovic, Adriana. 1986. Music of Yugoslav Gipsies. *Traditional Music of Ethnic Groups — Minorities, Proceedings of the Meeting of Ethnomusicologists on the Occasion of the European Year of Music 1985* 7(7):187–94.

Gómez-Peña, Guillermo. 1988. Documented/Undocumented. In *Multi-Cultural Literacy: Opening the American Mind,* trans. Rubén Martínez, ed. Rick Simonson and Scott Walker, 127–33. St. Paul, Minn.: Graywolf.

Gorov, Goro. 1983. *Strandzhanski folklor.* Sofia: BAN.

Grossberg, Lawrence, C. Nelson, and P. Treichler. 1992. *Cultural Studies.* London: Routledge.

Grudev, Nikolai. 1994. Pomatsite prizovani da boikotirat etnoizsledvaneto. *24 chasa* (Sofia) 4, no. 189 (20 July):4.

Gyurgyák, János, ed. 1990. Népiek és urbánusok — egy mítosz vége? *Századvég,* vol. 2.

Hajba, Ferenc. 1987. Nemzetiségi kombiné. *Népszabadság,* 14 May.

Halpern, Joel, and E. A. Hammel. 1969. Observations on the Intellectual History of Ethnology and Other Social Sciences in Yugoslavia. *Comparative Studies in Society and History* 11(1):17–26.

Hancock, Ian. 1987. *The Pariah Syndrome.* Ann Arbor, Mich.: Karoma.

Hedgbeth, Llewellyn H. 1975. Meyerhold's D.E. *Drama Review* 19(2):23–36.

Heim, Michael. 1972. Moravian Folk Music: A Czechoslovak Novelist's View. *Journal of the Folklore Institute* 9(1):45–53.

Heller, Ágnes. 1992. A szöveg és a nemzet. *Magyar nemzet,* 17 October.

Helsinki Watch. 1986. *Destroying Ethnic Identity: The Turks of Bulgaria.* New York: U.S. Helsinki Watch Committee.

Hemetek, Ursula. 1994. Muzik im Leben der Roma. In *Roma Das Unbekannte Volk: Schicksal und Kultur,* ed. Mozes Heinschink and Ursula Hemetek, 150–71. Vienna: Bohlau.

Héra, Mrs. István. 1981. Szervezeti gondok. In Széll, 126–30.

Herndon, Marcia. 1993. Insiders, Outsiders: Knowing Our Limits, Limiting Our Knowing. *World of Music* 35(1).

Hobsbawm, Eric, and Terence Ranger. 1988 [1983]. Introduction: Inventing Traditions. In *The Invention of Tradition,* ed. Hobsbawm and Ranger. Cambridge: Cambridge University Press.

Hofer, Tamás. 1984. Peasant Culture and Urban Culture in the Period of Modernization: Delineation of a Problem Area Based on Data from Hungary. In *The Peasant and the City in Eastern Europe,* ed. Irene Portis Winner and Thomas G. Winner, 111–28. Cambridge, Mass.: Schenkman Publishing Company.

Horváth, Zoltán. 1961. *Magyar századforduló. A második reform-nemzedék története, 1886–1914* [Turn-of-the-century Hungary: The history of the second reform generation]. Budapest: Gondolat.

Ilahije i Kaside: 450 godina Gazi Husrevbegove Medrese u Sarajevu (Stadion Bilino Polje, Zenica). [Videotape]. 1990. Sarajevo: Gazi Husrevbegova Medresa & Radio Sarajevo, Marketing.

Illasiewicz-Skotnicka, Elżbieta. 1996. "Powrót" czy "Podróż w nieznane": Pytanie o kulturowy wymiar integracji europejskiej. In Czekanowska 1996a, 41–47.

Jánosi, András. 1985. *Janosi Ensemble: Folk Tunes Arranged in Bartók's Music,* Hungaroton SLPX 18193.

———. 1988. *Hungarian Folk Music from Gyimes.* Hungaroton SLPX 18145.

Járdányi, Pál. 1943. *A kidei magyarság világi zenéje.* Kolozsvár: Erdélyi Tudományos Intézet.

Jurkovics, Tibor. 1987. *Új divat a magyarnota-rock. Szolnok Megyei Néplap,* 26 March.

Kagarlitskaya, Anna. 1990. Condemned to Solitude: A Conversation with Alfred Schnittke. In *The Best of "Ogonyok": The New Journalism of Glasnost,* ed. V. Korotich and C. Porter. London: Heinemann.

Kaplan, Robert D. 1993. *Balkan Ghosts: A Journey through History.* New York: Vintage.

Karpat, Kemal H. 1990. Introduction: Bulgaria's Methods of Nation Building and the Turkish Minority. In *The Turks of Bulgaria: The History, Culture and Political Fate of a Minority,* ed. Kemal H. Karpat, 1–22. Istanbul: Isis Press.

Katsarova, Raina. 1954. Folk Music: Bulgarian. *Grove Dictionary of Music and Musicians, Volume III,* 5th ed., ed. Eric Blom, 201–11. New York: St. Martin's.

Kaufman, Dimitrina. 1986. Koga horata rukoplyaskat: Vtora sreshta na instrumentalnite grupi za narodna muzika. *Bŭlgarska muzika* 37(10):38–42.

———. 1989. Kŭm problemi na instrumentalnata improvizatsiya v suvremennite svatbarski orkestri. *Muzikalni horizonti* 12/13:235–37.

———. 1990. Ot vŭzrozhdenskata chalgiya kŭm sŭvremennite svatbarski orkestri. *Bŭlgarski folklor* 16(3):23–32.

Kaufman, Nikolai. 1984. Istorichesko razvitie na obrabotkite na narodnata ni muzika. *Bŭlgarska muzika* 35(2):21–27.

———. 1987. Vtora natsionalna sreshta na instrumentalnite grupi za bŭlgarska narodna muzika. *Bŭlgarski folklor* 13(1):78–79.

———. 1989. Nyakoi predshestvenitsa na sŭvremennite orkestri na narodna muzika. *Muzikalni horizonti* 12/13:220–28.

Klibanov, Alexander. 1982. *History of Religious Sectarianism in Russia, 1860–1917*, ed. Stephen Dunn. Oxford: Pergamon.

Kodály, Zoltán. 1960 [1937]. *Folk Music of Hungary*. Budapest: Corvina.

Klima, Ivan. 1990. The Unexpected Benefits of Oppression. Paper presented at a conference, Czech Literature and Culture, 1890–1990, at New York University.

Kokareshkov, Aleksandŭr. 1986. Kŭm Vŭprosa za Traditsionnija Muzikalen Folklor i Sŭvremennostta. *Bŭlgarski folklor* 11(1):65–68.

Kostova, Yuliya. 1988. Za pravoto na rod i vyara, za myastoto na lichnostta i istoriyata. *Otechestven front*, 8 April, 12.

Kozma, Gábor. 1986. Alcázott dalok. *Vas Népe*, 1 November.

Kršić, Dejan. 1989. Dejan Kršić for New Europe (Slavic Soul). *Quorum* 3(26):604–7.

Kundera, Milan. 1982 [1967]. *The Joke*. New York: HarperCollins.

———. 1984. *The Unbearable Lightness of Being*, trans. Michael Henry Heim. New York: HarperCollins.

———. 1995. *Testaments Betrayed*. New York: HarperCollins.

Kurkela, Vesa. 1993. Deregulation of Popular Music in the European Post-Communist Countries: Business, Identity and Cultural Collage. *Worlds of Music* 35(3):80–106.

Kürti, László. 1989. Transylvania, Land beyond Reason: Toward an Anthropological Analysis of a Contested Terrain. *Dialectical Anthropology* 14:21–52.

Lagzi, Lajcsi. 1991. Interview. *Magyar Narancs*, 21 February.

Laing, Dave. 1978. *The Marxist Theory of Art*. Atlantic Highlands, N.J.: Humanities Press.

Lakodalmak sztárja: Kadlott Karcsi. 1987. *Szabad Föld*, 31 July.

Lampe, John. 1986. *The Bulgarian Economy in the Twentieth Century*. London: Croom Helm.

Laušević, Mirjana. 1993. Rascals and Shepherdesses: Music and Gender on a Bosnian Mountain. M.A. thesis, Wesleyan University.

————. 1994. Music and Politics in Bosnia. Paper presented at the annual meeting of the Society for Ethnomusicology and the American Folklore Society, Milwaukee, Wisc.

Lave, Jean, P. Duguid, and N. Fernandez. 1992. Coming of Age in Birmingham: Cultural Studies and Conceptions of Subjectivity. *Annual Review of Anthropology* 21:257–82.

Lázár, István. 1989. *Hungary: A Brief History*. Budapest: Corvina.

Lévai, Júlia. 1992. Personal communication. Budapest, Hungary.

Levin, Theodore. 1993. The Reterritorialization of Culture in the New Central Asian States: A Report from Uzbekistan. *Yearbook for Traditional Music* 25:51–59.

Liégeois, Jean-Pierre. 1986. *Gypsies: An Illustrated History*. London: Al Saqi.

Lineva, Evgeniia. 1911. Psalms and Religious Songs of Russian Sectarians in the Caucasus. In *International Musical Society Congress Reports*. London: International Music Society Congress.

Losonczi, Ágnes. 1968. Magyar nóta, népdal, dzsessz — és a közönség. *Valóság* 11(5):38–48.

————. 1969. *A zene eletenek szociologiaja*. Budapest: Zenemukiado.

Luković, Petar. 1989. *Bolja prošlost (Prizori iz muzičkog života Jugoslavije 1940–1989)*. Belgrade: Mladost.

Madzharov, Panaiot. 1983. *Strandzhanski narodni pesni: Iz repertoara na Kera Panaiotova Madzharova*. Sofia: Muzika.

Majorossy, Aladár, Andor Szenes, and Szilárd Darvas. N.d. Csipkés Kominé (Lace Slip). *3+2 Együltes: Halvany Öszi Rózsa*. Jugoton LSY 62089.

Malcolm, Noel. 1994. *Bosnia: A Short History*. New York: New York University Press.

Manga, János. 1969. *Hungarian Folk Songs and Folk Instruments*. Budapest: Corvina.

Manuel, Peter. 1993. *Cassette Culture*. Chicago: University of Chicago Press.

Markos, Edith. 1983. "Stephen the King" or Stephen the Superstar? *Radio Free Europe Situation Report*, 19 September.

Marushiakova, Elena, and Veselin Popov. 1993. *Ciganite v Bulgaria*. Sofia: Klub 90.

Marx, Karl, and Friedrich Engels. 1972. The German Ideology. In *Marxism and Art: Writings in Aesthetics and Criticism*, ed. Berel Lang and Forrest Williams, 39–47. New York: David McKay.

Mazo, Margarita. 1991. "We Don't Summon Spring in the Summer": Traditional Music and Beliefs of the Contemporary Russian Village. In *Christianity and the Arts in Russia*, ed. W. C. Brumfield and M. Velimirovich, 73–97. Cambridge: Cambridge University Press.

————. 1994a. Wedding Laments in North Russian Villages. In *Music-Cultures in Contact*, ed. M. Kartomi and S. Blum, 21–40. Basel: Gordon and Breach.

————. 1994b. Lament Made Visible: A Study of Paramusical Features in Russian Lament. In *Writings in Honor of Rulan Chao Pian*, ed. B. Yung and J. Lam, 164–212. Cambridge, Mass.: Music Departments of Harvard University and Chinese University of Hong Kong.

———. Forthcoming. Singing as Experience of Russian Molokans.

Millar, James R., and Sharon L. Wolchik. 1994. *The Social Legacy of Communism.* Washington, D.C.: Woodrow Wilson Center Press and Cambridge University Press.

Milošević, Vlado. 1964. *Sevdalinka.* Banja Luka: Muzej bosanske Krajine.

Moldován, Domokos, ed. 1976. *Hey, Galgamácsa Wouldn't Even Occur to Me: Songs, Folk Customs, and Folk Games from Galgamacs; The Songs of Dudás Juli.* Hungaroton SPLX 18021.

Moore, Williams. 1973. *Molokan Oral Tradition: Legends and Memories of an Ethnic Sect,* Folklore Studies No. 28. Berkeley: University of California Press.

Mosse, George L. 1985. *Nationalism and Sexuality.* New York: Howard Fertig.

Możeyko, Zinaida. 1991. Narodna estetika w otrażenii terminologii nositele avtentičnogo fol'klora. Paper presented at the Eighth European Seminar in Ethnomusicology, Geneva.

Muzsikás. 1986. *Muzsikás: Nem arról halnallik, amerről hajnallott. . . .* Hungaroton SPLX 18121.

———. 1993. *Muzsikás: Maramaros — The Lost Jewish Tradition of Transylvania.* Rykodisc HNCD 1373.

Nagy, Sz. Péter. 1990. *A népi-urbánus vita documentumai 1932–1947.* Budapest: Rakéta Könyvkiado.

Naidenova, Vera. 1988. Mudrostta na izbora. *Narodna kultura* (Sofia) 32, no. 14 (1 April).

Naselenie SSSR. 1989. Po dannym Vsesoiuznoi perepisi naseleniia 1989 goda. Moscow.

Noll, William. 1991. Music Institutions and National Consciousness among Polish and Ukrainian Peasants. In *Ethnomusicology and Modern Music History,* ed. Steven Blum, Philip V. Bohlman, and Daniel M. Neuman. Urbana: University of Illinois Press.

O'Brien-Rothe, Linda. 1989. *The Origins of Molokan Singing. The Molokan Heritage Collection,* vol. 4. Berkeley, Calif.: Highgate Road Social Science Research Station.

Ortutay, Gyula. 1972. Science and Politics. In *Hungarian Folklore: Essays,* 9–11. Budapest: Akadémiai.

Palinkas, Lawrence A. 1989. *Rhetoric and Religious Experience: The Discourse of Immigrant Chinese Churches.* Fairfax, Va.: George Mason University Press.

Papazov, Ivo. 1992a. Interviews and class discussions at the Department of Music, University of Texas at Austin, 4 May.

———. 1992b. Interview on National Public Radio's *All Things Considered,* 13 May.

———. 1994. Az vinagi sum si az. Interview conducted by Ilka Dimitrova, Rumyana Panaiotova, and Ventsislav Dimov. *Folk panair* (April):23–26.

Pareles, Jon. 1989. Clarinetist in His Element: Bulgarian Music Plus Rock. *New York Times,* 16 September.

Petkov, P. 1994. C profesionalizum za folklora. *Folk panair* (April):43.

Peicheva, Lozanka. 1994a. Bashao, Romi! *Folk panair* 1:8–9.

———. 1994b. Jashar Malikov. *Folk panair* 4:10.

Peicheva, Lozanka, and Ventsislav Dimov. 1994. Demokasetite (Za Edin Neizsledvan Fakt ot Sofiiskiya Muzikalen Pazar). *Bulgarski folklor* 20(4):25–34.

Pekacz, Jolanta. 1994. Did Rock Smash the Wall? The Role of Rock in Political Transition. *Popular Music* 13(1):41–49.

Perris, Arnold. 1985. *Music as Propaganda.* Westport, Conn.: Greenwood.

Petrás, Mária. n.d. *Ha folyóvíz lennék: Csángó énekek Moldvából* (If I were a river: Csángó songs from Moldavia]. Unlabeled cassette.

Petrović, Ankica. 1989. Paradoxes of Muslim Music in Bosnia and Herzegovina. *Asian Music* 20(1).

——. 1994. Music as the Subject of Political Manipulation in the Lands of the Former Yugoslavia. Paper presented at the annual meeting of the Society for Ethnomusicology and the American Folklore Society, Milwaukee, Wisc.

Pettan, Svanibor. 1992. Lambada in Kosovo: A Case Study in Gypsy Creativity. *Journal of the Gypsy Lore Society,* Series 5, 2(2):117–30.

Poulton, Hugh. 1989. *Minorities of the Balkans.* London: Minority Rights Group.

——. 1991. *The Balkans: Minorities and States in Conflict.* London: Minority Rights Publications.

——. 1993. The Roma in Macedonia: A Success Story? *RFE/RL Research Report* 2(19):7.

Preporod. March 1990. Sarajevo: Islamsko starjesinstvo Bosne i Hercegovine.

Punkin, Genko. 1988a. Nikoi ne sviri tolkova dobre! Razgovor c Dzho Boid. *Narodna kultura* 32, no. 1 (1 January):8.

——. 1988b. 7/8 (i drugi) za London i Nyu Iork. *Narodna mladezh* 44, no. 96 (24 April):1, 4.

Puxon, Grattan. 1973. *Rom: Europe's Gypsies.* London: Minority Rights Group.

Rădulescu, Speranţa. 1984. *Taraful Şi Acompaniamentul Armoniv în Muzica de Joc.* Bucharest: Editura Muzicală.

Ramet, Sabrina P., ed. 1994. *Rocking the State: Rock Music and Politics in Eastern Europe and Russia.* Boulder, Colo. Westview.

Rasmussen, Ljerka Vidic. 1991. Gypsy Music in Yugoslavia: Inside the Popular Culture Tradition. *Journal of the Gypsy Lore Society,* Series 5, 1(2):127–39.

Redfield, Robert. 1941. *The Folk Culture in Yucatan.* Chicago: University of Chicago Press.

——. 1947. The Folk Society. *American Journal of Sociology* 3(4).

——. 1968. *The Primitive World and Its Transformation.* Harmondsworth, England: Penguin.

Regev, Motti. 1989. The Field of Popular Music in Israel. In *World Music, Politics and Social Change,* ed. Simon Frith, 143–55. Manchester: Manchester University Press.

Rice, Timothy. 1982. The Surla and Tapan Tradition in Yugoslav Macedonia. *Galpin Society Journal* 35:122–37.

————. 1994. *"May It Fill Your Soul": Experiencing Bulgarian Music*. Chicago: University of Chicago Press.

Ricoeur, Paul. 1981. *Hermeneutics and the Human Sciences,* ed. John B. Thompson. Cambridge: Cambridge University Press.

Ronai, Esther. 1992. *Transylvania: Land Beyond the Forest* (video film). BBC production.

Ruf, W. 1994. Neue geistliche Musik in Deutschland. Paper presented at the Institute of Musicology of the University of Warsaw.

Ruskov, Lyuben. 1987. Kumovo Horo. *Narodna kultura* 2 (9 January):2.

Ryback, Timothy. 1990. *Rock around the Bloc: A History of Rock Music in Eastern Europe*. New York: Oxford University Press.

Sági, Mária. 1981. Sebő Ferenc és Halmos Béla útja avagy a Sebő együttes [The road of Ferenc Sebő and Béla Halmos: The Sebő ensemble]. In Széll, 14–22.

Samarin, James. 1975. *The Hieroglyphic of Mystery and Meaning*. Cudahy, Calif.: n.p.

Sárosi, Bálint. 1970 and 1978. *Gypsy Music*. Budapest: Corvina.

————. 1981. Professionelle und nichtprofessionelle Volksmusikanten in Ungarn. In *Studia instrumentorum musicae popularis* 7, ed. E. Stockmann, 10–16. Stockholm: Musikmuseet.

Schnebel, D. 1972. *Denkbare Musik-Schriften*. Cologne.

Schöpflin, George. 1979. Opposition and Para-opposition: Critical Currents in Hungary, 1968–78. In *Opposition in Eastern Europe,* ed. Rudolf Tokes, 142–86. London: Macmillan Press.

Scott, James. 1990. *Domination and the Arts of Resistance: Hidden Transcripts*. New Haven: Yale University Press.

Sebő, Ferenc. N.d. The Revival Movement and the Dance House in Hungary. Unpublished manuscript.

————. 1980. *Sebő Ferenc: Énekelt Versek.* Hungaroton SLPX 13877.

Seeman, Sonia Tamar. 1990. Continuity and Transformation in the Macedonian Genre of Calgija: Past Perfect and Present Imperfective. M.A. thesis, University of Washington.

Sekelj. 1993. *Yugoslavia: The Process of Disintegration*. Boulder: Social Science Monographs.

Senjković, Reana. 1993. In the beginning there were a coat of arms, a flag, and a "pleter." . . . In *Fear, Death, and Resistance (An Ethnography of War: Croatia 1991–1992),* ed. L. C. Feldman, R. Senjković, and I. Prica, 24–44. Zagreb: Institute of Ethnology and Folklore Research.

el-Shawan Castelo-Branco, Salwa. 1987. Some Aspects of the Cassette Industry in Egypt. *World of Music* 29(2):3–45.

Shchurov, V. 1994. Voice in Discussion. Tenth European Seminar in Ethnomusicology, Oxford, England.

Siklós, László. 1977. *Táncház*. Budapest: Zenemükiadó.

Silverman, Carol. 1984. Pomaks. In *Muslim Peoples: A World Ethnographic Survey,* ed. Richard Weekes, 612–16. Westport, Conn.: Greenwood.

——. 1986. Bulgarian Gypsies: Adaptation in a Socialist Context. *Nomadic Peoples* 21/22:51–61.

——. 1988. Contemporary Wedding Music in Bulgaria. Unpublished manuscript.

——. 1989. Reconstructing Folklore: Media and Cultural Policy in Eastern Europe. *Communication* 11:141–60.

——. 1995. Roma of Shuto Orizari, Macedonia: Class, Politics, and Community. In *East European Communities: The Struggle for Balance in Turbulent Times,* ed. David Kideckel, 197–216. Boulder, Colo.: Westview.

——. 1996. Music and Power: Gender and Performance among Roma (Gypsies) of Skopje, Macedonia. *World of Music* 38(1):1–15. Reprinted in *Music, Language and Literature of the Romany and Sinti,* ed. Max Peter Baumann. Berlin: International Institute for Traditional Music.

——. Forthcoming. Rom (Gypsy) Music. In *Garland Encyclopedia of World Music,* ed. James Porter and Tim Rice. New York: Garland.

Şimşir, Bilal N. 1990. The Turkish Minority in Bulgaria: History and Culture. In *The Turks of Bulgaria: The History, Culture and Political Fate of a Minority,* ed. Kemal H. Karpat, 159–178. Istanbul: Isis Press.

Singer, Milton. 1955. The Cultural Pattern of India. *Far Eastern Quarterly* 15:23–36.

——. 1972. *When a Great Tradition Modernizes.* New York: Praeger.

Slobin, Mark. 1971. Conversations in Tashkent. *Asian Music* 2(2):7–13.

——. 1982. *Old Jewish Folk Music: The Collections and Writings of Moshe Beregovski.* Philadelphia: University of Pennsylvania Press.

——. 1992. Micromusics of the West: A Comparative Approach. *Ethnomusicology* 36(1):1–88.

——. 1993. *Subcultural Sounds: Micromusics of the West.* Middletown, Conn.: Wesleyan University Press.

Smith, Anthony D. 1986. *The Ethnic Origins of Nations.* Oxford: Basil Blackwell.

Somfai, László. 1981. A Jánosi együttes "kemény folklór"-kísérelete. In Széll, 31–40.

Soulis, George. 1961. The Gypsies in the Byzantine Empire and the Balkans in the Middle Ages. *Dumbarton Oaks Papers* 15:142–65.

Sowińska, J. 1994. Przemiany kultury muzycznej Łużyczan. M.A. thesis, University of Warsaw.

Spivak, Gayatri Chakravorty. 1988. Can the Subaltern Speak? In *Marxism and the Interpretation of Cultures,* ed. Cary Nelson and Lawrence Grossberg, 271–313. Urbana: University of Illinois Press.

Staikova, Marina. 1988. Ekspresivnost, dramatizŭm, mŭzhestvo: Ivan Krŭstev (Manol). *Otechestven front,* 8 (8 April): 12.

Stalin, Josef. 1972 [1936]. Marxism in Linguistics. In *Marxism and Art: Writings in*

Aesthetics and Criticism, ed. Berel Lang and Forrest Williams, 80–87. New York: David McKay.

Stites, Richard. 1989. *Revolutionary Dreams: Utopian Vision and Experimental Life in the Russian Revolution.* New York: Oxford University Press.

Stockhausen, Karlheinz. 1966. *Telemusik.*

———. 1968. *Stimmung.*

Stokes, Martin. 1992a. *The Arabesk Debate: Music and Musicians in Modern Turkey.* Oxford: Clarendon Press.

———. 1992b. Islam, the Turkist State, and Arabesk. *Popular Music* 11(2):213–27.

Stoyanov, Georgi. 1988. Sudbovni prevratnosti ot istoricheskoto ni minalo: na ekrana: noviyat bulgarski igralen film "Vreme Razdelno." *Rabotnichesko delo* 62, no. 88 (28 March).

Sŭrnev, Tsan'o. 1988. Kontsertut. *Otchestvo* 3, no. 301 (26 April):23–25.

Sutton, R. Anderson. 1985. Commercial Cassette Recordings of Traditional Music in Java: Implications for Performers and Scholars. *World of Music* 27(3):23–46.

Szabolcsi, Bence. 1951. *A XIX. század magyar romantikus zenéje* [Nineteenth-century Hungarian Romantic music]. Budapest: Zenemukiado.

———. 1964. *A Concise History of Hungarian Music.* Budapest: Corvina.

Szász, János András. 1981a. A Vujicsics együttesről [About the Vujicsics ensemble]. In Széll, 52–62.

———. 1981b. Beszélgetés Olsvai Imrével [Conversation with Imre Olsvai]. In Széll, 93–107.

Szelényi, Iván. 1988. *Socialist Entrepreneurs: Embourgeoisement in Rural Hungary.* Cambridge, Mass.: Polity.

Szelényi, Iván, and Szonja Szelényi. 1991. Az elit cirkulácioja? *Kritica* (October):8–10.

Széll, Jenő, ed. 1981. *Huzzad, huzzad, muzsikasom . . . A hangszeres nepzene feltamadasa.* Budapest: Muzsak Kozmuvelodesi kiado.

Szemere, Anna. 1992. The Politics of Marginality: A Rock Musical Subculture in Socialist Hungary in the Early 1980s. In *Rockin' the Boat: Mass Music and Mass Movements,* ed. Reebee Garofalo, 93–114. Boston: South End Press.

Szeverényi, Erzsébet. 1988. Szórakoztató zenénk "sztalini müszaka." *Zenetudományi Dolgozatok,* 141–45.

———. 1992. Personal communication. Budapest, Hungary.

Tarasiewicz, Bogumiła. 1996. Tradycja a współczesność: Z badań nad kulturą muzyczną Łemków w Polsce. In Czekanowska 1996a, 387–406.

Taruskin, Richard. 1984. Some Thoughts on the History and Historiography of Russian Music. *Journal of Musicology* 3(4):321–39.

———. 1986. Stravinsky and the Painters. In *Confronting Stravinsky: Man, Musician, and Modernist,* ed. Jann Pasler. Berkeley: University of California Press.

———. 1993. *Musorgsky: Eight Essays and an Epilogue.* Princeton: Princeton University Press.

Todorov, Manol. 1985. Purva reshitelna krachka: Natsionalna sreshta na orkestrite za narodna muzika — Stambolovo '85. *Hudozhestvena samodeinost* 12:30–31.

Todorova, Maria N. 1996. The Ottoman Legacy in the Balkans. *Imperial Legacy: The Ottoman Imprint on the Balkans and the Middle East,* ed. L. Carl Brown. New York: Columbia University Press.

Tomova, Ilona, and Plamen Bogoev. 1992. Minorities in Bulgaria. Report to the December 1991 International Conference on the Minorities organized in Rome by the Lelio Basso International Foundation for the Rights and Liberation of Peoples. *The Insider* (February): 15-page insert.

Toth, Erzsebet. n.d. *Edesanyam rozsafaja.* Electrecord ST-EPE 01444.

Troitsky, Artemy. 1987. *Back in the USSR: The True History of Rock in Russia.* Boston: Faber and Faber.

Turner, Victor. 1988. *The Anthropology of Performance.* New York: PAJ.

Turner, Victor, and Edward M. Bruner, eds. 1986. *The Anthropology of Experience.* Urbana: University of Illinois Press.

Valkó, László. 1992. Interview. Budapest, Hungary.

Varsányi, Gyula. 1991. Vedett idő az értékes muzsikának. *Népszabadság,* 16 September.

Verdery, Katherine. 1983. *Transylvanian Villagers.* Berkeley: University of California Press.

———. 1991a. *National Ideology under Socialism.* Berkeley: University of California Press.

———. 1991b. Theorizing Socialism: A Prologue to the Transition. *American Ethnologist* 18(3):419–39.

Von Geldern, James. 1993. *Bolshevik Festivals, 1917–1920.* Berkeley: University of California Press.

"Vreme Razdelno" prez pogleda na zritelya. 1988. *Vecherni novini* (Sofia) 37 (17 April).

Vŭlchinova, Elisaveta. 1989. Svirdzhii (chalgadzhii) ot sredata na 19 vek: mezhdina forma mezhdu folklornata i gradska muzikalna kultura. *Muzikalni horizonti* 12/13:134–38.

Waterman, Christopher. 1990. *Juju: A Social History and Ethnography of an African Popular Music.* Chicago: University of Chicago Press.

Whitman, Lois. 1994. *Human Rights in the Former Yugoslav Republic of Macedonia.* New York: Helsinki Watch.

Wiora, Walter. 1958. Der Untergang des Volkslieds und sein zweitens Dasein. *Musikalischen Zeitfragen* 7:9–25.

Young, Pauline. 1932. *The Pilgrims of Russian-Town.* New York: Russel and Russel.

Zang, Theodore. 1989. *Destroying Ethnic Identity: The Expulsion of the Bulgarian Turks* (A Helsinki Watch Report). New York: U.S. Helsinki Watch Committee.

———. 1991. *Destroying Ethnic Identity: The Gypsies of Bulgaria* (A Helsinki Watch Report). New York: Human Rights Watch.

Zemtsovsky, Izaly. 1994. Socialism and Folklore. Paper presented at the conference "The Status of Traditional Arts and Music in the Former Soviet Union and Eastern Europe," Los Angeles.

Zender, H. 1991. *Happy New Ears*. Freiburg.

Zoltán, János. 1991. Nincs egyetlen barátom sem. *Riport,* 15 November.

Contributors

Michael Beckerman is Associate Professor of Music at the University of California, Santa Barbara, and has published on the work of Antonin Dvořák, Leos Janaček, Czech music, and topics in American music.

Donna Buchanan is Assistant Professor and Ethnomusicology Program Coordinator in the Department of Music at New York University. She has carried out extensive field research with Bulgaria's national folk ensembles since 1988.

Anna Czekanowska is Chair of the Institute of Musicology at the University of Warsaw and has published on the musics of Poland and Asia.

Judit Frigyesi is Assistant Professor of Music at Princeton University and has published on Béla Bartók and on Jewish music.

Barbara Rose Lange received the Ph.D. in ethnomusicology from the University of Washington in 1993 and is currently a Mellon Fellow at Cornell University. She has conducted research with Roma (Gypsies) and Hungarians in Hungary.

Mirjana Laušević is a Ph.D. candidate in ethnomusicology at Wesleyan University and received the Society for Ethnomusicology's Charles Seeger Prize for 1995.

Theodore Levin is the author of *The Hundred Thousand Fools of God: Musical Travels in Central Asia and Queens, New York* (1996). His recordings of music from Russia, Central Asia, and the Caucasus have appeared on the Nonesuch, Smithsonian/Folkways, Ocora, and UNESCO/Audivis labels. He teaches in the Music Department at Dartmouth College.

Margarita Mazo, a graduate of the Leningrad (St. Petersburg) Conservatory, is Professor of Music at Ohio State University. She teaches ethnomusicology and historical musicology (Russian music) and has published on Russian folksong and connections between Russian art and folk music.

Steluţa Popa is a researcher at the Institute of Ethnography and Folklore in Bucharest and has published on Romanian traditional music.

Ljerka Vidić Rasmussen has earned degrees in ethnomusicology from the Sarajevo Academy of Music and Wesleyan University. Her research interests include musics of the

Rom Gypsies and popular music in the former Yugoslavia. She teaches music at universities in the Nashville, Tennessee, area.

Timothy Rice is Professor of Music in the Ethnomusicology Department at UCLA. He has written extensively on Bulgarian and Macedonian music since his first field trip in 1969. He is a past editor of *Ethnomusicology* and has served on the Board of Directors of the Society for Ethnomusicology for four years as treasurer.

Carol Silverman is Associate Professor of Anthropology at the University of Oregon and has published on the music and folkways of Roma groups in Europe and the United States.

Mark Slobin is Professor of Music at Wesleyan University and former president of the Society for Ethnomusicology. He has published on the music of Afghanistan and Central Asia, Jewish music, and topics in the theory of ethnomusicology.

Catherine Wanner received her doctorate in 1996 from Columbia University and currently teaches cultural anthropology at Pennsylvania State University. She is working on a book entitled *Burden of Dreams: History, Memory, and the Making of National Identity in Post-Soviet Ukraine.*

Index

Library of Congress Cataloging-in-Publication Data

Retuning culture: musical changes in Central and Eastern Europe/edited by Mark Slobin.

p. cm.

Includes bibliographical references (p.   ) and index.

ISBN 0-8223-1855-5 (cloth: alk. paper).—ISBN 0-8223-1847-4 (pbk.: alk. paper)

1. Music—Europe, Central—20th century—History and criticism. 2. Music—Europe, Eastern—20th century—History and criticism. 3. Music and society. 4. Music and state—Europe, Central. 5. Music and state—Europe, Eastern.

ML240.5.R48 1996

780'.947'0904—dc20   96-27983   CIP M